The People's Republic of China After 50 Years

中

Studies on Contemporary China

The Contemporary China Institute at the School of Oriental and African Studies (University of London) has, since its establishment in 1968, been an international centre for research and publications on twentieth-century China. *Studies on Contemporary China*, which is edited at the Institute, seeks to maintain and extend that tradition by making available the best work of scholars and China specialists throughout the world. It embraces a wide variety of subjects relating to Nationalist and Communist China, including social, political, and economic change, intellectual and cultural developments, foreign relations, and national security.

Series Editor

Dr Frank Dikötter, Director of the Contemporary China Institute

Editorial Advisory Board

Professor Robert F. Ash
Professor Hugh D. R. Baker
Professor Elisabeth J. Croll
Dr Richard Louis Edmonds
Mr Brian G. Hook
Professor Christopher B. Howe

Professor Bonnie S. McDougall
Professor David Shambaugh
Dr Julia C. Strauss
Dr Jonathan Unger
Professor Lynn T. White III

The People's Republic of China After 50 Years

Edited by

RICHARD LOUIS EDMONDS

OXFORD
UNIVERSITY PRESS

This book has been printed digitally and produced in a standard specification
in order to ensure its continuing availability

OXFORD
UNIVERSITY PRESS

Great Clarendon Street, Oxford OX2 6DP

Oxford University Press is a department of the University of Oxford.
It furthers the University's objective of excellence in research, scholarship,
and education by publishing worldwide in

Oxford New York

Auckland Bangkok Buenos Aires Cape Town Chennai
Dar es Salaam Delhi Hong Kong Istanbul Karachi Kolkata
Kuala Lumpur Madrid Melbourne Mexico City Mumbai Nairobi
São Paulo Shanghai Taipei Tokyo Toronto

Oxford is a registered trade mark of Oxford University Press
in the UK and in certain other countries

Published in the United States
by Oxford University Press Inc., New York

© The China Quarterly 1999, 2000

The moral rights of the author have been asserted

Database right Oxford University Press (maker)

Reprinted 2004

ISBN 0-19-924065-5

Contents

vi   Contents

Notes on Contributors

JOHN P. BURNS is Chair Professor of Politics and Public Administration at the University of Hong Kong, where he has taught since 1977.

ELISABETH J. CROLL is professor of Chinese anthropology at the School of Oriental and African Studies, University of London.

ROBERT F. DERNBERGER received his Ph.D. from Harvard in 1965. He taught for three decades at the University of Michigan, retiring as professor emeritus of economics in 1997. He is currently director of the Centre for Asian Studies at the University of Aveiro in Portugal. He has published numerous articles and books, including *The Role of the Foreigner in China's Economic Development*; *Capitalism and the East Asian Miracle*; and an edited volume on *China's Development Experience in Comparative Economic Perspective.*

RICHARD LOUIS EDMONDS is editor of *The China Quarterly* and senior lecturer in geography with reference to China at the School of Oriental and African Studies in the University of London. He has written extensively on mainland China, Japan, Taiwan, Macau and Hong Kong, and is the author of *Macau* (1989) and *Patterns of China's Lost Harmony: A Survey of the Country's Environmental Degradation and Protection* (1994). Currently, he is working on environmental problems in China and transition issues in Macau.

MERLE GOLDMAN is a professor of Chinese history at Boston University. Her most recent books are *Sowing the Seeds of Democracy in China* and (with John K. Fairbank) the enlarged edition of *China: A New History* (1998).

BONNIE S. McDOUGALL is professor of Chinese at the University of Edinburgh. Her most recent work is as co-author of *The Literature of China in the 20th Century* (1998), and her current research is on Chinese concepts of privacy and the correspondence between Lu Xun and Xu Guangping.

JEAN C. OI is director of the Center for East Asian Studies and associate professor of political science at Stanford University. She is the author of *State and Peasant in Contemporary China: The Political Economy of Village Government* (1989); *Rural China Takes Off: Institutional Foundations of Economic Reform* (1999) and has a forthcoming co-edited volume, *Property Rights and Economic Reform in China* (1999).

PITMAN B. POTTER is director of the Institute of Asian Research at the University of British Columbia. He is also professor of law and director of Chinese legal studies at UBC's Faculty of Law. His teaching and research are focused on PRC and Taiwan law in the areas of foreign trade and investment, dispute resolution, intellectual property, contracts, business regulation and human rights. His publications include *Legitimation and Contract Autonomy in the PRC: The Contract Law of China* (1992), *Domestic Law Reforms in Post-Mao China* (1994), and *Foreign Business Law in China: Past Progress Future Challenges* (1995), as well as numerous articles on Chinese law and politics. He is also involved in arbitration work, and continues to advise governments and private companies on Chinese affairs.

LUCIAN W. PYE is Ford Professor of Political Science, Emeritus, at M.I.T.

MICHAEL SCHOENHALS is director of the Centre for East and Southeast Asian Studies, Lund University. He is the editor of *China's Cultural Revolution 1966-1969: NOT a Dinner Party*. His research interests range from the empirical plumbing of official CCP histories to the ideologically informed prefiguration of Western analyses of present-day China.

DAVID SHAMBAUGH is professor of political science and international affairs and director of the China Policy Program in the Elliott School of International Affairs at George Washington University, and non-resident senior fellow in the Foreign Policy Studies Program at the Brookings Institution in Washington, D.C. He formerly served as editor of *The China Quarterly* from 1991-1996. He has recently co-edited (with Orville Schell) *The China Reader: The Reform Era*, and (with James Lilley) *China's Military Faces the Future*. His new book, *Reforming China's Military*, will appear in 2000, as well as his edited volume, *The Modern Chinese State*.

DOROTHY J. SOLINGER is professor in the Department of Political Science at the University of California, Irvine. Her book, *Contesting Citizenship in Urban China: Peasant Migrants, the State and the Logic of the Market* and her co-edited book, *States and Sovereignty in the Global Economy* were both published in 1999.

MICHAEL SULLIVAN is fellow emeritus of St. Catherine's College, Oxford, and formerly Christensen Professor of Oriental Art at Stanford University. He has written a number of books on Chinese and Oriental art, his latest being *Art and Artists of Twentieth Century China* (1996).

MICHAEL YAHUDA is professor of international relations at the London School of Economics and Political Science. His recent publications include *The International Politics of the Asia-Pacific* and *Hong Kong: China's Challenge*.

The People's Republic of China after 50 Years

Richard Louis Edmonds

This volume assesses the state of the People's Republic of China on its 50th anniversary by asking leading scholars in various fields to give their views of developments since 1949 with emphasis on recent decades. With the exception of the contributions by Bob Dernberger and Michael Sullivan, the papers were presented and discussed at a conference co-sponsored with the Centro de Estudos Asiáticos of the Universidade de Aveiro in Aveiro, Portugal from 28 to 31 January 1999. *The China Quarterly* wishes to acknowledge the generous support of the Universidade de Aveiro, its Rector, Júlio Pedrosa de Jesus, and the efforts of the staff of the Centro de Estudos Asiáticos, in particular Pedro Vilarinho, António Miranda and Helena Costa.

As well as the comments of other paper writers, the contributions benefited from the participation and comments of Judith Shapiro, who teaches part-time at the Centro de Estudos Asiáticos, from notes of the proceedings compiled by Joanne Phillips of *The China Quarterly*, and from conversations with various Portuguese guests who attended the sessions. While not all aspects of the People's Republic were covered and many authors felt constrained by the limitation of space we allowed them, it is felt that these papers do provide a benchmark from which to measure the development of the People's Republic of China (PRC) and represent a refinement and update of work done in *The China Quarterly* to assess the PRC on its 40th anniversary.[1]

As an overview, Lucian Pye begins by pointing out that many early writers on the PRC in the West, including those who wrote in *The China Quarterly*, have now been proved to be more accurate in some of their pessimistic statements than others thought at that time. Pye presents two overarching themes for the first 50 years of the PRC. First, ideological conformity has restrained PRC intellectual and economic development. Secondly, the intertwined nature of the Party and the state has constrained politics and allowed the powerful to have economic advantage. The result is that China today is still searching for a national identity which can combine traditional and modern elements. In conclusion, despite recognizing many positive signs in recent years, Pye is "cautiously pessimistic" that the PRC will be able to meet the challenges that still lie ahead on China's long road to modernization.

In his discussion of national political reform, John Burns argues the regime is more resilient than we are led to believe by those who think it will fall or must democratize. The Chinese Communist Party (CCP) continues to remain small and elitist with a bureaucracy that remains fundamentally unchanged over the past 50 years. Related decision-making institutions, such as leading small groups, continue to be used by

1. *The China Quarterly*, No. 119 (September 1989), pp. 419–630.

the CCP, and it continues to control leadership of key social groups through appointment of Party members to lead these groups. Burns, however, does see the Party as relying more today on the law and notes other changes in China's internal environment. He then discusses the ways the CCP has adapted to these changes: opening up membership; moving towards a younger collective leadership; raising the standards for bureaucratic entry despite marked corruption; pursuing legal reform; strengthening the role of people's congresses; warily allowing labour unions to help solve unemployment problems; allowing non-state political groups to emerge while suppressing any challenge to the Party; and allowing the media to grow while continuing to try to control them. In conclusion, he notes that while the Party is adapting to change it seems least willing to adapt the links between state and society and this could pose problems for the future.

In his contribution, Michael Schoenhals notes the alteration from Mao Zedong's craving for "movements" (*yundong*) to Deng Xiaoping and Jiang Zemin's insistence upon market-based "stability" at all costs. For today's youth, "movements" appear archaic. In their day, however, they were a way of keeping a feeling of progress towards a brighter future alive, whereas the drive for the "stability" of later years suggests no progress. Schoenhals also draws out differences in the policies of Deng and Jiang by implying that ideology has become thinner under the latter than under the former. For Schoenhals the "moral left" does not pose a threat to the regime but instead can be seen as useful should reform fail. Attempts by reformers to use existing parties as alternatives to the Communist Party have failed and Schoenhals sees the CCP as remaining for quite some time – at least in name. Ultimately he sees political and environmental degradation as possibly more dangerous for the Party's future than political legitimacy.

Bob Dernberger divides his discussion on the economy into the Mao leadership years (1952–75), the Deng Xiaoping era (1978–95), and the initial years of Jiang Zemin and Zhu Rongji's leadership (1996–98). For the Mao years, he makes the point that while an essentially Soviet-style economic system was adopted, the Chinese did introduce modifications: more decentralization, which was positive; and self-dependency and reliance on mass movements, which he sees as negative. Dernberger notes that economic growth became not only more pronounced under Deng's leadership but also more steady. Under Jiang and Zhu, the international conditions for growth have become more difficult and there is now a need for the leadership to seek "new engines." Dernberger ends his macro-survey on an optimistic note, pointing out that Jiang and Zhu's administration has both a more realistic appreciation of the problems facing China today and a greater technical knowledge for dealing with them.

After noting the spectacular rise of grain production from 1979 to 1985, Jean Oi points out that it slowed and geographical disparities grew from the second half of the 1980s. She notes that the high opportunity costs connected with organic fertilizer application, made worse in those cases where IOUs are issued in lieu of payment, have not encouraged peasants to increase sustainable agricultural practices but have ushered in a period of unprecedented restructuring of the rural labour force and rural to urban migration. Oi points out the obstacles halting the privatization and full marketization of agriculture: fear of grain dependency upon international markets; peasants' wish to retain rights to land even if they do not farm it; and the government's desire to be able to force peasants back to the countryside in view of the urban enterprise lay-offs. In fact the move to force all sales of grain to be made via state grain stores in 1998 signals a retreat from rural marketization. At the same time there are trends towards rural industrial privatization, spurred on by government concern for revenues as the debts of collectively-owned firms mount. On the political front Oi sees the move to direct elections as a calculated way for the government to reduce peasant discontent. This is probably its most risky current rural policy, but non-action in politics could be even more costly. Overall, Oi sees such rural policy shifts as natural as the regime attempts to solve old and new problems in an increasingly complex countryside.

Dorothy Solinger traces the evolution of the PRC urban system. She tries to answer the question: is China today reviving the urban socio-economic systems that the founding leaders initially aimed to eliminate? Solinger looks at three facets of urban life: ownership, labour security and residency status – all of which had been social dividers prior to the founding of the PRC but were transformed in an attempt to create an urban proletarian realm. Solinger compares the current circumstances of these dividers, now blurred, with the situation in 1949, 1979 and 1989. Although changes have been significant, she does not think that the old divisions between public and private, state and non-state, and urban and rural have disappeared completely as the PRC turns 50.

The rural to urban discrepancy remains in my assessment of changes in the environment over the last 50 years, as the rural environment has been worsening at a faster pace since the mid-1980s. Keeping in mind that the population of the country has doubled and considerable efforts have been made to rectify environmental degradation over the past two decades, the overall picture remains pessimistic as the country has yet to devote enough resources to environmental protection. In the early years of the PRC, government was largely concerned with economic growth, although some health and wildlife measures were undertaken. The subsequent Great Leap Forward and the Cultural Revolution both produced disastrous ecological consequences. Contrary to common belief, the rebirth of environmental protection dates from the early 1970s. The rise to power of Deng Xiaoping was a mixed blessing, with some aspects of conservation improving but some systemic changes leading to a worsening of the environment throughout the 1980s. I conclude that the future remains highly problematic unless the government commits more resources to environmentally friendly forms of development.

In his contribution on foreign relations, Michael Yahuda gives a reminder of just what a change the establishment of the People's Republic was for the international status of China. He notes, however, that from 1949 to today, the leadership has never given a clear vision of how its newly achieved great power status will be used. Yahuda gives two reasons why China has difficulty coping with a great power identity, both historical: the legacy of being a great power prior to the mid-Qing dynasty, and the myth of the "century of shame and humiliation" prior to 1949. He sees a contradictory approach to foreign affairs emerging since the Tiananmen shootings: on the one hand, integration into the inter-national order on the global stage, and on the other, attempts to halt the foreign threat from "peaceful evolution" at home. Yahuda discusses relationships with neighbouring states but stresses the United States of America relationship. China continues to try to constrain the growth of American influence in the region and yet other Asian states see the American way as a basis for order. At the same time, Yahuda sees a significant contrast between positive developments with inland Asian states and hostile relations with maritime states. As of today, China's international role remains more one of a "spoiler" than a leader.

After a brief introduction to the importance of the People's Liberation Army (PLA) in the rise of the Communist Party to power and its role in Korean War, David Shambaugh's contribution looks in detail at reforms of China's military during the last decade. He focuses upon the new departures in strategy and training which emphasize short-term, local conflicts and more mobile forces, the reduction in troop strength (which is more visual than real), the beginnings of a possible bifurcation between the Party and the military, and the gradual upgrade of weaponry during the past decade. Despite modest modernization, restructuring and upgrad-ing during the 1990s, Shambaugh concludes that the PLA today is 20 to 30 years behind in state-of-the-art military technologies and equipment and the gap with the United States, Europe and Japan is actually widening. Today the military's long-term priorities are not completely clear, but it seems that capabilities to threaten Taiwan and to extend Chinese authority in the South China Sea are important. Thus Shambaugh feels that the PLA is acquiring the strength to pose regional attacks which could threaten Taiwan, Japan or other neighbouring states.

For Pitman Potter the achievements and limitations of the first decade of reform have set the pattern for post-1989 legal developments in China. Legal borrowing from the West remains constrained by the restraints such borrowing can put on state power. Rather, attempts are made to have the law protect the party-state. Legal intellectuals continue to be subject to the Party and lack legal training or career exposure. Despite this, Potter sees significant change in law-making, administration and dispute resol-ution institutions over the last decade although these institutions remain under heavy Party influence. Legal development in the economic growth sphere continues to outstrip growth in legal restraints on the political order. Potter discusses the substantial changes in property and contract relations as well as foreign economic relations. In contrast, criminal justice shows little change from a system which is designed to aid state security.

As Lisa Croll points out in her contribution, tensions have evolved in China's social welfare system during the 1990s as a result of expectations derived from the first 40 years of communist rule. Villagers appear to be responding to the lack of social services by resisting fees and taxes, setting up alternative kinship-based councils, and questioning the authority of the party-state. In urban areas, the erosion of welfare has been considerable during the 1990s, with the family picking up the responsibility at a time when family size is shrinking. Ironically, Croll concludes this erosion has resulted in an equalization of resources between state employees and other urban and rural residents. She points out that in rural areas, social security and welfare is reliant upon village enterprises which are increasingly as fragile as their urban counterparts. Overall there has been a move from a privileged enterprised-based urban system to an equally privileged system of rural enclaves based upon residence or share holding. Current trends suggest that in the future social security will not be employee-exclusive nor enterprise-based, but will be decentralized and increasingly provided by non-governmental organizations such as specialized commercial social insurance agencies. Croll concludes that whatever the government does it faces a dilemma, as it does not have the funds to run a centralized welfare system but can lose its authority if it withdraws from welfare provision.

Merle Goldman focuses on the role of intellectuals in the political scene since 1980. Even though intellectuals had more freedom to discuss political issues in the the 1980s than previously, they fared better after the 4 June 1989 crackdown than in the Mao years – no recriminations upon relatives or colleagues, no implicit threat of terrorism, and no need to participate actively in government-organized "movements." Goldman also traces the development of neo-conservative thought in the Jiang era and compares it to the neo-Maoist thought of the Deng era, as well as discussing the development of neo-Confucianist thought. The leadership made use of these philosophies in its appeal to nationalism as a unifying force in the mid-1990s. Goldman notes that dissidents in the 1990s have new ways of communication which are far harder for the government to control than the democracy wall of the late 1970s: e-mail, fax and mobile telephones. Today the government seems most concerned with intellectual involvement in worker unrest. Despite the continuing constraints, Goldman concludes that the post-Mao era has been the best period for intellectual dissenters since the founding of the PRC.

Michael Sullivan outlines the dramatic changes that have occurred in Chinese art over the last 50 years. He notes that many artists went to work for the new state in the 1950s – with little economic choice – and Soviet-style Western works became the dominant mode within a Western–Chinese painting dichotomy which has been ongoing for almost a century. Although there were periods of relative leniency when traditional painting showed some vigour during the Mao years, Sullivan notes Deng-era artists were slow to overcome the stifling of that earlier period. Exhibitions during 1979 and 1980, however, were a change of great significance as artists began acting as a group outside the formal artistic establishment. While there was a development of more daring and independent art during the 1980s, the Tiananmen shootings in 1989 did lead to a retreat from the scene by many major artists. Overall, however, artists of the 1990s have been more fortunate than writers because foreigners have been more eager to buy their work, freeing them from dependence upon a controlled domestic market. Sullivan concludes that art has become more creative in the 1990s despite calls from the Party to keep within certain bounds, and he feels that art is in a relatively vigorous state today.

Bonnie McDougall agrees with Michael Sullivan that the 1990s has been a hard time for artists and writers in the PRC. Despite this, the period is one during which certain writers have been able to commercialize their work and to write in freedom from overt political campaigns. McDougall feels political messages were more prominent in the fiction of the 1980s. She gives examples of fiction styles during the late 1980s and 1990s, many carnivalistic, others more orthodox, and feels that rotting bodies, foul language and family killings pervade this carnivalistic literature to a higher frequency than anywhere in the world at any time. She also points out that while many readers think modern Chinese novels bear witness to real situations, recent literature is just as historically unreliable as the socialist realism that preceded it. In conclusion, McDougall expects Chinese readers to be interested in writers who are not preoccupied with speaking on behalf of the people or Chinese civilization.

Overall, this volume presents a picture of a People's Republic of China which is not as healthy as optimists maintain nor in such a disastrous state as many pessimists have put forward. In particular, the experts have found many situations to be improving from their point of view in the last decade or two, but that these improvements, in and of themselves, pose problems for the current form of government. Increasingly, external developments will be shaping the pace of change in the People's Republic. The ability of the government to continue to respond in a measured fashion to change will be necessary if the People's Republic is to thrive in the 21st century.

An Overview of 50 Years of the People's Republic of China: Some Progress, but Big Problems Remain

Lucian W. Pye

In the very first sentence of the first article in the first issue of *The China Quarterly*, Howard L. Boorman, seeking to summarize the first decade of the PRC, wrote: "The man who faces his typewriter to set down a thousand words of coherent comment on the Communist revolution in China confronts not only a massive experiment in social engineering but also the fact that his interpretation of that experiment will expose as much of the author as it does of the revolution." Except that now it is a computer and not a typewriter, little is different for anyone who would try to summarize what is now 50 years of the PRC. True, enough time has gone by for us now to have not just the initial standard interpretations as to what transpired in China but revisions and then further re-revisions of the story, so that even though we cannot be so bold as to say that we now have the full truth, we probably are a bit closer.

As was common at the time, Boorman characterized the communist revolution as an "experiment," but from the current perspective it is hard to judge what definition of "experiment" might properly apply in the case of the PRC. Has it been an open-minded testing by trial and error, or is it more like an adolescent "experimenting" with drugs, only to get hooked? Or has it been a stubborn effort to confirm a known truth, much like the clumsy high school chemistry student who fruitlessly tries to "prove" Boyle's Law without success? And if the supposed "laws" of Marxism are not in fact the equal of Boyle's, what kind of an experiment is it to try stubbornly to prove the truth of Marxism? From the perspective of 50 years it is clear that the communist leaders were never engaged in a systematic and truly empirical set of experiments, but rather they have been "hooked" on an ideology which for decades they have stubbornly insisted embraced the "ultimate truth" and which, whether they still believe in it or not, they feel compelled to cling to as the justification for their monopolizing of power.

From the beginning scholars were confronted with the challenge of trying to understand a seemingly profound revolutionary process which was, however, confusingly encased in a grandiose ideology. They were understandably uncertain about what they should take as the baseline for measuring the pace and direction of change. Some tended towards starting with the conventional wisdom about Chinese society and culture, and then asked what were the limited changes the Communists could conceivably bring about. With a vivid vision of what China had been, they assumed that the ideology would have to bend to conform with Chinese propensities. Others started from what they understood to be the inflexible ideology and practices of Marxism-Leninism, and thus they expected Chinese realities to be significantly moulded in accordance with the doctrine. This reliance upon one form or another of abstract, theoretical formulations created some sharp divisions among scholars. For example, one of the earliest debates in the first decade of the PRC was over the question of whether there was such a thing as "Maoism" as a modified form of orthodox communism, or whether Mao's practices were in fact consistent with standard Leninism.[1] Neither approach prepared us for what was to happen, as it was the Chinese who became the champions of orthodoxy and were to denounce the Russians as the "revisionists."

The intellectual fashions at the time accentuated the vividness of theoretical speculation. The year the People's Republic was established was also the year that George Orwell published *Nineteen Eighty-four*, and in the next year Hannah Arendt came out with *The Origins of Totalitarianism*, which was followed shortly by Carl Friedrich and Zbigniew Brzezinski's influential *Totalitarian Dictatorship and Autocracy*. Thus, just as the Chinese Communist Party's regime was being founded, Western intellectuals were learning that it was old-fashioned to think in terms of the ancient category of autocracy, and that the way of the future was to employ the more elegant and disciplined model of totalitarianism.

Moreover, at that early juncture the Chinese propaganda machine began to call for "brain washing" (*xi nao*), and Westerners immediately felt that they understood what was involved, for at the time a book at the top of the best sellers list was Vance Packard's *The Hidden Persuaders* which made it clear how apparently innocent advertising practices could alter people's ways of thinking.[2] Moreover, at that time the authority of psychology was on the rise as the social sciences were being relabelled the behavioural sciences. Academic writings about communications theory, propaganda and psychological warfare all suggested that it was not unreasonable to believe that the Chinese people's thinking could indeed be systematically transformed to produce a country of "blue ants." The picture of an ideologically controlled population was then reinforced by the Chinese entry into the Korean War and their use of "human wave" attacks, with no apparent regard for the value of human life. The imagery of Chinese "hordes" in the Western press provoked a cynical U.S. Marine officer to ask "How many 'hordes' are there supposed to be in a platoon?"[3]

Given these general tendencies and the reverberations from the just

1. In an early, major debate, Karl A. Wittfogel argued that Mao's thoughts and actions were consistent with orthodox Leninism as applied to a backward, peasant-based country; see his: "The legend of Maoism," *The China Quarterly*, No. 1 (January–March 1960), pp. 72–86. Benjamin Schwartz in his "A Reply to Karl A. Wittfogel," *The China Quarterly*, No. 2 (Spring 1960), insisted that Mao had altered key tenets of Leninism precisely because of his peasant base of power.

2. Academic understanding of Chinese thought control practices was also greatly advanced by Robert Lifton's *Thought Reform and the Psychology of Totalism: A Study of "Brain-washing" in China* (New York: W.W. Norton, 1961).

3. Official U.S. Marine Corps history as quoted in Alexander George, *The Chinese Communist Army in Action* (New York: Columbia University Press, 1967), p. 4.

inaugurated Cold War with the Soviet Union, it is impressive that so much scholarly work of the first years turned out to have been remarkably sound. Richard Walker's *Red China: The First Five Years* was thought by some at the time to have been unnecessarily shocking, especially his numbers for "class enemies" killed, but subsequent official Chinese figures showed that he had underestimated the casualties. Among others, Doak Barnett lucidly analysed Chinese domestic and foreign policies; Franz Schurmann perceptively depicted the close interrelationship of ideology and bureaucracy at the core of Chinese administrative practices; and Roderick MacFarquhar, while serving as the first editor of this journal, fathomed the political manoeuvres behind the Hundred Flowers campaign and the Anti-Rightist movement.

The drama of a "New China" and the palpable sense of a nation with renewed vitality which accompanied the establishment of the PRC easily convinced both participating Chinese and foreign observers that China was about to realize its long promised return to greatness. The break with the past seemed much too dramatic to allow the new regime to fall into the pattern of high hopes and crashing disappointments that had been the cyclical story of China from the initial Reform Movement of 1898, and then the 1911 Revolution, the May Fourth Movement and the founding of the Nanking Government of 1927. However, before the first decade was over it had become apparent that the road ahead for China was not going to be either straight or smooth. Almost immediately a major problem for understanding PRC developments became the propensity of the system to make sudden and unexpected changes in direction.

The Deadening Effects of Ideological Conformity

The first such difficult intellectual adjustment came as the CCP made the transition from being an isolated Party in Yan'an, striving for power, to becoming the ruler of all of China, in a world that was also sharply divided ideologically. People who had been thinking in terms of "peasant reformers" were suddenly confronted with a dogmatic ideological movement. Mao's early declaration that China would "Lean to one side" in foreign affairs was matched by his cry for the Party to "Learn from the Soviet Union" domestically. The initial "younger brother–elder brother" relationship was set in place when Mao, barely two months after standing at Tiananmen and declaring the founding of the People's Republic, took off for a three-month visit to Moscow, not getting back until March 1950.[4] (The ideological significance of Mao's visit can be appreciated by imagining what Nehru's legitimacy as a Third World leader would have been if he had made such a prolonged visit to Washington immediately

4. We now know from Soviet and Chinese documents that for more than two years before Mao finally visited Moscow, he and Stalin had been in frequent communication about such a visit and that there had been nearly half a dozen suggested dates. Mao was anxious to go, but Stalin was hesitant for fear that the visit could not be kept secret and thus Mao would have been "named a Moscow agent." See Michael M. Sheng, *Battling Western Imperialism: Mao, Stalin and the United States* (Princeton: Princeton University Press, 1997), ch. 8.

after India's independence.) The adoption of the Soviet model extended from the introduction of the First Five-Year Plan to the practice of using the "unit" or *danwei* as the mechanism for social and political control of the urban population.

Today as we look back on 50 years of the PRC, it is clear that a dominant theme throughout its history has been the sovereign role of ideology. It was an unrelenting, mobilizing and disciplining force during the Mao era, and it has been something that the leaders of the reforms have not been able to abandon for all their reputed pragmatism. The land reform programme, which shook the countryside as the Party came to power, gave the rural people dramatic instruction in class warfare and the supreme importance of being ideologically "correct." The Three-Antis and the Five-Antis Campaigns then taught the city people that class identification and knowing the right ideological slogans would be critical in determining who would benefit and who would suffer under the new rulers. The learning experience, however, became even trickier in 1956 when Mao initiated the Hundred Flowers Campaign by calling upon the intellectuals to "bloom and contend" by expressing their criticisms, but when the response was not as flattering as the Chairman expected, the intellectuals were suddenly punished with the Anti-Rightist Campaign of 1957 which sent tens of thousands of China's best educated talent to rural labour, and paralysed China's intellectual life for more than three decades.

Although China's Confucian political culture had stressed the importance of ideological orthodoxy for the well-being of society, with Mao's rule the Chinese public discovered that ideology was now a matter of first importance in determining the individual's fate. Ideology now decreed that everyone had to be consigned to fixed categories according to his or her class background. This was more than a revival of the importance of family, which had been slowly eroding with the 20th-century advances of modernization. Now family background carried a class identification that was so strict that it created a virtual caste system. What one's father or even grandfather had been determined one's chances in life. When combined with all the social controls inherent in *danwei* membership, the life chances of Chinese became more restricted than at any time in their history. The anger at being so constrained exploded into the passionate battles of the Cultural Revolution.[5]

The sovereignty of ideology also meant that people had to join the mass movements of the day, and they could not opt out or take a passive view about what their leaders were declaring the ultimate truth of the

5. For an perceptive comparison of the economic roles of the traditional Chinese family and the "socialist family" (the *danwei*) of the PRC see Wang Fei-ling, *From Family to Market: Labor Allocation in Contemporary China* (Lanham, MD: Rowman & Littlefield, 1998). The evolving importance of the *danwei* is analysed in Xiaobo Lu and Elizabeth Perry (eds.), *Danwei: The Changing Chinese Workplace in Historical and Contemporary Perspective* (Armonk, NY: M.E. Sharpe, 1997). The anger and frustration over class background identifications which exploded in the Cultural Revolution is the central theme of Lynn T. White III, *Policies of Chaos: The Organizational Causes of Violence in China's Cultural Revolution* (Princeton: Princeton University Press, 1989).

moment to be. Initially it was thought that ideological conformity would guarantee security, but after the Hundred Flowers and the Great Leap Forward, people learned that the Party line could unexpectedly change, and those who had been the most conspicuous champions of abandoned positions could suffer punishment. The game thus changed, and people learned to hold in reserve their real thoughts and to act opportunistically according to changing circumstances.

Then came the Great Proletarian Cultural Revolution which forced nearly everyone to take positions and to clash with colleagues and neighbours in a mad struggle to be on the winning side and to avoid years of exile in the countryside. Mao's ultimate madness had devastating consequences for the Chinese public spirit. By the time the Gang of Four was arrested and Deng Xiaoping had opened the country to outside contacts, faith in the doctrines of Marxism-Leninism-Mao Zedong Thought had largely evaporated and cynicism reigned. But neither Deng nor his successor Jiang Zemin was prepared to abandon Marxism-Leninism as the only legitimate ideology for the Chinese people.

Thus, at its 50th anniversary the People's Republic of China still adheres to a single ideology, and the authorities in Beijing continue to demand that the Chinese people give at least lip service to that doctrine and make no attempts to challenge it. Fifty years of coping with an oppressive ideology has had profound consequences for China's public life. The stifling of spontaneity has produced a pathetically low intellectual level of public discourse. Intellectuals in particular have had to retreat into the security of their private worlds. Operating in an atmosphere in which openly expressing thoughts can have dangerous consequences has made self-censorship the norm for even the most established intellectuals. Consequently for half a century China's intellectual life has been one of the most vacuous and sterile in all the world. For more than two generations China has not produced any charismatic, creative thinkers. The repression of intellectual life has been particularly troublesome for China because of its great political tradition of scholar officials.

The relatively relaxed political mood of both Deng's and Jiang's rule has encouraged more and more professors and think-tank researchers to test the limits of freedom, and to exploit any hints of greater openness. Some, choosing co-optation, have put themselves into what the Hungarian writer Miklos Haraszti called the "velvet prison," accepting rewards from the authorities in return for performing internationally as respected intellectuals while not openly challenging or embarrassing the regime. Others have sought the patronage of powerful leaders who may have their reasons to disassociate themselves from the negative consequences of the "reforms" – such as the rise of corruption, economic insecurity and inequality – and who thus favour some criticisms of the current scene. Still other intellectuals are constantly engaged in subtle twisting of the words that the leadership uses, turning them to mean more than intended. Thus when Jiang Zemin at the 15th Party Congress of 1997 said, "we should promote democracy, improve the legal system and build a socialist country ruled by law," some intellectuals, anxious to push the boundaries, chose to ignore his following statement that the Four Cardinal Principles must continue to prevail. They began to write about the nature of the "rule of law," changing Jiang's term "rule by law" to "rule of law."[6] By artfully using quotations of Deng and even Mao, such intellectuals have exploited any possible opening in their efforts to break China out of its sterile bind of ideological conformity.

Although outside observers can rightfully welcome any and all signs of greater freedom in China, the continued prohibition of free public dialogue is having incalculably damaging consequences for China's national development. Marxism-Leninism-Mao Zedong Thought may have few true believers in China, but the continued insistence that it reigns as the official ideology prevents the Chinese people from getting on with the task of defining for themselves a new national identity.[7] China desperately needs a new public dialogue in order to give substance to a coherent and respectable spirit of nationalism. Having to pretend to a doctrine they do not respect causes the Chinese to be understandably hypersensitive to foreign criticisms. The Chinese today feel that they have not been getting the respect that is their due in the light of all the positive changes since the end of Mao's rule, but they are unable to articulate exactly what ideals, principles and values they believe their country stands for, and for which others should respect them.

Politics Confined to the State and Party Hierarchies

A second dominant theme in the history of the PRC, and closely associated with the problems of ideological orthodoxy, has been the constricted nature of politics which has had to operate within the confines of the two intertwined bureaucratic hierarchies of the Party and the state.[8] Indeed, the attempt to integrate a disciplined Party based on a binding ideology with a bureaucratically structured governmental apparatus set the stage for a very constrained form of politics revolving around inner Party struggles. The mass campaigns that produced ritualized popular participation never constituted real politics. Instead the combination of the imperative for secrecy, the denial of authority for technical specialists

6. Because of a quirk in their language, it is not surprising that the Chinese may have some difficulties distinguishing "rule by law" from "rule of law" since both are pronounced in Chinese in exactly the same way, with the same tones, *fa zhi shi*, but written with different characters. The word play in trying to change "rule by law" to "rule of law" was skilfully carried out by Li Shenzhi, former head of the Marxism-Leninism Institute of the Chinese Academy of Social Sciences, in his essay in *Political China: Facing the Era of Choosing a New Structure*, edited by Shi Binhai, senior editor of *The China Economic Times*, who was detained shortly after publication. (Reported by Erik Eckholm, "China's fine art: linguistic survival," *New York Times*, 20 September 1998.)

7. On the problems of Chinese national identity, see Lowell Dittmer and Samuel S. Kim, *China's Quest for National Identity* (Ithaca: Cornell University Press, 1993; and Jonathan Unger (ed.), *Chinese Nationalism* (Armonk, NY: M.E.Sharpe, 1996).

8. On the Chinese political system, see Kenneth Lieberthal, *Governing China: From Revolution Through Reform* (New York: W.W. Norton, 1985).

and the pretensions of a centralized bureaucracy limited what passed as national politics to relations among the top elite.

An atmosphere of fear, verging at times on terror, permeated all the recesses of elite politics. For the involved cadres the stakes were exceedingly high for any misstep could trigger terrifying punishment. Everyone was kept in line by intimidation.

The intimidating character of elite politics compelled the participants to use code words and Aesopean language in signalling power alignments and debating policy differences. Major shifts of policy were often initiated by no more than the cryptic utterances of the paramount ruler. Mao Zedong's statement that "Communes are good" was enough to set the whole countryside to work communizing their lives as cadres sought to carry out the Chairman's apparent wishes. Deng's utterance that "To get rich is glorious" and his January 1992 Southern Tour, during which he praised the Special Economic Zones, was enough to signal to the entire country that the economic reforms should be accelerated.

An early and lasting feature of the politics of fear under Mao was the purging of elite ranks through factional struggles.[9] Throughout Mao's rule high-level cadres knew that differences over policy and ideological emphasis could lead to career crises, and therefore security depended upon having a powerful patron and trusted associates. The Party ideals of conformity and consensus, however, made it a crime to have any personal relationships or special friendships. In theory everyone was everyone else's comrade.[10] Even within Zhongnanhai, the leadership compound, Politburo members did not engage in private socializing for fear of raising suspicions that they might be up to something. In the fearsome atmosphere it was impossible to live up to the ideal of comradeship. The cadres felt a compelling need for personal protection. With great care they created their private networks which became the power bases for political struggles. Factions thus became the power groupings for inner Party politics in defiance of the Party ideal. With the Cultural Revolution the existence of factions could no longer be denied, what with the publicized struggles between the "two lines" and then the attacks against the Gang of Four, and Hua Guofeng's "Whatever" faction.

The practice of building personal networks for personal security and advancement during the Mao era has continued into the less fear-filled reform period. What started when politics was in command, and led to factional strife, became under the new regime, with economics in command, the flagrant involvement of officials in the economy, often for personal gain. The skills developed in the operations of factional

9. On the role of factions in Chinese politics, see Andrew Nathan, "Policy oscillations in the People's Republic of China, a critique," *The China Quarterly*, No. 68 (1976), pp. 720–733; Lowell Dittmer, "Patterns of elite strife and succession in Chinese politics," *The China Quarterly*, No. 123 (1990), pp.405–430; Lucian W. Pye, *The Dynamics of Chinese Politics* (Cambridge, MA: Oelgeschlager, Gunn and Hain, 1981).

10. Ezra Vogel, "From friendship to comradeship: the change in personal relations in Communist China," in Roderick MacFarquhar (ed.), *China Under Mao: Politics Takes Command* (Cambridge, MA: MIT Press, 1969).

politics, and the informal norms of cadre behaviour, set the stage so that when the whole PRC system shifted towards stressing economic activities, the cadres' leadership skills and reputations left them still in charge. Although changes in the system as a whole have been dramatic, changes in the actual behaviour of officials has not been so great. Even when ideological politics dominated, the more successful cadres always got the best material benefits the country offered, for they could command the best housing, more perquisites, such as the use of the only cars in the country, and better schools for their children. With the reforms officials continue to exploit the advantages that political power offers in an economy that is semi-socialist, semi-capitalist. Officials who were the most secure in their informal networks, and who were the most skilled in wielding power, were also favourably positioned to obey Deng's decree that "To get rich is glorious." Party and state officials have not held back in helping themselves when "privatizing" state assets, or when establishing such "collectives" as the village and township enterprises (VTEs).[11] Although the Chinese public appears increasingly distressed over what it perceives to be a shocking rise in corruption, in actual fact during the presumed "purer" times of Mao's rule officials also benefited more than others in getting the best of what society had to offer. Thus, throughout the 50 years of the PRC the political elite has also been the economically advantaged.

Pragmatism, Blinded by Exuberance, Hits the Wall of Reality

With the passing of Mao and the arrival of Deng's reforms, there were high hopes that China would be able to break out of the grip of ideological conformity and elite bureaucratic politics. The country was ready for new ideas and pragmatic solutions to problems. The changes have indeed been astonishing, and for the masses of the Chinese people the first years of Deng's "reforms" did bring dramatic improvements in their lives. In the 20 years of the reforms 200 million people were lifted out of poverty, but 20 million still live below the line, which in 1995 was set at $95 a year.[12] At the same time the country was caught up in a spirited enjoyment of consumerism as families became the proud owners of washing machines, television sets, bicycles, and for some even cars. More than a million people in both Shanghai and Beijing carry around cellular phones. Tens of thousands of students have gone abroad to study. People who had been through hard times are convinced that their children will have far better lives. These social and economic changes have

---

11. For how the structure of incentives for local Party leaders produced the motivating force behind the highly successful VTEs, see Jean C. Oi, *Rural China Takes Off: The Institutional Foundations of Economic Reform* (Berkeley: University of California Press, 1998).

12. Deputy Prime Minister Wen Jiabao quoted in the *China Daily*, 19 October 1998. According to the World Bank's standards of $1 a day for measuring poverty, more than 200 million fall below the line.

provided space for the emergence of some nascent forms of civil society.[13]

The transition from a planned to a market economy has, however, also produced a host of winners and losers so that China has become increasingly a land of contradictions and inequalities. China is now characterized by both prosperous coastal cities and poverty-plagued interior provinces, rich entrepreneurs and masses of urban unemployed. Over time the economic problems have seemed to pile up, and there are no easy solutions in sight. President Jiang Zemin recognized that Deng did not have all the answers for the economy, and he thus called for "reforms within the reforms" with Prime Minister Zhu Rongji in charge.[14] Deng's great success was in eliminating the stifling agricultural communes and freeing the farmers to work for themselves. However, in spite of the improvements in agricultural production and the mushrooming of semi-collectively organized VTEs, there are over 120 million rural migrants flowing into China's over-crowded cities.[15] By October 1998, the problems of the rural economy were back at the top of the agenda so that at the plenum of the 15th Party Congress it was proposed that the state should help with marketing and support services, a retreat in the abandonment of socialism.

The urban scene has undergone a dramatic cosmetic make-over, as fancy hotels and skyscrapers have been hurriedly erected, financed largely by Overseas Chinese capital. Yet all is not well, for the construction has been driven by a troubling real estate bubble. In the Pudong area of Shanghai cranes are to be seen everywhere, but buildings finished in 1997 have only 20 per cent occupancy. Indeed, behind the glitter of the urban construction, the Chinese economy is plagued with massive problems as the transition to a market economy is far from complete. Of the registered urban population, over 65 per cent still work for the state in one way or another, 45 per cent in state industries and another 20 per cent in government offices. The intractability of the huge, inefficient state-owned enterprises, and a state-run banking system more debt-ridden than any in Asia, means that China is moving towards economic crisis.[16] Instead of the second round of reforms solving the difficulties, the problems have only intensified, so that by 1998 the four leading banks had non-performing loans that were 25 to 40 per cent of their total loans, and only 0.7 per cent of the total credit available in China was going to

13. Deborah Davis *et al.* (eds.), *Urban Spaces in Contemporary China* (New York: Cambridge University Press, 1995); and Arthur Lewis Rosenbaum (ed.), *State and Society in China: The Consequences of Reform* (Boulder: Westview Press, 1992).

14. For an appraisal of the post-Deng leadership see Bruce Gilley, *Tiger on the Brink: Jiang Zemin and China's New Elite* (Berkeley: University of California Press, 1998).

15. On the increasing problems of the reforms in rural China, see Scott Rozelle, "Stagnation without equity: patterns of growth and inequality in China's rural economy," *The China Journal*, Issue 35 (January 1996), pp. 63–92.

16. The crisis of the state-owned enterprises is well analysed in Edward S. Steinfeld, *Forging Reform in China: The Fate of State-Owned Industry* (New York: Cambridge University Press, 1998). Nicholas Lardy has detailed the appalling problems of the banking system in *China's Unfinished Economic Revolution* (Washington D.C.: Brookings Institution Press, 1998).

private firms. The extraordinary high savings rate of the Chinese people – nearly 40 per cent – provides nearly 60 per cent of the banks' assets, amounting to $600 billion in deposits, but constituting liabilities the banks could not possibly meet if there should be even a minor run on them.[17] There is no judging how long this state of affairs can continue. Foreign bankers were shocked in early 1999 when the government allowed Gitic (Guangdong International Trust and Investment Corporation), with $4.5 billion in debts, to go into bankruptcy without favouring its international creditors.[18]

Faced with the danger that China would be the next to be caught up in the Asian economic crisis, Zhu Rongji has had to pull back from his initial plan to eliminate 50 per cent of the people in both the state and the Party bureaucracies. The urban situation was grim enough with rising unemployment stemming from people who thought that they had life-time jobs being dismissed from the faltering state enterprises. If their ranks were to be swelled by dismissed officials and cadres, who thought that they were part of the elite and who have shown leadership skills, the conditions for political instability could become ominous. The slowdown has left uncertain when or how the reforms will be completed. The leadership as a group is torn in two directions: it knows that it has serious problems and that action is called for, but at the same time it is timid in moving for fear of losing power. Zhongnanhai can thus be described as a hot-bed of cold feet.

Instead of unqualified support for further reforms, the Jiang regime, with heightened concern for its monopoly on power, has reverted to contradictory policy vacillations. In the first half of 1998 there was a conspicuous relaxing of controls and even some tolerance for unorthodox and critical views. The signs of increased freedom gave new life to the intellectual, artistic and publishing circles.[19] Books critical of official corruption and calling for democracy were for sale, and a fledgling China Democracy Party was allowed to organize quietly. But then in the autumn, repression suddenly returned with the authorities declaring the Democratic Party illegal and arresting and sentencing its three most prominent members – Xu Wenli, Qin Yongmin and Wang Youcai – to prison terms of more than ten years. In early January 1999, the Propaganda Department closed down some book publishers and newspapers, and sent warning signals for scholars to be less openly critical. Yet the regime was not prepared to become as repressive as it had been after Tiananmen, and thus in a contradictory way it allowed new leaders of the Democratic Party to plan national meetings.

In sum, the regime is still groping to find a formula for solving China's massive problems of both economic and political modernization. Thus,

17. "China's economy," *The Economist*, 24 October 1998, p.26.
18. "Bankruptcy the Chinese way," *New York Times*, 22 January 1999. The collapse of Gitic was followed in less than a month by the closing of five other leading investment trust corporations.
19. Geremie Barmé, *In the Red: Contemporary China Culture* (New York: Columbia University Press, 1999).

after a half century of heroic efforts and massive human sacrifices, China is today, in a fundamental sense, back to where it was in 1949, or even earlier in 1911, in the sense that the country is still in search of a modern national identity which can combine elements of its great traditional civilization with features of modernity. The road down which Mao and the CCP took China turned out to have been a disastrous one. Now China must desperately try to catch up to where it once was and to where it rightfully should be. In spite of the dramatic economic growth that came with Deng's initial reforms, China's economy rests on rocky foundations, and the country is still without a clear collective sense of direction. The task of building a modern economy and society out of the ruins of communism is a daunting one as can be seen from the pathetic condition of Russia, and from the fact that East Germany, with all the help it has received from a prosperous West Germany, still lags far behind. The Chinese officials know the problems the country faces, but in their urgency they are still prone to pin hopes on grandiose solutions which are bound to fail.[20]

Thus on the occasion of the 50th anniversary of the regime it is impossible to foresee whether China is heading in the direction of more liberal public life, or whether it will turn down a blind, nationalistic path which would again cut the country off from full participation in world affairs. Civil society is gradually forming; increased education has produced an enlightened middle class; awareness of the standards of the outside world has touched the urban masses; rural and village people have been learning the practices of local elections; and the National People's Congress is no longer an unqualified rubber stamp – all developments that hold out hope for the country. But unfortunately the historic record of China's modernization efforts calls for the reining in of optimism and the adoption of what may be called a "cautiously pessimistic" position. The impressive responses of the Chinese people to the openings that came in the post-Mao era prove that they are capable of producing a modern society and polity, if it were not for the autocratic tendencies of their leaders. The Chinese also have a great tradition of muddling through, of seeking out a method (*xiang banfa*), of accepting what is approximately correct (*chabuduo*), and of living with a host of contradictions. Things are never as black or white, as good or as bad, as Westerners tend to expect them to be. Yet, there is no escaping the horrendous problems China faces with its only partially transformed economy. China must still go through many difficult days before it can achieve its long-sought goal of becoming a fully modern nation-state.

---

20. For example, State Councilor Wu Yi announced an infrastructure programme to meet the massive deficiencies in transportation and power generation, and also to stimulate the economy, but for which he gave a totally unrealistic figure of 10 trillion *yuan* ($1.2 trillion) for the years 1998 to 2000, a sum that would be equal to about 40% of the cumulative gross domestic products for those years. Nicholas Lardy, "China chooses growth today, reckoning tomorrow," *Asian Wall Street Journal*, 30 September 1998.

The People's Republic of China at 50: National Political Reform*

John P. Burns

After 50 years of revolutionary transformation and uneven consolidation, and a generation of economic re-structuring, the political institutions of the People's Republic of China remain essentially Leninist. The Chinese Communist Party (CCP) continues to enjoy monopoly power, and independent media, autonomous trade unions and other manifestations of civil society are almost wholly absent. Yet the environment within which the Party now operates has changed fundamentally. Marxist-Leninist parties in power around the world have collapsed and to stay in power the CCP has abandoned central planning for market economics. Living standards and literacy rates have improved dramatically and ordinary people now have more control over their own lives. Some analysts have suggested that as a result of these changes, the regime is facing imminent institutional collapse.[1] Others have suggested that the regime cannot but democratize.[2] This article argues that the regime is more resilient than either of these interpretations allows. In spite of the formal trappings of Leninism and its neo-authoritarian political reform programme, the CCP has adapted to the new situation. The reforms, which date from the early 1980s, have considerably strengthened the country's political institutions. Although there is disagreement on the content and pace of reform, China's elite with few exceptions appears to agree that further political reform is necessary. Yet the Party is caught in a dilemma: if it moves too slowly, it could fail because it cannot meet the demands of the people; if it moves too quickly, it could fail because it further undermines its already weakened position.

Characteristics of China's Leninist Polity

After 50 years of CCP rule, China's political system continues to exhibit the characteristics of a mature Leninist state. According to the 1982 state constitution, Party rule is legitimized by the "four basic

* The author gratefully acknowledges the help of Michael Schoenhals, David Shambaugh and other participants attending the Aveiro Workshop and the support of the Hong Kong Research Grants Council and the University of Hong Kong in the production of this article.
1. See especially, Pei Minxin, *From Reform to Revolution: The Demise of Communism in China and the Soviet Union* (Cambridge, MA: Harvard University Press, 1994). See also Zheng Shiping, *Party vs. State in Post-1949 China: The Institutional Dilemma* (Cambridge: Cambridge University Press, 1997). Andrew Walder writes of the party-state's political decline brought about by the CCP's abandonment of the command economy on which Leninist party rule was based. See Andrew Walder, "The quiet revolution from within: economic reform as a source of political decline," in Andrew Walder (ed.), *The Waning of the Communist State: Economic Origins of Political Decline in China and Hungary* (Berkeley: University of California Press, 1995), pp. 1–26.
2. See, for example, Edward Friedman, *National Identity and Democratic Prospects in Socialist China* (Armonk, NY: M.E. Sharpe, 1995).

principles." Chief among these is the principle that asserts the hegemony of the CCP. Others continue to define the state as a people's democratic dictatorship, the economy as socialist, and the defining ideology as Marxism-Leninism-Mao Zedong Thought. These values, which champion organizational concepts such as democratic centralism and the mass line, resonate with the language of 1940s and 1950s Party documents. There have been some modifications, but they have been relatively minor.[3] Thus in 1987, then Party Secretary General Zhao Ziyang re-characterized China's economic system as being in "the primary stage of socialism," a move that permitted the Party to introduce market-oriented policies, protect private property and encourage private entrepreneurship to develop the economy. Still, 50 years on, China's constitution continues to legitimize a monist political system, formally recognizing the hegemony of the CCP. Moreover the Party continues to repress all attempts to organize challenges to its authority.

As it was by the mid-1950s, the CCP today remains relatively small and coherent. First, it continues to be an elite rather than a mass party. In 1998, it had 62 million members, or approximately 5 per cent of the total population. Although Party membership has grown as a percentage of the population (0.83 per cent, 1.7 per cent and 2.2 per cent of the population in 1949, 1956 and 1959 respectively[4]), the relative size of the Party has been kept deliberately small. Membership continues to be very selective. Surveys indicate that it continues to be highly sought after,[5] although perhaps not as much as it was in 1949–50. Secondly, evidence of the Party's discipline in 1998 was its ability to ensure that its nominees were elected to national and local government and people's congress posts in more than 98 per cent of cases.[6] Party discipline may have declined in recent times, undermined for example by corruption. Still, given its vast size, in comparative terms the CCP is still relatively tightly disciplined.[7] Indeed, in 1999 it may be more disciplined than it was in the early 1950s, flush with victory and absorbing huge numbers of new recruits.[8]

The organization of the Party bureaucracy has also remained fundamentally unchanged for more than 50 years. First, the system that centralizes power in the Politburo and in territorial Party secretaries and their committees continues unchanged. Secondly, the Central Committee and local territorial committees continue to set up general offices and

3. See *Wenhui bao* (Hong Kong) 16 January 1999.

4. Ying-Mao Kau, "Patterns of recruitment and mobility of urban cadres," in John W. Lewis (ed.), *The City in Communist China* (Stanford: Standford University Press, 1971), p. 109.

5. See a survey conducted among university students in Shanghai, in which 81% expressed a desire to apply for Party membership. Xinhua, 12 May 1998, in Foreign Broadcast Information Service, *Daily Report – China* (FBIS-CHI-98-132), 12 May 1998.

6. Xinhua, 2 August 1998, FBIS-CHI-98-223, 11 August 1998.

7. There have been significant lapses of Party discipline, usually associated with leadership disputes, such as during the Cultural Revolution.

8. In 1949 the party grew by 50%. Growth rates declined in 1950 and 1951 (to 11 and 16% respectively) but they were still high. Only in 1952 in the wake of severe discipline problems did the CCP cut back recruitment to 4%. It shot up again in 1954 to 23%. Zheng Shiping, *Party vs. State*, p. 268.

organization, propaganda and united front work departments.[9] The functions of these departments have also remained remarkably constant although the scope of their authority has varied with periodic decentralization and re-centralization. The structure of provincial Party committees in the late 1980s, for example, closely resembled committees set up in the mid-1950s.[10] From 1952 to 1996, although the state went through six major rounds of restructuring (mainly streamlining), the impact of the reforms was relatively modest and in no sense did they change the character of Party or state institutions.[11]

Thirdly, authorities continue to rely on decision-making and policy-implementing institutions, such as Party leading small groups.[12] The leadership system within the Party continues to give primacy to Party secretaries and higher level territorial committees. Formally, the Party continues to value collective leadership and democratic centralism. That is, there appears to have been relatively little organizational innovation or re-invention of the CCP.

Since 1949, the CCP has maintained itself in power through its control over leadership selection in all strategic groups and control of the military. The fundamental principle of personnel administration laid down in the 1920s that "the Party manages cadres" has continued to guide organization work since 1949. The 1990 Central Committee *nomenklatura* lists, the most recent ones available to me, reveal that the Party continues to rule through its control of leadership selection not only of government agencies at all administrative levels but of the legislature, judiciary, the military, strategic economic enterprises, the media and mass organizations such as the All-China Federation of Trade Unions.[13] Recent evidence, such as the appointment of Li Changchun as Party secretary in Guangdong, indicates that the Party's power of appointment continues to be effective. The broad scope of its personnel authority is typical of Leninist parties in power. Similarly, its control of the People's Liberation Army is exercised through institutions[14] headed by Party Secretary General Jiang Zemin.

The Party's method of rule has changed since the 1950s. No longer

9. See Kenneth Lieberthal, *Governing China: From Revolution through Reform* (New York: Norton, 1995), pp. 155–182 for a discussion of the Party's formal organization. Party committees also routinely established investigation departments until 1983 (thanks to David Shambaugh).

10. Shanghai shi bianzhi weiyuanhui bangongshi (ed.), *Shanghai dang zheng jigou yange (Evolution of Shanghai Party and Government Organizations)* (Shanghai: Shanghai renmin chubanshe, 1988), pp. 69–70 and 207. See also Zheng Shiping, *Party vs. State*, pp. 86–88.

11. Liu Zhifeng (ed.), *Di-qi zi gaige: 1998. Zhongguo zhengfu jigou gaige beiwanlu (The Seventh Reform: Background to the 1998 Organization Reform of the Chinese Government)* (Beijing: Jingji ribao chubanshe, 1998). According to Liu, earlier reforms occurred in 1952–53, 1958–59, 1960–65, 1982, 1988 and 1993.

12. The role of the CCP Secretariat has changed, however.

13. J. P. Burns, "Strengthening central CCP control of leadership selection: the 1990 nomenklatura," *The China Quarterly*, No. 138 (June 1994), pp. 458–491.

14. Such as Party committees in the PLA, the General Political Department and the discipline inspection system. See David Shambaugh. "The soldier and the state in China: the political work system in the People's Liberation Army," *The China Quarterly*, No. 127 (September 1991), pp. 527–568.

able to rely on the charisma of Mao Zedong and ideological campaigns (see Michael Schoenhals' contribution), both of which were severely discredited during the Cultural Revolution, the current leadership has relied on a mix of remunerative and coercive incentives on the one hand, and patriotism on the other. More rational bureaucratic rule has replaced campaigns.

After 50 years of rule, the Party shows no more tolerance of opposition than it did in the 1950s although the methods used to silence dissent may have changed somewhat. The December 1998 sentencing to long prison terms of Wang Youcai, Xu Wenli and Qin Yongmin, organizers of a fledgling opposition, the China Democratic Party, for trying to overthrow the state is a case in point. The state has also punished labour activists such as Zhang Shanguang for trying to set up an autonomous trade union and has banned on the mainland books such as *Political China: Facing the Era of Choosing a New Structure*[15] that discuss the need for and prospects of political reform. The authorities have relied more on the law to deal with these cases than secretive administrative or police measures, which probably were more common in the 1950s. In another departure from previous practice, since the 1980s a growing number of dissidents such as Wang Dan and Wei Jingsheng have been exiled. That is, although the methods used to combat dissent and opposition may have changed, the Party is still firmly committed to maintaining its hegemonic position.

In many fundamental respects, then, China's political system remains wedded to its Leninist origins. Yet, the environment in which it operates is now much less supportive of this kind of political system.

The Changing Environment

Both China's external and internal environments have changed substantially since 1949. During the last decade, change has been especially significant in the external environment. First, the collapse of Leninist parties in the Soviet Union and Eastern Europe robbed the CCP of allies and some legitimacy. This development underscored the importance of appropriately handling the relationship between economic and political reform and probably re-enforced the leadership's view that any political reform programme must suit China's national characteristics, that is, preserve the monopoly position of the CCP.[16] Secondly, the Party's decision to integrate China's economy with the world economy not only boosted economic development but opened up the country to new sources of information and managerial technologies, and contributed to the pluralization of Chinese society.[17] Thirdly, the diffusion of modern

15. See *SCMP*, 1 November 1998 for a list of banned titles.
16. See, for example, Jiang Zemin's report to the 15th Party Congress, summarized in Xinhua, 11 September 1997, FBIS-CHI-97-254, 12 September 1997.
17. See the literature on emerging civil society in reformist China. Gordon White, *Riding the Tiger: The Politics of Economic Reform in Post-Mao China* (Stanford: Stanford University Press, 1993), ch. 8, and Jude Howell, *China Opens Its Doors: The Politics of Economic Transition* (London: Lynne Rienner, 1993).

technology has meant that virtually every urban household and over 90 per cent of rural households now own a television set[18] and that more than 2 million computers are linked to the internet.[19] With this has come exposure to new ideas that has made governing China more complex. Finally, based largely on its successful economic development, as Michael Yahuda's contribution shows, China has emerged as a major player on the world scene that must be taken seriously by the United States and other world powers. The country's new international position has undoubtedly reinforced the leadership's self confidence that it can effectively manage affairs of state both at home and abroad.

The internal environment has also changed dramatically during the last 50 years. First, as a result of 20 years of economic reform, the country has witnessed years of high economic growth and rising living standards.[20] Indeed, it is probably true to say that a new middle class is emerging, composed of entrepreneurs and professionals, especially in China's cities. Secondly, China has also undergone rapid urbanization and industrialization. Thus from 1952 to 1997 China's total population living in cities grew from about 12 to 30 per cent,[21] while the number of people engaged in agriculture has fallen from 70.5 per cent in 1978 to 47.5 per cent in 1997.[22] Finally, literacy rates have also risen sharply during the last two decades.[23]

These rapid changes have placed many more resources in the hands of ordinary people. They are freer to live where they like,[24] choose their own occupation, buy goods and services from a variety of public and private providers, and travel. Indeed, managing China's new "mobile population," estimated at some 80 million people, has become a new and major pre-occupation of the state.[25] The state continues to try to control what people may publish and read, with whom they may associate, and under what conditions they may speak in public.

The last two decades of economic restructuring have been accompanied by considerable dislocation. First, they have resulted in rising unemployment (officially put at 3 per cent of the urban work force,[26] but unofficially estimated to be as high as 20 per cent). Secondly, the reforms have also been accompanied by a huge increase in the incidence of corruption.[27] Other sources of discontent include enterprises failing to pay

18. State Statistical Bureau, *China Statistical Yearbook 1998* (Beijing: China Statistical Publishing House, 1998), p. 324.
19. *SCMP*, 18 January 1999. See also Xinhua, 15 January 1999.
20. *China Statistical Yearbook 1998*, p. 324.
21. *Ibid.* p. 105.
22. *Ibid.* p. 132.
23. *SCMP*, 25 November 1998.
24. On the relaxation of the household registration system, see *Zhongguo qingnian bao* (*China Youth*), No. 1 (January 1997), in FBIS-CHI-97-046, 1 January 1997.
25. See *Renkou yu jingji* (*Population and Economy*), No. 101 (25 March 1997), in FBIS-CHI-97-121, 25 March 1997.
26. *China Statistical Yearbook 1998*, p. 127.
27. *Liaowang* (*Outlook*), No. 4 (26 January 1998), in FBIS-CHI-98-057, 26 February 1998.

or providing too little wages, pensions or severance pay; the growing gap between the rich and poor;[28] arbitrary and increasing taxes and levies imposed mainly by rural local governments; and families displaced by urban renewal projects and commercial developments without adequate compensation, often in collusion with local government officials. Still, according to a survey carried out by the State Economic Structure Reform Commission in 1997, some 83.9 per cent of urban residents approved of the reforms, although only 65.9 per cent were satisfied with their results.[29]

People have expressed their discontent to government officials through a variety of means, both legal and illegal. On the one hand, they have attempted to present their case to officials through existing channels, such as local leaders, people's congresses, the media and official trade unions. When formal legal channels failed, people have turned to other methods of protest. By the late 1990s protest demonstrations and violence were becoming more commonplace throughout China.[30] Protesters demanded compensation for stock swindles, reduced fees and taxes, the elimination of corruption, increased compensation for giving up their housing, abandonment of enterprise privatization, and payment of stipends for laid-off workers. For all of 1997, officials reported that farmers had engaged in more than 10,000 cases of "unruly incidents" ranging from demonstrations and petitions to efforts to surround and damage government offices.[31] The Party has reacted to these incidents with a renewed call for stability. Indeed, by the end of 1998, stability had once again become the single most important goal of the Party leadership.

Political Reform

China's leaders have recognized the need for political reform of some kind since 1952. In the 1950s and early 1960s, the Party attempted to re-structure the state on several occasions, and to establish a system of people's congresses, provide for basic-level elections and establish legal institutions.[32] In the wake of the Cultural Revolution, Deng Xiaoping put political reform on the Party's agenda in 1980. By then it came to mean reform of the leadership system, constitutional reform and the creation of

28. *Gongren ribao* (*Workers Daily*), 10 December 1997, in FBIS-CHI-98-042, 11 February 1998 and *Renkou yu jingji*, No. 107 (25 March 1998), in FBIS-CHI-98-174, 23 June 1998.

29. Reported in *Zhongguo qingnian bao*, 13 February 1998, in FBIS-CHI-98-160, 9 June 1998.

30. See *Ming bao* (Hong Kong), 7 June 1998, in FBIS-CHI-98-159, 8 June 1998; *SCMP*, 12 November 1998, 8 November 1998, 10 November 1998, 15 October 1998, 2 October 1998, 22 November 1998; *Zhengming*, No. 243 (1 January 1998) in FBIS-CHI-98-135, 15 May 1998; and Hong Kong AFP, 7 September 1998, in FBIS-CHI-98-250, 7 September 1998.

31. *SCMP*, 8 November 1998.

32. See James R. Townsend, *Political Participation in Communist China* (Berkeley: University of California Press, 1969), pp. 103–144. During the Cultural Revolution authorities re-structured the State Council and established revolutionary committees.

new institutions within the CCP to supervise discipline.[33] It was again on the agenda in 1986 and 1987. During the 13th Party Congress then Party Secretary General Zhao Ziyang called for the establishment of a new civil service system, separating the functions of the Party and government, further perfecting the people's congress system, and strengthening the rule of law.[34] A decade later, during the 15th Party Congress, Jiang Zemin again placed political reform on the Party's agenda, retreating somewhat from earlier proposals.[35] His proposals included: further development of democracy within the system of people's congresses and in co-operation with the democratic parties; strengthening the legal system; restructuring government to separate it from economic enterprises; streamlining government departments and agencies and improving the civil service system; and improving the system of democratic supervision.[36] Not surprisingly, at no time have Party authorities considered any proposals that would have threatened the CCP's monopoly position. Official calls for reform were punctuated by the pro-democracy and anti-corruption protests of 1978–79, 1981, 1986 and 1989. During these years the Party's attention turned from reform to repression.

The Impact of Political Reform

China's economic reforms and the CCP's on-again, off-again approach to political reform have had an impact on the country's political institutions. There are clear signs that the political system has adapted to the new circumstances and that China's political system is becoming increasingly institutionalized. Institutionalization here means increased structural differentiation, more regularized decision-making processes and more state autonomy from society.

Adaptation can be said to have occurred in two different arenas: internal and external. Internal adaptation[37] has happened in the following areas: the backgrounds of Party members; the characteristics of the leadership; the incentive systems and selection criteria for the bureaucracy; and reform of the legal system. The impetus for these came from elite shock at the consequences of the Cultural Revolution and the obvious need to find successors. External adaptation refers to the extent to which interaction between state and society has changed. External adaptation has occurred in the following areas: people's congresses and

33. Deng Xiaoping, "On the reform of the system of Party and state leadership" (18 August 1980), in Deng Xiaoping, *Selected Works of Deng Xiaoping 1975–1982* (Beijing: Foreign Languages Press, 1984), pp. 302–325.

34. Zhao Ziyang, "Advance along the road of socialism with Chinese characteristics," *Beijing Review*, No. 30, Vol. 45 (9–15 November 1987) (insert).

35. Xinhua, 12 September 1997, in FBIS-CHI-97-254, 12 September 1997. In the wake of the 4 June 1989 episode, the Party abandoned "separating Party and government functions" and revised its proposals for separate management methods for "political" and "professional" civil servants.

36. Xinhua, 12 September 1997, in FBIS-CHI-97-254, 12 September 1997.

37. See Bruce Dickson, *Democratization in China and Taiwan: The Adaptability of Leninist Parties* (London: Oxford University Press, 1997).

political participation; trade unions and mass organizations; non-state social and political groups; and the media. Less progress at institutionalizing change has been made in this arena, however.

Internal adaptation: changing Party member backgrounds. The background of Party members has changed substantially over the past 50 years. In the mid-1950s, for example, peasants still formed over 60 per cent of Party membership. They were recruited mostly during mass campaigns, which heavily relied on political criteria such as class background. Generally, they had a low level of education and lacked specialized knowledge.[38] In 1979, on the eve of the reform era, approximately half the CCP's then 37 million members had joined the Party during the Cultural Revolution era (1966–76).[39] During those years the Party recruited from among poor peasants and urban workers and emphasized the values of class struggle, egalitarianism, public ownership, central planning, and reliance on normative and coercive incentives. Indeed these values were present already by the mid-1950s. By 1998, another 20 million Party members had been recruited from more diverse social backgrounds using decidedly different criteria that emphasized economic development, some people getting rich first, mixed modes of ownership, reliance on market forces and remunerative incentives. The nature of the Party's values have changed as a result, legitimized by new ideologies. Many current local leaders joined after the Cultural Revolution.

Although whether private entrepreneurs should be admitted has been controversial during the reform era, apparently a growing number of China's wealthy business elite have managed to join the CCP. Business members of the National People's Congress and the Chinese People's Political Consultative Conference have also increased. Indeed, 80 private businessmen and women were delegates to the Ninth NPC. Research into the behaviour of China's business elite indicates that becoming a Party member is perceived by them to be an important avenue of success.[40]

Leadership rejuvenation. When the fourth generation of leaders takes over from Jiang Zemin, the founding father generation, which has so dominated Chinese politics, will have completely passed from the scene. Because no single leader will have the authority of either Mao Zedong or Deng Xiaoping, who dominated the political scene from the mid-1950s to 1997, the pressure to maintain collective leadership at the top will grow.[41] However, China's leaders have made little progress in institutionalizing collective leadership. Leaders are still chosen through a secretive process

38. Hong Yung Lee, *From Revolutionary Cadres to Party Technocrats in Socialist China* (Berkeley: University of California Press, 1991), pp. 56-57.

39. Zheng Shiping, *Party vs. State*, p. 268.

40. See Richard Robison and David S.G. Goodman (eds.), *New Rich in Asia: Mobile Phones, McDonalds, and Middle Class Revolution* (London: Routledge, 1996).

41. See *Zhengming*, No. 255 (1 October 1998), in FBIS-CHI-98-290, 17 October 1998, which argues that collective leadership was "harmonious" in mid-1998.

that depends heavily on factional political alignments and not on elections.

Political reform has, however, improved the quality of China's leaders. The third and fourth generations are as young as the leaders who took power in the 1950s, reversing a trend towards older leaders that character-ized the 1960s and 1970s. Beginning in 1980, but especially since 1982, the Party abolished the life tenure system for Party and government functionaries.[42] Current leaders are also much better educated and much better informed about the world than those of two decades ago.[43] By the 1990s, most leaders had spent their youth in school and although school-ing was interrupted during the Cultural Revolution, education credentials have become important since 1980. Political reform has undoubtedly increased the capacity of China's leaders.

Bureaucratic rejuvenation. Political reform has brought several significant changes to the bureaucracy. First, with civil service reform the CCP disaggregated "state cadres" into a business elite, government officials and employees of not-for-profit institutions. Different manage-ment methods are being developed for each sector. Separate incentive systems are also in operation, so much so that becoming a government official is now considerably less materially attractive than previously,[44] especially for those living in China's coastal areas. Secondly, since 1993 civil servants in China have once again been selected through open competitive examinations. This is designed in part to raise the quality of the civil service and in part to demonstrate to the public that civil service jobs are only available through open competition and not through per-sonal connections (*guanxi*) or "the back door."[45] These changes should improve the quality of the civil service.

While authorities were attempting to reform the personnel system, perennial abuses continued to emerge. For example, from 1996 to 1998 the press published numerous cases of officials selling government jobs.[46]

42. Melanie Manion, *Retirement of Revolutionaries in China: Public Policies, Social Norms, Private Interests* (Princeton: Princeton University Press, 1993).

43. Li Cheng and Lynn T. White III, "Elite transformation and modern change in mainland China and Taiwan: empirical data and the theory of technocracy," *The China Quarterly*, No. 121 (March 1990), p. 15.

44. In one random sample survey carried out in Nanjing, respondents were asked to rank occupations according to prestige. Civil servants ranked 24th out of 50 occupations. The top positions went to university teachers, mathematicians, middle school teachers, engineers, doctors, architects and so forth. Individual traders (*getihu*) and prostitutes scored at the bottom. *Shehui*, No. 1 (January 1997), p. 8. Other surveys, such as one carried out among Peking University students in 1997, indicated that 27% of respondents hoped to work for "Party or government units," 23% for joint venture enterprises (*sanzi qiye*), 13% for institutes of higher learning, 10% for research institutes, 8% for state-owned enterprises, and 1% for middle schools. A further 16% were reported as "other." *Zhongguo qingnian bao*, 5-10 June 1997.

45. Interview, Ministry of Personnel, 22 July 1996.

46. *Liaowang*, No. 10 (March 1997), in FBIS-CHI-97-071, 10 March 1997; *Renmin ribao*, 24 March 1998, in FBIS-CHI-98-097, 7 April 1998 Xinhua, 23 June 1998, in FBIS-CHI-98-179, 28 June 1998; *Renmin ribao*, 17 January 1996, in FBIS-CHI-96-034, 17 January 1996; and *SCMP*, 22 September 1998. The problem is so serious that it has received Politburo

Corruption at unprecedented levels in the history of the People's Republic has further undermined the legitimacy of the regime. Although thus far only one Politburo member (Chen Xitong) has been convicted of corruption, and political infighting was probably as much a factor in this case, corruption allegations have reached to the vice-minister or vice-governor level.[47] Tens of thousands of cases of corruption are reported and investigated each year and the numbers are growing.[48] Corruption especially at local level remains a serious problem that has undoubtedly undermined attempts to rejuvenate the bureaucracy.

As China moves towards a market economy, its civil service must assume the position of a neutral regulator. This is a new role for China's government officials, entirely unheard of since 1949. Reformers have taken steps to implement civil service neutrality by forbidding them to engage in business (although their relatives are not so controlled) and, more recently, by requiring civil servants at and above deputy county (section) level to declare their assets and business dealings.[49] Authorities have also sought to boost neutrality by rotating leading civil servants once every five years.[50] The extent to which these regulations have been implemented is unknown.

If China's six attempts to streamline central and local government since 1952 have largely failed,[51] the more important policy of changing the functions of the state to suit a market economy has met with some success. Indeed, by 1999 the functions of the state had witnessed significant change. For example, the state has taken on market regulatory functions that are entirely new, in organizations such as the China Securities Regulatory Commission, set up to regulate the country's stock and futures markets. Major reforms of the banking system, and insurance and social security system are also under way.

Legal reform. China's political system is still based on personal rule rather than on the rule of law.[52] However, since 1979, legal reform has continued. From 1979 to 1997, China enacted 311 laws, and issued 700 sets of regulations and 4,000 sets of administrative rules covering a wide range of political, economic and social activities.[53] Among these, rules on the regulation of securities and futures markets, consumer protection, intellectual property, banking and insurance are almost entirely new. Institutions to enforce the regulations have also been established. Al-

---

footnote continued

attention. See *Ming bao* (Hong Kong), 28 October 1998, in FBIS-CHI-98-301, 28 October 1998.

47. See the case of Guangdong's Yu Fei in *Xin bao* (Hong Kong), 16 October 1998, in FBIS-CHI-98-296, 23 October 1998.

48. *Liaowang*, No. 4 (25 January 1998), in FBIS-CHI-98-057, 26 February 1998.

49. Xinhua, 24 March 1997, in FBIS-CHI-97-083, 24 March 1997.

50. Xinhua, 7 August 1996, in FBIS-CHI-96-162, 7 August 1996.

51. See J.P. Burns, "Restructuring the Chinese government: 1993–1996: a preliminary assessment" (unpublished paper).

52. According to one view attributed to Lord Dicey, the rule of law means that the state is treated as just another actor.

53. Xinhua, 31 March 1997, in FBIS-CHI-97-139, 19 May 1997.

though the number of lawyers practising in China has increased substantially (there were 8,265 law firms and 100,200 practising lawyers in 1997[54]) they still fall short of the 150,000 the state estimates are required.[55] New laws, such as the State Compensation Law, enacted in 1995, give citizens the right to sue the state, and these are being used with increasing regularity. According to a survey carried out in 1997, people are not satisfied with the extent to which others in society "have the habit of operating within the law."[56]

As Pitman Potter's contribution shows, China has made some progress towards institutionalizing the legal system. First, specialist competencies in legal drafting have been developed within the National People's Congress and the Legislative Affairs Office of the State Council.[57] As a result, the comprehensiveness and quality of Chinese law have undoubtedly improved. Secondly, political leaders have made reform of the judiciary a high priority. Policies include improving the quality of judges (only since 1983 were they required to have "legal professional knowledge"[58]), making judicial proceedings more transparent,[59] curbing judicial corruption, and prohibiting judicial, procuratorial and public security departments from engaging in business.[60] These measures, still not implemented, are aimed at improving the impartiality of the judiciary. Because local authorities appoint local judges, the judiciary continues in many cases to protect local interests at the expense of justice.[61] As the importance of the law in dispute resolution has increased, enforcing judicial decisions has become more difficult.[62]

External adaptation: people's congresses and political participation. The system of people's congresses, set up in 1954, has remained fundamentally unaltered to the present day. People's congress membership is screened through the Party's *nomenklatura* system, control that continues to be effective. Only Party authorities may convene the congresses, a principle the CCP re-emphasized during the 4 June 1989 disturbances. As a result, people's congresses in their own right continue to be unable to

54. Xinhua, 31 March 1997, in FBIS-CHI-97-139, 19 May 1997.
55. *SCMP*, 6 January 1994.
56. Survey carried out in urban areas by the State Economic Structure Reform Commission and reported in *Zhongguo qingnian bao*, 13 February 1998, in FBIS-CHI-98-160, 9 June 1998.
57. See M. Scott Tanner, "The erosion of Communist Party control over lawmaking in China," *The China Quarterly*, No. 138 (June 1994), pp. 381-403.
58. See Albert H.Y. Chen, *An Introduction to the Legal System of the People's Republic of China* (Singapore: Butterworths Asia, 1992), p. 109. See also Xinhua, 15 April 1998, in FBIS-CHI-98-106, 16 April 1998.
59. See Xinhua, 15 July 1998, in FBIS-CHI-98-196, 15 July 1998.
60. Xinhua, 31 July 1998, in FBIS-CHI-98-217, 5 August 1998.
61. *Liaowang*, No. 7 (17 February 1998), in FBIS-CHI-98-044, 17 February 1998, and *Zheng-fa luntan* (*Politics and Law Forum*), No. 73 (February 1997), in FBIS-CHI-97-115, 1 February 1997.
62. *Guangzhou ribao* reported in *SCMP*, 1 April 1998. According to the head of the Guangzhou Municipal Court, in 1997 verdicts in 6,000 cases were not enforced, an increase of 31% over 1996. The judge also reported cases of government bodies intimidating the court and of police lobbying to overturn criminal convictions. In one case, a procuratorate official turned up to pay the debts of a convicted criminal.

hold the government politically accountable. Accountability is exercised through the Party. Even in this environment, the National People's Congress has been strengthened in recent years. For example, authorities have established new standing committees to examine such items as the state budget.

The CCP limits popular participation in people's congress elections. Universal suffrage is available only for elections at the lowest adminis- trative levels. In 1988, for example, the CCP began again to popularize village committee elections aimed at preserving stability and fighting corruption.[63] Villagers are now better educated and the Party more often offers them a choice of candidates in these elections. Still, it continues to control the elections through its control of the nomination process.[64] Although the media in China occasionally report cases of candidates being elected who are not nominated by the Party, such cases are relatively rare.

In spite of their Leninist trappings, recent research into political participation in Beijing has revealed that "political involvement ... is far higher than many students of political participation have believed." Shi Tianjian's study argues that elections in the 1980s put nominated candi- dates under public scrutiny and provided people with an opportunity to show their displeasure with candidates to higher authorities.[65] As a result, local leaders have adopted styles designed to build popular support. Local government offices now have telephone hot-lines, advertised in local newspapers, and invite citizens to call with suggestions or to report abuses. Mayors of China's cities appear on television and radio pro- grammes and host radio talk shows taking calls from the public. China's local leaders are now much more knowledgeable about the use of the media and the importance of public opinion.

Trade unions and mass organizations. The Leninist paradigm contin- ues to dominate China's official trade unions. Just as it has done for the past 50 years, the Party controls union budgets and the selection of union leaders. For the most part, the function of the official All-China Feder- ation of Trade Unions, to which all unions must affiliate, is to assist in the implementation of Party policy. During economic restructuring, it has championed the Party's policy that has resulted in mass lay-offs of workers, an unpopular position.[66] As a result, pressure to form illegal unions has grown and local governments, pressed to find jobs for the unemployed, have often tolerated them because they promised to help solve the unemployment problem.[67] The leadership's fear of a

63. Xinhua, 25 June 1998, in FBIS-CHI-98-176, 25 June 1998.
64. The press reports that cases of "self-nomination" are growing in village elections. "This has helped ordinary farmers, who are not CCP members and never served as a village cadre to become strong competitors for membership in the villagers' committee," said Xinhua, 22 April 1997, in FBIS-CHI-97-112, 22 April 1997.
65. Shi Tianjian, *Political Participation in Beijing* (Cambridge, MA: Harvard University Press, 1997), pp. 176-77 and 278-79.
66. *SCMP*, 16 November 1998.
67. CCP circular on "wild-cat unions" quoted in *SCMP*, 4 June 1996.

"Solidarity-type" labour movement in China has led officials to crack down on illegal unions. Labour activists have been arrested throughout the country.[68]

Non-state social and political groups. Party policy during the 1950s was to penetrate society and either co-opt and control social groups or eliminate them. So successful was the policy that the boundaries between state and society faded away. By the mid-1950s, the authorities only permitted officially sanctioned social groups. All others, such as religious groups, were suppressed. With economic reform, a more complex plurality of interests has emerged, people now have more resources and are more demanding of government. During the late 1980s individuals set up genuinely non-state social organizations that were tolerated by officials. Authorities cracked down on many of these organizations in the wake of the 4 June 1989 incident.

During the late 1990s politically oriented social groups re-emerged and attempts were made for the first time since 1949 to establish an opposition party, the China Democracy Party. Encouraged by what they perceived to be a more politically relaxed atmosphere in Beijing, dissidents tried to register the new party in November 1998.[69] At about the same time, Chinese authorities issued new quite restrictive regulations on the registration and management of social groups[70] and a month later the leaders of the new party were gaoled for attempting to overthrow the state.[71]

Although the activists in 1998 demanded democracy and a multi-party system as many had done during the Hundred Flowers Campaign in 1956, they have made little impact. Recent research indicates that China does not provide particularly fertile ground for unorthodox or oppositional points of view. A nation-wide random sample survey carried out in 1990 reveals that the Chinese are among the least tolerant of viewpoints and political activities of opponents of the regime of seven countries surveyed.[72] In the political landscape in China today, a credible alternative to the CCP simply does not exist. The Party's dominant position is likely to continue for the foreseeable future.

The media. Since the 1950s, with considerable fluctuation, there has been an explosion of publishing in China. By 1998, publishers were producing more than 2,000 daily and weekly newspapers and 8,000

68. *SCMP*, 4 June 1996, 2 November 1998 and 28 December 1998; AFP (Hong Kong), 29 March 1998, in FBIS-CHI-98-088, 29 March 1998.

69. *Xin bao* (Hong Kong), 10 November 1998, in FBIS-CHI-98-314, 10 November 1998. In October, activists set up an Anti Corruption Watchdog Group in Henan, which was promptly banned. AFP (Hong Kong), 14 October 1998, in FBIS-CHI-98-287, 14 October 1998.

70. Xinhua, 3 November 1998, in FBIS-CHI-98-309, 5 November 1998.

71. *SCMP*, 23 and 28 December 1998.

72. The countries were Australia, Germany, the United Kingdom, the USA, Austria and Italy in Andrew J. Nathan and Shi Tianjian, "Cultural requisites for democracy in China: findings from a survey," *Daedalus*, Vol. 122, No. 2 (Spring 1993), p. 112.

periodicals and magazines for public distribution. The country had more than 3,000 radio and cable television stations, over 1,000 broadcasting stations and 565 publishing houses.[73] The CCP's Propaganda Department continues to preside over the media, enforcing the policy that the media's role is to assist in the implementation of Party policy. The Party itself continues to own directly scores of newspapers and magazines, such as *Renmin ribao, Guangming ribao* and publications published by local Party committees.

During the 1980s and 1990s, the Party's degree of supervision over the media has varied. In the late 1980s, for example, authorities tolerated critical intellectual dailies such as *Shijie jingji daobao* (*World Economic Herald*), published in Shanghai. In the wake of the 4 June 1989 disturbances, however, the Party cracked down on these liberal publications.[74] Since then, authorities have tolerated and, indeed, used the media to further Party policies, such as the fight against corruption.

With so many media and with new pressures to commercialize publishing, maintaining Party control is a daunting task, sometimes resulting in the arrest and imprisonment of journalists.[75] Similar strong measures were taken against offending journalists during campaigns such as the Anti-Rightist Campaign in 1957. By the 1990s, however, authorities more often relied on the legal system to discipline errant journalists. Yet by the late 1990s the content of the media in China showed much more variety than it did in the mid-1950s.

Still, 50 years on, the Party continues to control the media through propaganda departments, New China News Agency's monopoly, State Council bureaucracies and the official All-China Federation of Journalists. Attempts to make journalism more professional and independent of Party control have largely failed. In the 1990s, just as in the 1950s, journalists were admonished to study Marxism-Leninism-Mao Zedong Thought, establish a mass viewpoint and accept correct media guidance. However, they were also admonished to defend citizens' rights under the law, ensure the truthfulness of the news and not to engage in corrupt practices.[76]

Conclusion

From the vantage point of the late 1990s, it is obvious that the Chinese political system has adapted to its changing environment. Unlike the mid-1950s, the Party is more "middle class," and its leaders are better educated and more highly differentiated. Public officials with higher capacity are performing new functions in an environment in which the law has become increasingly important. Government decision-making is

73. *Dagong bao* (Hong Kong), 17 April 1998, in FBIS-CHI-98-110, 20 April 1998.
74. See Burns, "Strengthening central CCP control of leadership selection," pp. 465–66.
75. *Hong Kong Standard*, 11 October 1998, in FBIS-CHI-98-286, 13 October 1998. See also *Ming bao*, 12 September 1998, in FBIS-CHI-98-255, 12 September 1998, and AFP (Hong Kong), 14 September 1998, in FBIS-CHI-98-257, 14 September 1998.
76. Xinhua, 26 January 1997, in FBIS-CHI-97-018, 26 January 1997.

increasingly based on rational considerations as authorities struggle to develop the economy in a market. There has been less adaptation in the links between state and society. But even here, as Shi Tianjian has pointed out, citizens are able to use traditional institutions such as people's congresses to participate in politics. In conclusion, then, China's formally Leninist political institutions continue to be relevant and useful, and citizens have been able to make them "work."

Currently the legitimacy of the CCP is based on the performance of China's economy and, more recently, patriotism. The legitimacy of the Party could be undermined by continuing high levels of corruption, on the one hand, and a serious economic downturn, on the other. As China's leaders are aware, a sharp downturn in the fortunes of China's citizens after almost a generation of high growth and prosperity is a recipe for instability. Further reform of the institutions linking state to society is now required within the general demands of maintaining stability.

Political Movements, Change and Stability: The Chinese Communist Party in Power

Michael Schoenhals

Actually we could have picked a different name, such as the Chinese People's Party, the Revolutionary Party, the Liberation Party – any of these would have been OK. But no matter what, our intention remains to resolve the "property" (*chan*) issue. What are we fighting for? What is our goal all about? Getting "property" – not private property, but public property. For everybody to get rich, for everybody to lead a good life. That's why there has to be a revolution.[1]

This declaration concerning the name and political programme of the party that assumed power in Beijing on 1 October 1949 was made, not by Deng Xiaoping – as readers familiar only with the last 20 years of China's history might be inclined to believe – but by Lin Biao, commonly regarded as one of the CCP's most unrepentant "Leftists." My point in citing it here is not merely to add something of the unexpected to this introduction but to remind the reader that the intellectual rights to the programme that launched a "revolution ... for everybody to get rich, for everybody to lead a good life" was the collective property of the founders of the PRC.

It is one of the ironies of history that the most important member of the 1949 CCP leadership was also the one who, in retrospect, may have been least committed to that simple programme. Mao Zedong had a much "grander" vision of where the people of China ought to go once they had, as he proclaimed on 30 September 1949, "stood up."[2] Simply "getting rich" was not a challenging enough proposition to him. It was "wrong," he insisted, without mentioning names, only to raise slogans about "family prosperity" and the like.[3] Mao wanted to achieve something different and for the next 26 years, the rest of the Party leadership followed him – reluctantly at times and not always fully comprehending what drove the CCP Chairman. Visions of a "new society"? The realization of "communism"? The total eradication of "bourgeois rights"? Near the end of his life Mao complained bitterly about how his "old comrades" had failed to understand his own brand of revolution: "they don't comprehend, they object, they even resist," he insisted.[4]

Where the rest of the Central Committee found it hardest to follow Mao had been in the matter of what constituted the rationale for initiating

1. Lin Biao's address to the Seventh National Congress of the CCP on 22 May 1945, excerpted in *Liu Shaoqi jiqi yilei pianzi zai gongyun luxian shang de fandong yanlun zhaibian (Selections from the Reactionary Statements of Liu Shaoqi and Swindlers Like Him Concerning the Worker's Movement Line)* (Lijiang, 1973), p. 7.
2. *Jianguo yilai Mao Zedong wengao (Mao Zedong Manuscripts Since the Founding of the Nation)*, 13 vols. (Beijing: Zhongyang wenxian chubanshe, 1987–98), Vol. 1, p. 10.
3. *Ibid.*, Vol. 2, p. 579.
4. *Ibid.*, Vol. 13, p. 487.

and sustaining, as Mao insisted upon doing, near constant "movement" in the field of politics. Where Jiang Zemin today – and Deng Xiaoping before him – insists upon absolute stability at any cost, Mao had craved and repeatedly engineered instability, even chaos. Movement in the realm of politics, so Mao had argued, ignited and fuelled development and momentum in the economic realm. Yet when unable simply to quote or paraphrase the Party Chairman, his "old comrades" never quite succeeded in expressing the same idea.

It was thus perhaps only to be expected that the members of the founding generation who outlived Mao ended up discarding the most counter-intuitive aspects of his thinking after 1976. Today it is no longer vulgar "goulash communism" to maintain that the goal of the revolution should be "for everybody to get rich, for everybody to lead a good life." And to admit to a preference for political stability over movement – not to mention chaos – has been the only correct standpoint of a self-respecting Party member for the past 20 years. A fundamental re-evaluation of how politics and economics relate in instrumental terms has occurred. As the PRC turns 50 the creation of a permanent and ideally self-sustaining *market-driven* momentum in the economic sphere constitutes the Party's main means for achieving and ensuring political stability.

Movement

The word "movement" (*yundong*), that once occupied such a prominent place in the political lexicon of the CCP, has become an archaism. Today's younger generation recognizes it at best as something distant that parents refer to in passing while complaining about the past, or possibly lamenting the present, depending on how the Party's reform policies have hit them. At the end of the 1990s, senior Chinese politicians grappling with everything from political corruption to economic recession warn against the grave dangers of "having movements"; yet 40 years earlier, the Chairman of the CCP had insisted that everything had to be done by way of movements and that movements were indispensable.[5]

In its original sense, the CCP movement was the intentional "shattering of all regular standards" (*dapo changgui*). It involved the temporary suspension of whatever laws, norms and rules applied at "regular times." This induction of a state of flux served two purposes, of which the first, according to Mao, was the prevention of an undesirable strain of wealth creation – named revisionism and unidentified in China prior to 1949 – wherein a "better life" came at the price of a serious loss in "revolutionary spirit." Only by having movements was it possible to ensure that "economic construction" proceeded along genuinely socialist lines; the so-called practice of "managing the economy according to

5. *Ibid.*, Vol. 7, p. 433.

economic principles," so the Party press insisted, resulted in little other than the revival and/or spread of capitalism.[6]

Referring to flux, uncertainty and the negation of that which was "regular" as movement also served a crucial purpose on the cognitive level, at least initially. As a metaphor reiterated over and over again, the term movement helped maintain the illusion that Chinese society was moving forwards, or *progressing*, in a direction away from the dreary here-and-now towards a brighter and better future. In this sense, the CCP catch-word of the 1990s – stability – is clearly inferior, implying as it might that China is in fact going nowhere. It is not surprising that CCP propaganda, having abandoned movement, today speaks of "development" (*fazhan*) more than ever, especially in conjunction with the beautiful vista that political stability is said to open up.

If anyone was to have suggested to Mao Zedong that his movements merely represented illusory progress, it would not have fazed the CCP Chairman. To Mao, even chaos was progressive. In 1969 he proclaimed: "It seems as if where things are really chaotic, that's where they're really better. We've been at it for decades, and that's our experience."[7] Such ideas were elevated to the level of a theory, the rationale of which hinged completely on one's understanding of words like "socialist" and "revolution." If one shared Mao's understanding, then it may have made sense to claim – as the Party media did – that "by far the most important way of developing socialist production" is "by way of grasping revolution in politics and ideology."[8] If not, comprehending Mao's "development strategy" became truly difficult. His insistence upon mediating all economic activities through political movements was so total, his wife was able to claim she "never heard the Chairman mention pushing the national economy forward."[9] Whereas early drafts of the CCP constitution produced by Zhang Chunqiao and Yao Wenyuan for adoption by the Ninth National Congress had stated that it was one of the essential tasks of the *communist party* (not merely the PRC government) to "build China into a strong socialist country with modernized agriculture, industry, national defence and science and technology," by the time Mao had finalized the text, that famous formulation was gone, not to reappear in programmatic party (as opposed to State Council) texts until 1977.[10]

6. *Renmin ribao* (*People's Daily*), 25 August 1967.
7. Contemporary transcript of Mao's speech on 13 April 1969 in the possession of the author.
8. *Renmin ribao*, 25 August 1967.
9. *Zhonggong zhongyang wenjian* (*CCP Central Document*) Zhongfa (1977), No. 37, p. 175.
10. Early drafts of the 1969 CCP constitution are in *Zhengdang xuexi ziliao III* (*Material on Party Rectification and Study III*) (Beijing: Zhongguo kexueyuan geming weiyuanhui zhengzhibu, 1968), pp. 1–17. The adopted texts of the 1969, 1973 and 1977 CCP constitutions are in *Zhongguo gongchandang dangzhang huibian* (*Collected Constitutions of the CCP*) (Beijing: Renmin chubanshe, 1979), pp. 206–233.

Stability

In the wake of the CCP's most total movements, serious doubts began to surface in the minds of some of Mao's colleagues who expressed themselves cautiously in favour of trying something called simply "regular" work. Thus Deng Xiaoping in 1962 said: "It is not good to have movements so frequently. The result of this has been that much of the regular work of departments and work units has been interrupted ... We should learn some valuable lessons from our experience over these years."[11] And Chen Boda in 1969 stated: "We still have to develop production successfully and raise labour productivity. We cannot simply engage in movements, movements, and nothing else."[12] But such views were anathematized as "revisionism." The idea that there could possibly be such a thing as "revolutionary revisionism" was derided as a joke by Zhou Enlai during an attack on Chen Boda in 1972.[13]

In private, the best informed members of the CCP's repressive apparatus were the most explicitly critical. Mao's brand of politics, they argued, had made the nation "wealthy" in quotation marks only, while in a very real sense it had kept ordinary citizens poor. For the duration of the 1960s, China's economy had remained stagnant; the peasantry lacked food and clothing, and workers had their wages frozen.[14] This is how, in 1971, a deputy section chief with the PLA Air Force chose to characterize the CCP Chairman and the intellectual cronies with whom he surrounded himself:

They have replaced Marxism-Leninism with pseudo-revolutionary verbiage which they use to deceive and fool the minds of the Chinese people ... The real target of their revolution is the Chinese people, and bearing the brunt are the military and anyone who holds views different from theirs. Their socialism is in actuality social fascism. They have turned China's state machinery into a kind of meat-grinder in which everyone is butchering, and trying to do away with, everyone else.[15]

In the PRC today, the document from which this quotation is taken, the infamous so-called "Outline of Project 571," is regarded by some as a programme of proto-reformers who, had history given them a chance, would have initiated a reform programme similar to but pre-dating Deng Xiaoping's by almost a decade.

The Third Plenum of the 11th CCP Central Committee in December 1978 became the crucial gathering of survivors of the PRC founding generation that sanctioned the change away from Mao's brand of politics. Not only was "class struggle" made a thing of the past; after one last futile attempt by a moribund propaganda apparatus to eradicate "spiritual

11. *Selected Works of Deng Xiaoping* (Beijing: Foreign Languages Press, 1992), Vol. 1, p. 308.
12. "Chen Xiaonong (ed.), *Chen Boda yigao: yuzhong zishu ji qita (The Late Chen Boda's Writings: Personal Accounts from Prison and Other Items)* (Hong Kong: Cosmos Books, 1998), p. 114.
13. According to a reliable official source.
14. *CCP Central Document* Zhongfa (1972), No. 4, appendix 2, pp. 2–11.
15. *Ibid.* p. 5.

pollution" with the help of a movement, that most Maoist instrument of revolution was history as well. As Deng Xiaoping and others began the search for a way of "managing the economy according to economic principles," key aspects of the original programme on which the CCP had assumed power were revived. As the PRC turns 50, the National People's Congress is now considering a resolution of the property issue raised by Lin Biao that would give constitutional protection to private as well as public property rights.[16]

The Moral Left

In public statements concerning the relationship between political stability and economic development, Jiang Zemin today maintains that the first is a precondition for the second.[17] Yet he nevertheless acts as if the reverse were the case, and this makes him a more predictable political actor in the eyes of the West than both Mao and Deng had ever been. Whereas the behaviour of the latter two was such that an entire esoteric science ("Pekingology") had to be created to explain it, Jiang's behaviour no longer seems all that alien. He aspires to shore up support for what he does by giving what in a democracy would be his electorate the impression that they are better off with him than without him.

Not only is Jiang a very different Communist Party leader; the CCP, too, is no longer the party that Deng took over from Mao. Many newly recruited Party members are so totally unconcerned with "communism," they might as well have joined the KMT, had it given them similar advantages. A recent survey conducted under the supervision of the Zhejiang provincial CCP Organization Department discovered that a full 32.6 per cent of Party-member respondents were "unable to figure out (nongbuqing) the essence of Deng Xiaoping's theory for building social- ism with Chinese characteristics."[18]

Does this inability to summarize, in orthodox theoretical terms, the essence of present policy reflect a lack of understanding of that same policy or merely a disinterest, among CCP members, in policy matters? It is undoubtedly the case that the CCP's current strategy as outlined in Jiang Zemin's report to the 15th Party Congress has its strongest and most powerful supporters inside the CCP, but here too – as in society at large – there are those who challenge it. Of particular significance is the emergence of what could be termed a "moral left." Lacking the cohesion of a political faction, the moral left is essentially a combination of forces contesting present policies and practices on moral grounds. It encom- passes the Contemporary China Research Institute which, in addition to

16. *China News Digest*, 30 January 1999.
17. See Guo Dehong *et al.*, *Dang he guojia zhongda juece de licheng* (*The Course of Major Policy Decisions of the Party and the State*), 6 vols. (Beijing: Hongqi chubanshe, 1997), Vol. 6, pp. 479–480.
18. Zhonggong zhongyang zuzhibu yanjiushi (ed.), *1997 zuzhi gongzuo yanjiu lunwen* (*1997 Selected Organization Work Research Papers*), 4 vols. (Beijing: Dangjian duwu chubanshe, 1998), Vol. 1, p. 35.

funding some of the best research inside China on the history of the PRC, provides a safe haven for the publishers of *Contemporary Trends of Thought*, a bimonthly voice of frustration in which pseudonymous authors insist that not to ask oneself whether today's reform policies as such are socialist or capitalist (*bu wen xing she xing zi*) is to forget that there is a difference between being a master or a slave, a man or a monster.[19] The moral left also includes closet social democrats who are searching for a morally superior alternative to the inhumane cut-throat capitalism that seems to characterize the "primary stage of socialism." In parts of China falling behind in the race to "become rich," the moral left has a natural constituency among those to whom the late Mao Zedong still appeals for his purported egalitarianism and the relative absence of economic corruption associated with his rule.

The moral left does not pose a threat to stability – and by extension to the current Party leadership – in organizational terms, as it lacks even a semblance of cohesion. The celebrated "ten-thousand character tractates" (*wanyanshu*) emanating from the Contemporary China Research Institute may resonate with the sentiments of many a disappointed, discontented and dissatisfied Party member, but their authors are not convincing contenders for Jiang Zemin's position. In strict ideological terms the moral left is both a challenge to the present leadership and a rhetorical resource into which it can – and is likely to – tap in the event of a dramatic failure of "reform," in which case even Jiang Zemin may be forced to claim some of its arguments as his own.

"Liberalization"

Deng Xiaoping's decision to promote a market economy has produced significant numbers of quasi-independent Chinese intellectuals without firm economic ties to the state. On the basis of Western historical precedent, this new social stratum is expected to challenge a communist party which, by definition, is "anti-market." Yet in the case of the PRC, this expectation may well be based on a false premise, since China's Communist Party no longer conforms to traditional, Marxist definitions.

Since the late 1980s, intellectuals interested in actively changing the present system have begun to join China's smaller "democratic" parties on the assumption that one may transform those parties from within to a point where they, one day, could perform the role of a genuine and legal political opposition to the CCP. Yet this has proved extremely difficult. The experience of a Revolutionary KMT member recruited two years after 4 June 1989 is probably typical: an assistant professor aged 40, he became by far the youngest member of his city district branch (the next youngest was 53). Initially joining on the assumption that working from within the Revolutionary KMT would be a superior alternative to the open defiance of the CCP that had ended so tragically in Tiananmen

19. *Dangdai sichao*, No. 5, 1998, p. ii.

Square, he quickly found out that not only were his fellow party members more orthodox in their Marxism than most CCP members, they were also totally unwilling to accept even the most moderately worded dissidence. Although he stopped paying his party dues in 1993, hoping in this way to force the Revolutionary KMT to accept his wish to resign, he has been unable to secure a formal confirmation of withdrawal.[20]

In 1998, an altogether new activist option appeared to have been granted not just China's intellectuals but any citizen who cared to become involved in politics: the right to set up a new political party. This unprecedented and in a purely domestic context somewhat inexplicable "liberalization" prompted a handful of bold and brave individuals to register branches of the China Democratic Party in a number of provinces and cities. True to form, the CCP eventually rounded up the people involved, accused them of threatening stability, and threw them in gaol. The lesson to be learned from this is that China's present stability does indeed coincide with a near total absence of movement towards anything resembling a genuine multi-party system. After 50 years, the PRC is still a place where Mao Zedong's notorious "black pigs, white pigs" thesis – slightly more obscure than Deng Xiaoping's feline variant, but equally poignant – still sums up the Party's treatment of challenges to its one-party monopoly: "It doesn't matter if a pig is white or black: once you've slaughtered one, you know how to do it!"[21] Of course, the metaphorical "slaughter" of political dissidents under Jiang Zemin has assumed new and moderately humane forms utterly unimaginable under Mao, including banishment to the capitalist West.

Urban Inequality

The CCP's decision to employ the forces of the market in an attempt to maintain political "stability" has also fostered the emergence of an increasingly well-to-do urban middle class. At the same time, it has alienated the working class that, in theory, the Party was meant to represent in the first place. A full 12 million Chinese workers lost their jobs in 1997, and a similarly large number are likely to have met the same fate in 1998.[22] Although fighting unemployment has become a number one social priority, the problems created by the CCP's decision to "manage the economy according to economic principles" after decades of doing quite the opposite are daunting to say the least. Herein, then, lies the most serious threat to the political stability that the CCP so craves.

China's workers have a sense of entitlement and strong residue of stubborn faith in the CCP in the sense that they hope the Party will feel a paternal obligation to take care of them. For the past 20 years, the CCP

20. Interview on Lund University campus, 10 January 1999.
21. See *Peng Zhen guanyu siqing yundong de liu pian jianghua (Six Speeches by Peng Zhen on the Four Cleanups Movement)* (Beijing: Zhonggong Beijing shiwei bangongting, 1966), p. 3.
22. *China Rights Forum*, Spring 1998, pp. 38–40.

has made efforts not to undermine this faith. In the 1980s, the Central Committee General Office came down firmly on Party bodies who had launched slogans such as "Let cadres in party and government organs get rich as quickly as possible too," lest such slogans should be "misinterpreted."[23] In Shanghai – where thousands of workers facing redundancy may view "deepening economic reform" as something more akin to a threat than an opportunity – the Party's municipal Organization Department in the 1990s put out the slogan: "Make the people happy, let the people rest assured!"[24] It is difficult to think of a less communist-sounding slogan. No longer carrying pictures of Chairman Mao, the working class of the 1990s is expected to be happy ever after in the market place.[25]

The solution to the problem of urban working class unrest provoked by economic change is so daunting, no single – much less simple – solution is presently in sight. The CCP has few other choices than to persist in its present ad hoc practice of pacification by payoffs and sometimes force. Members of China's moral left, not surprisingly, claim that much could be gained from reverting to an analysis of the problem in the kind of terms drawn up by Mao Zedong, that is by acknowledging that post-1979 CCP recruitment policies and reform have put "the bourgeoisie inside the party." But even the most articulate proponents of this argument are unable to do much more than recycle old ideas associated with the Gang of Four. And, as establishment historians point out, those ideas have all been tried and proved unworkable in practice.

Rural Inequality

The rural poor – not least the millions recruited into the People's Liberation Army – had brought the CCP to power in 1949 and their values were very much in evidence in the Party's policies of the early 1950s. These values resurfaced in Deng Xiaoping's 1979 formula which spoke of letting a majority of Chinese become "comparatively well off" (*dadao xiaokang shuiping*) by the year 2000.[26]

In the 1990s, glaringly uneven economic development in parts of rural China has been identified by both the CCP and foreign observers as a serious threat to political stability. Yet it is important to note that, as recent studies show, increases in rural inequality since 1988 have in fact been proportionally smaller than increases in urban inequality over the

---

23. Guojia tigaiwei bangongting (ed.), *Shiyi jie san zhong quanhui yilai jingji tizhi gaige zhongyao wenjian huibian (Collected Important Documents on Reform of the Economic System since the Third Plenum of the Eleventh Central Committee)*, 3 vols. (Beijing: Gaige chubanshe, 1990), Vol. 2, p. 692.

24. *1997 Selected Organization Work Research Papers*, Vol. 4, p. 114.

25. John Lennon and Paul McCartney, *Revolution I* and *Ob-La-Di, Ob-La-Da* (London: Northern Songs, 1968).

26. *Xuanchuan dongtai 1985 nian xuanbianben (Selections from Propaganda Trends 1985)* (Beijing: Jingji ribao chubanshe, 1986), pp. 181–83.

same period.[27] Also, glaring inequalities are by no means new in the PRC countryside: prior to 1979 they had *defined* the political realm, with certain social strata being what Vivienne Shue has called "automatic class enemies."[28] That this punitive classification of selected individuals and their kin impeded economic development was recognized already in the 1960s by rural cadres who claimed – and were criticized by superior Party organs as a result – that "land reform depended on the poor peasants, production depends on the middle peasants" and "construction assumes people with technical skills and education, hence it disqualifies the poor peasants."[29] The extent to which the trend of the 1990s represents a simple inversion of the past, with economic inequalities now finding articulation in the political realm, is still unclear. Also unclear is the likelihood of a serious threat to "stability" on a nation-wide scale arising in rural China. In the past, highly placed CCP officials had noted that even when rural cadres treated their subjects "worse than Tibetan serf owners," such abuse rarely provoked rebellion (*zaofan*).[30] Still, the CCP is taking no chances and has recently clamped down hard on disturbances in parts of rural Hunan and Sichuan.[31]

In the interest of maintaining stability and forestalling further disturbances, Jiang Zemin's CCP leadership is busy attempting to alter both actual economic inequalities in rural China and – equally important from a political point of view – popular perceptions of its own responsibility for the emergence of those same inequalities. Dealing with inequalities is proving difficult, and the success of redistributive tax reforms, inter-regional co-operation schemes and revamped poverty-relief programmes is far from certain. Possibly even more difficult is bringing about a change in popular perception of the Party as being the root of the problem. In parts of rural China, the local population has in a sense abandoned the CCP altogether, instead pinning its hopes for the future on traditional clan networks, self-styled chambers of commerce, even secret societies. Perceived as hopelessly corrupt and morally bankrupt, first local officialdom and now even the highest levels of the CCP are reduced to the role of a target of discontent, resistance and violence. There is a growing consensus among foreign observers that the CCP expects democratically elected village assemblies to become channels for the peaceful articulation of popular discontent, but whether this expectation is realistic or not remains to be seen.[32]

27. Azizur Rahman Khan and Karl Riskin, "Income and inequality in China: composition, distribution and growth of household income, 1988 to 1995," *The China Quarterly*. No. 154 (June 1998), p. 241.

28. Vivienne Shue, *Peasant China in Transition: The Dynamics of Development Toward Socialism 1949–1956* (Berkeley: University of California Press, 1980), p. 23.

29. *CCP Central Document* Zhongfa (1963) No. 347, p. 39.

30. Michael Schoenhals, "Yang Xianzhen's critique of the Great Leap Forward," *Modern Asian Studies*, Vol. 26, No. 3 (1992), p. 604.

31. *New York Times*, 2 February 1999.

32. For more on the topics of rural violence and village elections, see Jean C. Oi's contribution to this volume.

Conclusion

Despite all that has happened since Lin Biao more than 50 years ago noted that the name of the CCP was by no means sacred, the Party has not changed its name. A *Red Flag* propagandist discussing its appropriateness once admitted that perhaps the "Democratic Party" or the "Socialist Party" would be more "realistic" or "practical" – given that the CCP in fact does not practise communism – but he suspected that nobody would consider, much less accept, a name change on those grounds.[33] In many European countries, it took an event of the magnitude of the "fall of communism" to bring about a change in the name of national communist parties; in China, the "CCP" appears likely to remain for quite some time. Mao's revolution may be over, but his party has succeeded in re-inventing itself.

What the CCP appears desperate to achieve next is a new kind of legitimacy. Ten years ago, Western political scientists commenting on the likelihood of it surviving in power for yet another decade called the CCP's lack of legitimacy a factor of major uncertainty. Even when, in retrospect, the precise wording of their predictions merely highlight the proto-scientific nature of political science, their common-sense observations retain their persuasive power. The point made by David Bachman in "The people's unfinished revolution: Communist China at 40" hardly appears less valid today than it did in 1989, even though history has invalidated the evidence cited to back it up: "The lack of legitimacy does not necessarily mean that the CCP will fall from power in the near term; there are a number of illegitimate political systems in the world, such as in South Africa, which show no sign of disappearing soon."[34]

That the way in which the members of the CCP leadership – the men and women supposedly still committed to a revolution for the sake of giving the Chinese people a "good life" – see and act upon the world will change is certain. Equally certain is that such change will occur only slowly, at a pace that can be counted in generations rather than years. Meanwhile, it may be something quite different from a loss of legitimacy that will decide the CCP's future in power. Despite their differences, the developmental models – if one may indeed characterize them thus – of the CCP prior to and since the Third Plenum of the 11th Central Committee share the same fundamental flaw. The relative ease with which the shift from one to the other was accepted can in part be traced to the fact that the metaphorical matrix linking act, agency and purpose remains unchanged. To this day, CCP leaders still act as if through some thermodynamic miracle, ordered manipulation of one realm of experience will generate predictable results in another. This is simply not the case. Bread and circus, pen and sword, politics and economics, revolution and construction, "getting rich" and "political stability": the relationship between the elements of each pair is infinitely more complex and chaotic

33. *Xueshu yanjiu dongtai (Academic Research Trends)*, No. 15 (1980), pp. 8–9.
34. *Fletcher Forum of World Affairs*, Vol. 14, No. 1 (Winter 1990), p. 17.

than the CCP has so far been prepared to acknowledge. Add to this flawed cognitive map the kind of entropy represented by an unpredictable international environment and a deteriorating physical environment, and popular legitimacy may turn out to be one of the CCP's lesser worries.

The People's Republic of China at 50: The Economy

Robert F. Dernberger

The dynamic growth of the Chinese economy over the past 50 years under the policies and administrative management of the People's Republic of China must rank among the most important developments of the 20th century. When I began my serious study of China's economy in the early 1950s, Western economists were preoccupied with a single question, "how are they ever going to feed all those Chinese?" Today, after 50 years in power, we must respect and even admire not only their ability to feed a population that has more than doubled in size, but also to provide the Chinese consumer with watches, washing machines, sewing machines, colour television sets, and tape and video recorders. A small, but significant and rapidly expanding, share of China's consumers is using mobile phones, computers and even private cars.

Yet a retrospective account of this amazing story of economic development, with special emphasis on the last decade, is not easy to provide in a few thousand words. The problem is that China's economic evolution over the last half of the 20th century is a story of path-dependent and very dynamic change. Furthermore, China's economic growth could be discontinuous with frequent changes in direction. To tell the story with time trends over a period of years would not reflect the true picture in any particular year, while an accurate telling of the story for any particular year would fail to capture the dynamic changes in any other year.

However, the fundamental economic institutions and policies, as well as the resulting economic developments during the period in which Mao Zedong was the supreme political leader (1952–75) can be readily distinguished from those in the period of Deng Xiaoping's leadership (1978–95). And, inasmuch as we want to place the greatest emphasis in our retrospective evaluation of developments in the economy on the more recent past, the years 1996 to 1998 can be viewed as the initial years of the economic policy regime of Jiang Zemin and Zhu Rongji.[1]

The Economic Policy Regime of Mao (1952–1975)

A major distinguishing feature of this period was the adoption and implementation of the Soviet-type economy as China's economic system. Thus, the farmers of 40 centuries ultimately found themselves as members of a production team within a commune, losing title to their land and

1. It is important to note that our use of these terms to represent discrete periods of economic institutions and policies is a matter of convenience and is not meant to imply that the institutions or policies were the products of these individuals. As the paramount political leader(s) of the PRC at the time, they were obviously involved in the discussions and decisions that lead to the adoption of these institutions and policies, but the extent and nature of that involvement is not the focus of this article.

working in work groups for work points, which were a claim on a share of the net income of their team. Markets were replaced by the plan as the means for allocating resources and investment. Banks, domestic and foreign trade, and enterprises of any importance were nationalized and placed under the control of managers appointed by the state. Central planners set targets for outputs of the enterprises, determined how those outputs should be produced, and who was to get them. Prices remained for the purpose of transactions, but served as bookkeeping entries, not as values to be used in economic decisions. The main objective of such an economic system was economic growth. This was to be achieved by mobilizing forced savings under the control of the planners.[2] Pursuing a strategy of extensive economic growth in which growth was not demand driven but investment and supply driven, the Chinese planners were able to pursue directly both rapid growth and a rapid restructuring of the economy.

This describes the basic Soviet-type economic system, but the Chinese introduced several modifications which make it quite different from the norm. They quickly recognized that their level of development and bureaucratic administrative capacity precluded a strict implementation of the Soviet-type economy. Thus as early as 1957 they introduced a considerable degree of decentralization, whereby the central directives were meant as guidelines for lower levels to interpret and implement in light of their specific conditions. In this manner, the Chinese system of planning was much looser and much more dependent on local cadres' initiative and management skills than in the Soviet Union. Then too, to overcome the lack of horizontal contacts between suppliers and users in the Soviet-type economy, the Chinese relied on lower-level conferences among suppliers and users of particular products to work out delivery contracts and schedules. In short, the lower-level cadre in China had considerable on-the-job management training and entrepreneurial responsibility well before Deng's economic policy regime began.

On the negative side, however, two other Chinese adaptations of the Soviet-type economic model were counter-productive and helped to bring Mao's economic policy to an end. First, there was the extreme emphasis given to self-dependent economic development: nationally, regionally, provincially, even within the enterprise. Internationally, this policy limited China's participation in the global economy just at the time when global technological developments and economic growth were generating tremendous benefits to the developing economies pursuing an export promotion policy. The second adaptation of the Soviet-type

2. These forced savings were achieved by means of assigning the peasant output quotas and setting the prices of that output relatively low. The prices of inputs for industrial enterprises were also set relatively low. The output of consumer goods was priced relatively high and the restricted supply of essentials distributed by rationing. The profits of the state enterprises, i.e. their revenue from sales minus their costs, were rather large (the rate of profit often being greater than 50% sometimes even over 100%) and went to the state as revenue in its budget. These were just disguised indirect taxes on the population, which were put into the hands of the planners to finance their investment programme.

economic model was even more costly than the first: the reliance of mobilization campaigns and mass movements to achieve a rapid transition to true socialism. Two leading examples of this strategy were the Great Leap Forward (1958–59) and the Cultural Revolution (1966–69).

The Great Leap Forward began the peasants' steady transition to a more equitable distribution of income at the local level, but an equity achieved by shared poverty. The resulting decline in output and the famine that followed is estimated to have cost the Chinese ten years of positive growth. Then, when the Chinese economy was revived by the mid-1960s, Mao unleashed the Cultural Revolution that tried to overthrow the established functioning of the economic system for the sake of implementing true socialist norms of behaviour and objectives. The pursuit of self-dependence threatened to isolate China from the rest of the world and was leading the Chinese economy to a dead end. In the early 1970s, Zhou Enlai and Deng Xiaoping were empowered to bring the institutions of China's Soviet-type economy back to life. But it was too little, too late. By 1976, with the death of Mao and the arrest of his most radical followers soon after, Mao's economic policy regime came to an end.

Despite the counter-productive economic policies of the Maoist period, the Chinese economy during 1952–75 did exhibit some important accomplishments. The foremost of these was a record of impressive economic growth and rapid restructuring of the economy. From 1952 to 1975, China's gross domestic product (GDP) grew at an average annual rate of 6.7 per cent and the secondary sector (industry) increased its share of GDP from 20.9 to 45.7 per cent.[3] However, the reliance on repeated mass campaigns that were often growth inhibiting rather than growth enhancing produced wild variations about this positive growth trend. In fact, the average annual absolute deviation from the average annual growth rate was so large that the former was larger than the latter.

There are, of course, the well-known problems associated with the Soviet-type economic growth strategy. Growth obtained by simply mobilizing forced savings into a relatively high rate of investment in fixed capital involves inefficiencies and these inefficiencies grow over time. For example, at the beginning of the period (the first half of the 1950s), the Chinese were able to obtain a one *yuan* increase in annual output from an investment in gross capital formation of 2.51 *yuan*, but by the end of

---

3. For the sake of brevity I have tried to limit my reliance on factual statements to those that can be found in the more readily available and popular sources on developments in the Chinese economy. These include: State Statistical Bureau (PRC) and the Institute of Economic Research, Hitotsubashi University (Japan), *The Historical National Accounts of the People's Republic of China, 1952–1995*, printed and distributed by the Institute of Economic Research, Hitotsubashi University, 1997; State Statistical Bureau, *Statistical Yearbook of China*, the published hard-cover copies of 1991, 1992, 1993, 1994, 1995 and 1996 and the CD ROM version of the 1997 and 1998 volumes; *Chinese Economic Trends*, published quarterly by the Development Research Centre of the State Council, People's Republic of China.

the period (the first half of the 1970s) it took 5.49 *yuan*.[4] Then there is the problem of the neglected sectors in a Soviet-type strategy of growth. Central planners do best at what they directly control – forced savings, the allocation of those savings and the development of an industrial sector. They are much less able to plan and direct the activities of the farmer, the foreigner and the consumer according to their plan. These weak spots of the Soviet-type economic model and strategy are clearly shown in the record of economic developments under Mao. The record is especially bad in regard to the growth of personal consumption. While GDP was growing at 6.7 per cent a year in 1952–75, per capita household consumption expenditures were growing by only 2.2 per cent. Further-more, by 1975, the per capita consumption of grain, cooking oil and some meats was lower than it had been in the 1950s, while the number of Chinese living below the poverty line was growing.[5]

The Economic Policy Regime of Deng (1978–1995)

It is doubtful that any modifications, such as the campaigns to improve the management of the state-owned enterprises or adjustments in the rate and allocation of investment, as was tried in the 1970s and very early 1980s, could save the Soviet-type economic regime of Mao. Fortunately, his death in 1976 and the arrest of his most radical followers shortly thereafter provided an opportunity for a change in both leadership and the economic development strategy. While some within the leadership wanted to continue Mao's policies, the Third Plenum of the 11th CCP Central Committee in November and December of 1978 heralded the emergence of Deng Xiaoping as the supreme leader in China and the launching of Deng's economic policy regime.

Deng obviously focused on eliminating the most serious economic problems inherited from Mao. Agriculture was the most pressing of these problems and local cadres and peasants were allowed to abandon the communes and restore household farming. Except for a few key crops, such as grain and cotton, farm outputs began to be traded on relatively free markets. The state today still claims residual ownership rights in the land and retains the right to interfere in the markets as first purchaser of any farm output, as well as the right to control excessive price changes. Nevertheless, "farmers," with use rights to their land and ownership rights in their produce, now dominate rural China's market economy. To close the growing gap between the level of technology and efficiency in the Chinese economy and that in the developed economies of the world,

4. Calculated by means of three-year moving averages with a one-year lag between investment and output.

5. To give credit where credit is due, during the Mao era, the Chinese did provide for widespread educational opportunities, better access to medical and dental care, more opportunities for women, a significant social welfare package for the urban worker – those favourable accomplishments associated with most Soviet-type economies. In addition, they achieved the significant industrialization of the Chinese economy with a remarkable degree of self-sufficiency.

Deng's policies opened the Chinese economy to foreign trade and investment. In addition, China moved quickly to join those institutions that managed the rapidly growing global economy. In the urban-industrial sector, markets for most industrial products replaced the planned allocation of those goods. In other words, state-owned enterprises (SOEs) were forced on to the markets, where they had to buy their inputs and sell their outputs. Furthermore, non-state enterprises, both domestic and foreign, could be created to compete with the state-owned enterprises in those markets.

As a result of these initial changes, it soon became clear that complementary changes in the monetary and fiscal sectors were needed as well. While the state remains responsible for investment in infrastructure and other key projects, most investment activity has been removed from its budget and is now financed by self-provided funds, bank loans, sales of stock[6] and foreign investment. The People's Bank of China has been made the central bank, which sets the reserve requirements of the banks, buys and sells bonds or sets the rediscount rate, to regulate the money supply, much as does the Federal Reserve System in the United States. The rest of the banking system became commercial banks, engaging in normal banking activities for their customers. The development of a market economy, with non-state enterprises, saw a dominant share of transactions and profits made and earned by units outside the direct control of the central government. To preserve the revenue base of the central government, therefore, the tax system had to be revised to provide for higher direct taxes on individuals, uniform taxes on enterprises no matter what their ownership form, and the introduction of a value added tax on all economic activity. In addition, to ensure that the central government received its share of the taxes collected, certain taxes were to be collected directly at their source by agents of the central government.

Deng's economic policies are best viewed as a process, and this process of building a "socialist economy with Chinese characteristics" was far from complete when Deng died in 1997. The nature of the problems inherited by the current leadership as a result of the incomplete process of economic policy changes as the PRC celebrates its 50th anniversary is presented in the final section of this article. However, an assessment of the economic results achieved during Deng's rule must be presented before proceeding to that discussion to provide some balance to the rather negative assessment that follows.

The dominant objective of Mao's economic policy regime was to achieve high growth rates, but the growth rate of GDP during the Deng era was 9.8 per cent, or approximately 1.5 times the average annual growth rate under Mao. The structure of the economy was also adjusted under Deng. The tertiary sector (services), the sector seriously neglected

---

6. Although it is common to refer to these sales as sales of stock on China's new stock markets, these are really sales of debt obligations with unspecified property rights to the enterprise's assets and assign no direct management control over those assets.

during Mao's rule, regained some, but still not all, of its normal share for an economy at China's level of economic development, increasing from 23.7 per cent of GDP in 1978 to 30.7 per cent in 1995.

The change in economic policy from Mao to Deng involved a significant decentralization of decision-making throughout the economy and a withdrawal of the state from interference in the daily life of the people. Despite concerns over the threat of chaos and instability involved in reliance upon markets, the abandonment of centrally directed mass movements in favour of reliance upon markets actually reduced the average absolute deviation in the annual rate of growth by more than 50 per cent. As for the greater efficiency of a market over a Soviet-type economy, it took 5.49 *yuan* of investment in gross capital formation to obtain an increase of one *yuan* in annual output in 1973–75, but took only 1.38 *yuan* in 1992–95. This very favourable growth in efficiency was obviously related to China's growing participation in the global economy under Deng. By the end of 1995, China was the world's seventh largest participant in world trade and direct foreign investment had gone to 233,564 enterprises in China, the foreigner accounting for 40 per cent of the US$639 billion invested in those enterprises. Finally, the greatest achievement of the change in economic policy regime was the change in the livelihood of the average Chinese. Whereas per capita household consumption expenditure (in constant prices) was growing by only 2.2 per cent a year during the Mao era, the annual rate of growth increased to 7.3 per cent a year under Deng.

The Economic Policy Regime of Jiang and Zhu (1996–1999)

The Deng era has a most impressive list of accomplishments. As pointed out in other articles in this volume, however, the process of creating a stable "socialist market economy with Chinese characteristics" on a self-sustaining path of economic growth in not only incomplete but problematic. Jiang Zemin and Zhu Rongji must fine-tune many of the earlier policies that were boldly introduced by Deng. They must also develop new economic policy innovations to remove remaining constraints on China's self-sustained economic growth. Finally, they must solve some very serious economic problems inherited from Deng's policies. Focusing on these problems can give a much better appreciation of the economic condition of the Chinese economy as the PRC turns 50 than listing the impressive accomplishments achieved under Deng. As is true with people anywhere in the world, the recent past soon becomes a "golden age" of history, while the question the Chinese now demand answered by their leaders is "what have you done for us lately?"

The first major area of present concern is the decline in the rate of growth of the economy. The average annual rate of growth under Deng was 9.8 per cent and, for the period as a whole, it exhibited a strong positive time trend. However from 1992 to 1997 the average annual growth rate (in constant prices) of GDP shows a very strong negative time trend of 1.17.[7] The explanation for this downward trend is straight-forward: the sources of growth relied upon to achieve the rapid growth rates in the Deng era are no longer readily available in the economic policy regime of Jiang and Zhu.

In the early 1980s, the restoration of household farming and markets in the rural economy resulted in a one-off shift of very significant propor-tions in the production of agricultural products, then accounting for approximately one-third of China's gross domestic product. Once China's agricultural sector had been restored to household farming for the market, growth in this sector slowed.[8] Industry replaced agriculture as the leading growth sector when Deng's regime allowed the creation of non-state-owned enterprises in the mid-1980s. The result was a very rapid growth of output in what became known as the TVEs (township and village enterprises), community enterprises that had rather mixed owner-ship including the local government, former cadres, private individuals, and other local enterprises and banks. By 1985, the TVE sector accounted for 14 per cent of the labour force and produced a gross output equivalent to 30.7 per cent of China's GNP. In 1984–94, this sector's output grew at an average annual rate of 33.9 per cent. By the mid-1990s, however, it was growing at a much slower pace, and the industrial output of township enterprises even declined in 1996. This was a result of increased competition from the rapidly growing number of other TVE enterprises, the lack of access to bank credit, which was diverted mostly to the state-owned sector, and the softening of domestic demand for their output.

Fortunately, a third source of growth continued to sustain China's declining, yet substantial, growth rate in the mid-1990s: the foreign sector. In 1985–97, China's exports grew at an average annual rate of 27.7 per cent (in current prices). Over the same period, foreign direct investment (actually utilized) in China was growing at an annual average rate of more than 30 per cent. However, this source of growth was also coming to an end by the mid-1990s. In part because of the weakening of domestic demand and difficulties encountered by the foreign investor, the growth in foreign direct investment declined to below 10 per cent in 1996 and 1997, and slowed even further in 1998. Despite the Asian financial crises, Chinese exports did continue to grow rapidly in 1998, but only because of the decline in competition from those economies hit by the crises and the ability of the Chinese to shift exports destined for those economies rapidly to the United States and European Union. Neither of these conditions is expected to hold during 1999, when the full impact of the Asian crises should affect China's export trade, reducing

7. The growth rate of GDP was 14.2% in 1992, 13.5% in 1993, 12.6% in 1994, 10.5% in 1995, 9.6% in 1996 and 8.8% in 1997.

8. Jean Oi's article in this volume evaluates the current leadership's efforts to resolve the problem of the Chinese farmers' property rights in land as a means for restoring incentives in this sector. However, as serious as this problem may be, the current leadership should appreciate that no modern economy in the world has been able to rely on household farming in a market economy without price supports or an income policy. There is no indication that either is a part of Jiang and Zhu's policy.

the contribution of export promotion in sustaining the rapid growth of China's economy. Throughout Deng's rule, the growth of private incomes and private consumption demand helped sustain China's economic growth, but after years of large increases in private consumption, that source of growth is also running out as the growth in domestic consumption is stagnating. In short, the leadership of Jiang and Zhu must seek out new engines of growth to sustain the high growth rates enjoyed by the Chinese under Deng.

A second area of serious concern is the difficulty in obtaining further increases in efficiency. The gains in efficiency under Deng were the result of the shift from a planned to a market economy and the rapid growth of non-state-owned enterprises. The state-owned enterprises were not privatized and have been retained as one of the remaining means by which China's economy can be termed a "socialist market economy." Forced on to the market and faced with competition, the SOEs have suffered ever-growing losses. In 1978, their pre-tax profits per 100 *yuan* of gross output were 24.9 *yuan*, in 1990 they were 12 *yuan* and in 1997 they were 10.4 *yuan*. In 1998, the number of SOEs suffering losses was increasing, as was the size of their losses. This worsening position was putting the financial position of both the state and the banking sector at risk.[9]

It was in recognition of these threats that the Jiang Zemin and Zhu Rongji leadership decided it was time to tackle seriously the problem of the SOEs.[10] This will involve the widespread privatization of the smaller SOEs, the merger of some, and a significant increase in the closing of the most inefficient. Each of these moves will create large-scale unemployment, a most unwelcome challenge to the leadership of Jiang Zemin and Zhu Rongji as the PRC turns 50.[11] In addition, some of the larger SOEs in key sectors will undoubtedly remain state-owned, but with improved management so as to minimize their losses. The record of the repeated efforts to improve the management of the SOEs over the past two decades, however, is not very impressive.

A third major area of concern is the insolvency of the banking system. The SOEs suffering losses were kept afloat by bank loans, with funds made available to the banking system by the state or by the savings deposits of the people.[12] The banking system accumulated a large share of its assets in loans to the SOEs and as the latter suffered ever-growing losses, many of these loans became unrecoverable. As long as the interest

9. These losses were putting the state at risk by becoming a "dead-weight" loss in the budget. In 1976, while the profits of the SOEs had declined to the point where they were no longer reported in the budget, the revenue from their income tax exceeded the expenditures on subsidies to the loss-making SOEs by 17.43 billion RMB. In 1997, however, the net flow in the budget due to these two items was a negative 2.49 billion. For the explanation of how these losses were putting the banking system at risk, see the explanation in the text below.

10. This resolve of the Jiang and Zhu leadership to "bite the bullet" and truly reform the SOEs is discussed more fully in Dorothy Solinger's article in this volume.

11. Elisabeth J. Croll discusses the problem of growing unemployment of the urban labour force in her article in this volume.

12. This transition from supporting the SOEs with *forced* savings to supporting them with the *voluntary* savings of the people is one of the more remarkable aspects of the success of Deng's policies.

was repaid, however, the loans were simply rolled over when they became due. As the amount of bad loans grows and the share of those loans, which are no longer paying interest, also grows, the banking system becomes more and more insolvent. If people ever demanded their money in a run on the banks, they could not be paid without a large injection of funds from the state. Furthermore, by using their available funds for loans to the SOEs, credit made available by the high rate of private savings is made unavailable to the more efficient non-state sector. Even if the SOEs are to be privatized, who will buy their debt obligation, and if they are closed who will pay off their bank loans? The only answer, of course, is to close the inefficient SOEs, write off their bad debts and recapitalize the banking system, but who will provide the capital?

In the absence of a well-developed capital market, the recapitalization of those SOEs that will remain state-owned and the recapitalization of the banks will undoubtedly be the responsibility of the state. But a fourth major area of concern is the state's own budget problems. As a result of the decentralization of control over economic activities and the rapid growth of the non-state sector, the budget revenue of the central government had declined to only 10.7 per cent of GDP in 1995. The new financial and tax system introduced in 1994 was designed to reverse this trend and did halt the decline, but had only increased the share of the state's revenue in GDP by one percentage point by 1997. Thus, it is no surprise that the central government runs a deficit in its budget, financed by bank credits (printing money) and by bond sales.

Although the actual deficit is relatively small, the fiscal problems of the state are compounded by the fact that over 40 per cent of its expenditures are net transfers from the central to local governments. Adding to the potential burden of recapitalizing the SOEs that are retained and the banks, there is the need for tremendous investment in the infrastructure. This sector was seriously neglected during the attempts at self-sufficiency under Mao and lagged behind overall growth of the economy under Deng. Although the current leadership of Jiang and Zhu recognize the need to give the development of infrastructure priority, they seriously underestimate the amount of investment required and overestimate the amount of that investment that will be provided by foreigners. To meet its various obligations, the central government will need to continue the reform of the tax system aimed at increasing its revenue as a share of GDP. These efforts must be accompanied by renegotiations of its contract with local governments to increase the central government's share of the total revenue received by government units at all levels.

To this list of four serious problem areas in the economy as the PRC celebrates its 50th anniversary can be added problems of increasing corruption and the worsening regional and class-size distribution of incomes. Compared with the popular perception of the past successes of Deng, this is a rather sober appraisal of the economic problems inherited by the post-Deng leadership. But other considerations can be introduced to qualifying this pessimistic conclusion, as most authors of articles included in this volume have done. The identification of Jiang Zemin and Zhu Rongji in the designation of the economic policy regime of Jiang and Zhu denotes some very important changes when compared with the use of Mao and Deng in identifying the economic policy regimes of earlier periods. These two men are much less dominant in the coalition leadership from which they derive their power than was true of Mao or Deng. Yet, although they lack the credentials of veterans of the Revolution, they also lack much of the ideological baggage – often economically counter-productive – possessed by their predecessors.

Zhu Rongji confronts China's current economic problems with a growing number of other able leaders who share his vision of China's economic future. And this generation of leaders is more educated, they often were trained as engineers, and they have earned reputations as problem-solvers and administrators. They know what China's economic problems are and have the technical knowledge to solve them. The fundamental unknown is whether or not they can sustain their purpose and retain the political support of the Chinese people as they proceed. Finally, we can take hope in referring to a sentence in the concluding paragraph of Lucian Pye's overview article in this volume: "Things are never as black or white, as good or as bad, as Westerners tend to expect them to be."

Two Decades of Rural Reform in China: An Overview and Assessment

Jean C. Oi

China's countryside has been the target of dramatic change since 1949.[1] The CCP directed redistribution in land reform, the transformation away from private farming to collectivization, and, most recently, the move back to household production. Throughout the PRC's 50 years, agriculture and peasants have paid for the regime's ambitious programme of industrialization, as the price scissors consistently favoured the urban over the rural producers. The state struggled with its food producers over the grain harvest, using ideology and organization to maximize both the production and extraction of the surplus from the countryside.

The regime's concern for food security remains unchanged, but beginning in the late 1970s it abandoned the previous system of collective production, diversified the rural economy away from grain production and turned to economic incentives to spur growth. By the mid-1980s household production was firmly in place, agriculture output grew and, most impressively, rural industry went from almost nothing to become the fastest growing sector in the entire economy, with output increasing more than 20 per cent a year. More than 200 million peasants were lifted from extreme poverty by government procurement price increases (by as much as 50 per cent from the Mao period), free market development and new income opportunities.[2] Net income rose from less than 150 *yuan* in 1978 to close to 400 *yuan* in 1985, and reached approximately 2,000 *yuan* by 1997.[3] In real per capita terms, rural incomes increased by 63 per cent between 1985 and 1997.[4]

Such impressive economic results gave the regime a tremendous boost in legitimacy, but the process of reform had just begun. China reformed around the system of central planning to avoid the thorny issues of the "big bang" approach.[5] But for the last decade or more, policy makers have had to confront the dilemma of incomplete reform as well as deal with the consequences of successful reform. On the agricultural front, after stunning success in raising grain production immediately after the reform began, by the second half of the 1980s grain production dropped as new, more lucrative job opportunities lured rural labour away from agriculture. On the industrial front, after almost a decade of booming

1. I would like to thank the participants of the workshop held in conjunction with this volume at the Centro De Estudos Asiáticos, Universidade de Aveiro, Portugal, for their helpful comments. Special thanks go to Scott Rozelle for his critical reading of an earlier draft of this paper. I also want to thank Cai Yongshun for research assistance.
2. Scott Rozelle, Albert Park, Vincent Benziger and Changqing Ren, "Targeted poverty investments and economic growth in China," *World Development*, Vol. 26, No. 12 (December 1998) pp. 2137–51.
3. *Zhongguo tongji nianjian 1998 (China Statistical Yearbook 1998)*, p. 345.
4. Albert Nyberg and Scott Rozelle, "Accelerating China's rural transformation," World Bank Working Paper Series, Washington, D.C., forthcoming.
5. See, for example, articles in Andrew Walder (ed.), *China's Transitional Economy* (Oxford: Oxford University Press, 1996).

growth, township and village enterprises began to show serious problems by the early 1990s. Regional inequalities became more rather than less evident, as the coastal areas continued to pull ahead of the still desperately poor central and western regions, creating two disparate faces of the Chinese countryside. The peasant discontent in some instances erupted into unrest, mostly in the poor agricultural regions of the country that had benefited little from the reforms.

What the existence of these problems says about how far the rural reforms have succeeded is ambiguous. Any assessment of China's rural reforms depends on the yardstick one uses. For example, one could view the results primarily from an economic perspective, looking at growth rates and yields per hectare of land, or from the perspective of inequality and stratification, or from that of political stability, and in each case the outcome will differ. Similarly, does one compare the results to what other developing nations have been able to achieve or does one focus on China's remaining problems? The mass of rural residents have raised their standard of living, but there remain another 50 million (about 6 per cent of the rural population) who still live in abject poverty. Incomes on average have increased steadily at around 5 per cent a year since 1991, but this also means that those who have failed to benefit from these increases feel that much poorer by comparison.[6]

China faces the problems of consolidation of reform, which is more challenging than its initiation.[7] The insulation provided by initial policy successes begins to give way to growing problems and discontent. After a decade of transition, by the 1990s, the "trickle-down" theory underlying Deng's policy of "let some get rich first" has come under increasing question as those who have fallen behind in the first phase of reform become anxious and those who have failed to benefit lose patience. What makes these problems particularly challenging for the current Chinese communist leadership is that the initial reforms, while not complete, have significantly altered the economic and political context. Policies that were effective during earlier periods may no longer work.

This article provides an overview and assessment of the major rural reforms of the last 20 years. It views these reforms from the perspective of the social, political and economic goals of the regime. What will become evident is the increasing number of trade-offs that the regime has had to make as its policy agendas have become increasingly complex and interrelated. What looks economically irrational and inefficient may be essential for political and social stability.

Reform in Agriculture: An Old Story in a New Context

Beginning in the late 1970s and culminating in the early 1980s, the initial phase of rural reforms worked remarkably well to solve the

6. Nyberg and Rozelle, "Accelerating."
7. See Joan Nelson, "The politics of economic transformation: is Third World experience relevant in Eastern Europe?" *World Politics*, Vol. 45, No. 3 (April 1993), pp. 433–463.

incentive problems that had plagued Maoist agriculture. Production boomed to the point where peasants for the first time had difficulty selling grain to the state. Unfortunately, this increase was short lived. After 1985 the state once again worried about grain supply, as production increased only about one per cent per year.[8] While some have attributed the initial increases in grain production to the change in property rights from collective to household production, others have blamed the same system for the decreases after 1985. The problem, these latter analysts argue, is the incompleteness of property rights reform, that is, ownership remains collective and peasants do not have secure rights over the land they are working. This keeps peasant investment in and enthusiasm for agriculture low.[9]

Household contracting allocated peasant households the right to manage the land they worked and rights to the residual income from that land, but not the right of alienation, that is the right to dispose of the land. This prohibited peasants from selling their land, but more disturbing, it left the collective – either the village or in some cases the village small group – with the right to take that land and redistribute it to someone else. The original land contracts provided no commitment that those who invested to improve the land would be the long-term beneficiaries of such investments.

The general principle regulating land distribution was that if a household lost or gained a member, then it would have a portion of its land adjusted accordingly. However, it was left ambiguous as to when there would be a redistribution, whether it would be a minor adjustment or a major redistribution where everyone's land would be re-allocated, and whether families would get back the same plots. Government-sponsored surveys found that since the initiation of the household responsibility system, nation-wide, between the late 1970s and the mid to late 1990s, the majority of villages (at least 80 per cent) had adjusted land allocations at least once, and some did five times or more.[10]

Not all research comes to the same conclusion about the importance of secure property rights. Some suggests that peasants may not always want long contracts.[11] The insecurity problem is not an issue in villages where social norms prompt all households to invest at least minimal amounts of

8. Nyberg and Rozelle, "Accelerating."

9. See, for example, Roy Prosterman, Tim Hanstad and Li Ping, "Can China feed itself?" *Scientific American*, November 1996, pp. 90–95.

10. See Office of Fixed Investigation Points in Pural China (Nongcun guding guancha dian bangongshi), "Dui dier lun tudi chengbao gongzuo de guancha fenxi" ("An observation and analysis of the second round of land contracting"), *Jingji yanjiu cankao* (*Reference of Economic Research*), No. 73 (1997), pp. 32–42; and Office of Fixed Investigation Points in Rural China, "Dangqian nongcun tudi chengbao jingying guanli de xianzhuang ji wenti" ("The current situation and problems of the management of land contracting in the countryside"), *Nongcun jingji yanjiu cankao* (*A Reference for the Study of the Rural Economy*), No. 5 (1998), pp. 28–30.

11. Kung and Liu, for example, note that some "villagers prefer short-term contracts ... because off-farm employment remains unstable and farming therefore serves as the last resort should these more lucrative alternatives become suddenly unavailable." James Kai-sing Kung and Shouying Liu, "Farmers' preferences regarding ownership and land tenure in post-Mao China: unexpected evidence from eight counties," *China Journal*, No. 38 (July 1997), pp. 33–64.

effort and fertilizer. In such villages, even if there were a land readjustment, each household could be reasonably assured that it would get a comparable, if not the same, plot of land.[12]

Betting that lengthening the land contracts would at least ameliorate the problems in agriculture, the state took a decisive step towards granting peasants more secure property rights, but stopped short of privatizing ownership. The state increased the length of land leases in 1993 to at least 30 years, and for some more marginal lands, termed the "four types of barren land" – barren hills, slopes, ditches and beaches – lease rights could be 50 years or more.[13]

Whether this extension of property rights will be sufficient to increase enthusiasm for farming is questionable. Regardless of the security of rights over the land, the returns from agriculture, particularly grain production, rank at the bottom compared to other income opportunities in China's new economic context.[14] Although the state has raised grain prices a number of times since 1979, and finally abolished food rationing in the early 1990s, the government remains intent on keeping grain prices low and supply stable for the urban areas. After the glut of grain in 1983–84, a 1985 ruling said that peasants would receive a higher price for their quota sales to the state, but they would no longer receive a high over-quota sale price for any over-quota sales. The free markets were not much relief as prices plummeted with increased supply. Grain prices have continued to fall sharply during the good harvests, such as occurred in 1991 and 1992. In 1997, according to one report, the market price of grain in one area dropped by 40 per cent.[15]

The situation is worse when one considers the costs of production and the relative lack of infrastructural and technological support in the wake of decollectivization, especially low investment in the development of water supply, which is essential to maximize benefits from fertilizer. Throughout the period the costs of production have steadily increased. On average for all agricultural products, production costs have increased close to 15 per cent per year between 1984 and 1996.[16] The re-emergence of the scissors effect, which was only temporarily mediated by the 1979 price increases, inclines peasants to invest less time and fewer resources in their allocated plots of land. Peasants can use organic fertilizers, and this is what the state encourages because of their long-term benefits to the

12. Cai Yongshun, "Peasant and farmland use in five Chinese villages," M. Phil. thesis, Hong Kong University of Science and Technology, Division of Social Science, 1997.
13. See Chen Xiwen, "Ba-wu nongye" ("Agriculture in the Eighth Five-Year Plan") in *Zhongguo nongye nianjian 1996* (*China Agricultural Yearbook 1996*), pp. 19–20.
14. James Kung, "Equal entitlement versus tenure security under a regime of collective property rights: peasants' preference for institutions in post-reform Chinese agriculture," *Journal of Comparative Economics*, Vol. 21, No. 2 (1995), pp. 82–111; Kung and Liu, "Farmers' preferences regarding ownership."
15. Gao Youqing, "Taiping xiang bufen nongmin weihe gandang hei hukou" ("Why were some peasants in Taiping town willing to have a black household registration"), *Neican xuanbian* (*A Compilation of Selected Internal Materials*), No. 21 (1998), pp. 16–17.
16. Lu Nan, "1980–1996 nian nongye shengchan chengben he nongye laodong shengchanlü wenti" ("Issues of agricultural costs and the rate of agricultural labour productivity between 1980 and 1996), *Jiage lilun yu shijian* (*Theory and Practice of Price*), No. 9 (1997), pp. 23–28.

soil and higher yields, but use has decreased. This may not be a result of insecure property rights but simply of decreased supply and the high opportunity costs associated with collection and application.

The low rate of return is further aggravated when the procurement system goes astray and peasants are given only an IOU and told to wait for actual cash payment, sometimes for months, when they deliver their grain for sale to the state. The state hopes to end IOUs with the establishment of the Agricultural Development Bank, which is separate from the Agricultural Bank, to channel procurement funds directly to the state granaries to prevent localities from illegally mis-allocating funds earmarked for procurement.

A Losing Battle: New Aspirations of China's Peasants

As the years of reform have passed, the economy has become more diversified and peasants have more freedom of choice and movement. There are signs that regardless of the extension of land contracts, increasing numbers of peasants are becoming, at best, only part-time farmers, and some would prefer to leave farming entirely.[17] By 1996 China had over 23 million rural enterprises, employing over 135 million people, about one-third of the rural labour force.[18] These jobs absorbed a substantial portion of the surplus labour created with the decollectivization of agriculture.

It is true that only a relatively small portion of China's countryside, concentrated mainly along the eastern coast, has many rural industries. But the existence of alternative lucrative income opportunities, even if limited, has restructured the aspirations of the entire rural labour force. Approximately 60 million rural residents migrate annually in search of higher paying jobs. Some migrate to cities, others to richer, more industrialized rural areas where villagers are too busy working in industry to farm.[19]

Regional inequality existed during the Mao period as well, but the differences were less sharp. Most importantly, the state could effectively use administrative means to prohibit peasants from leaving their assigned villages to find better job opportunities. The rural reforms set into motion in the late 1970s, particularly decollectivization and the re-opening of markets, effectively ended the state's ability to control migration. Originally, when the reforms began, peasants were required to have authorization (zhengming) before they could leave their home villages, but in practice this was only loosely enforced, if at all. In China today, peasants

17. Chu Yelai, "Neimenggu xuduo nongmin qigen waichu dailai xin wenti" ("New problems arise because peasants leave land for off-farm work in Inner Mongolia"), *Neican xuanbian*, No. 27 (1998), pp. 21–22.

18. The 135 million represents a 46% increase in jobs from 1990 alone. *Zhongguo tongji nianjian 1997*, p. 6.

19. See Solinger in this volume and Elisabeth J. Croll and Huang Ping, "Migration for and against agriculture in eight Chinese villages," *The China Quarterly*, No. 149 (March 1997), pp. 128–146.

have the freedom to leave the fields and leave the countryside in search of opportunities.

Most, if not all, modernizing countries would see such a massive movement of the population from agriculture as a positive development – it is a phenomenon all industrializing countries face. But in China, successful rural industrialization has created a disjuncture between the new realities of the Chinese countryside and the government's expectations towards its rural population. The state maintains land and grain policies formulated for a period when it could keep all people registered as peasant households on the farms, actively working the land and growing grain.

The consequence is policy incoherence where off-farm jobs, the source of rural income increases, continue to mushroom and the rural labour force is allowed to be increasingly mobile, but the regime stubbornly adheres to its original policy of household responsibility contracting that allocates land to approximately 70 per cent of China's population that is registered as "peasants." Each peasant household, regardless of whether it wants to farm, is allocated land, required to cultivate that land and pay all taxes and fees, and to sell to the state a set quota of grain associated with each plot. Little land actually lies fallow, but an increasing amount is not worked with the care and investment of time and inputs that would produce maximum yields. Those who are now only part-time farmers find it burdensome either to spend their off-farm earnings to buy market-priced grain to meet state-mandated grain sales quotas or to leave the older and weaker members of their families to farm the family's land allocation. How effectively they can do the latter often depends on how much mechanized assistance is available for the heavier work.

Underlying Agenda for Collective Ownership of Land

The problem is not that the state is unaware of the problems with its land policy. The State Planning Commission and the Ministry of Agriculture have discussed large-scale rural urbanization and population reclassification to change the status of 300 million peasants into residents of rural towns by 2010.[20] The question is why the leadership clings to a seemingly outdated land policy.

There is no economic reason why all rural residents must farm to ensure China a sufficient grain supply. While some worry that China might empty the world's food basket, it can import more grain. Those only concerned with economic efficiency might wonder why China doesn't simply privatize the ownership of land and allow a true market in land to develop. It could then subsidize those who do farm to ensure profitability and rely on scientific advances in farming to increase yields. Such subsidies and division of labour were already under way in the most

20. Lin Zhaomu and Shao Ning, *Kua shiji de fazhan silu yanjiu* (*Research on Thoughts on Development at the Turn of the Century*) (Beijing: Zhongguo jihua chubanshe, 1995), p. 59.

highly industrialized villages like Daqiuzhuang, near Tianjin, where as early as the 1980s, only a few households that were designated to farm were able to produce sufficient grain to feed the entire community and allowed the village to meet its grain sales quotas to the state.

In China, equal land distribution and the desire to keep as many peasants as possible growing at least some grain is a political rather than an economic issue. But ideological rigidity does not seem to be the primary force driving this policy choice. More important are the political obstacles and underlying agendas that collective ownership of land can serve within the broader context of the regime's programme of gradual reform.

First, and perhaps foremost, China, like Japan in the past, does not want to be dependent on imports of grain. Just as the regime wanted all areas of the country to be self-sufficient in grain during the Mao period, forcing everyone to "take grain as the key link" regardless of whether they were suited to growing grain or not, China's long-standing concern about food security and supply turns a positive development – the restructuring of the rural labour force – into a worry for the regime. On the one hand, China needs and wants to diversify the rural economy and develop rural industry: those small factories that dot China's countryside, which now produce more than half its total industrial output, account for a sizeable portion of its exports and have been responsible for the bulk of the rise in rural incomes. Yet the regime is deeply ambivalent about the prospect of increasing numbers turning agriculture, and particularly grain production, into a sideline activity; there are millions of peasants who have migrated to the cities or found employment in rural industries.

Secondly, even if the state is not worried about food security, it must worry about a political backlash from the bulk of rural households if it tries to take land away from the peasants. While rural households have a decreased interest in working their land, most seem unwilling to give it up. Some pay outsiders to farm their land, simply to maintain their rights to that land, which remains their security. The growth of rural industry does not overshadow the fact that nation-wide, even though the proportion has decreased, agriculture still accounts for about 60 per cent of rural household income.[21]

Thirdly, the state needs to have an economic cushion for the peasants as it begins to tackle the state-owned enterprise problem, where it has created massive lay-offs. The threats to stability are that much greater in the shadow of the Asian financial crisis. The millions who have previously found work in the urban centres are going to find it increasingly difficult to keep their jobs as more and more of the urban population becomes unemployed. Authorities can more easily justify telling rural

21. Agricultural Investigation Group of the State Statistical Bureau, "Nongchanpin shengchan bodong dui nongmin shouru de yingxiang" ("The impact of fluctuations in agricultural production on peasant income"), *Jingji gongzuozhe xuexi ziliao* (*Study Materials for Economic Workers*), No. 31 (1998), pp. 6–18.

migrants to leave the cities and factories, both in urban and rural areas, if these individuals can return to farming.

Retreat from Grain Markets

The state concern about food security and supply is further evident in its policies towards grain markets. The regime has consistently shown signs of unease with the grain market that emerged after the reforms began. Throughout the 1980s and 1990s, grain markets were closed when state grain procurements were being collected. Only after the peasants had met their state obligations of grain could they sell it on the open market. Nevertheless, for most of the 20 years the state allowed a substantial force of private grain traders to traverse the countryside, buying directly from the peasant households. Concurrently, the state encouraged its state grain stations to pay market prices to compete with the private grain traders for peasant grain.[22]

But in 1998, the state took a step that signalled new concerns and anxiety over grain supply that had not been seen for most of the previous 20 years. It reversed earlier policies and declared that state grain stores should be the *sole* procurer of grain from the peasants. Private grain traders are allowed to operate, but they can only buy grain from the state grain stores and are forbidden to buy directly from the peasants.[23] While details of this are still sketchy, the state's actions indicate a clear retreat to administrative prohibitions and more, rather than less, state intervention in the market, in an attempt to re-create the state's Maoist era monopoly.[24] It remains to be seen how viable this policy will be in the new context. As is well known, local officials are good at the "selective implementation of policies."[25] The key is how costly this policy will be to local interests. Apart from the convenience and savings to the producers of having private traders go to the farms, there remains the issue of price. Will these reforms provide peasants a more stable price? If so, will grain prices throughout the system increase, thus fuelling inflation?

Reform of Rural Industry: From Collective Ownership to State-sponsored Privatization

In contrast to land and grain policy, the leadership has more room to manoeuvre in the case of rural industry. Changing ownership forms within rural industry directly affects a much smaller proportion of the population. The regime has moved fairly quickly and decisively to

22. See Albert Park, "Reforming state–market relations in rural China," *Economics of Transition*, Vol. 6, No. 2 (1998), pp. 461–480, and Terry Sicular, "Establishing markets: the process of commercialization in agriculture," in Andrew Walder (ed.), *Zouping in Transition: The Process of Reform in Rural North China* (Cambridge, MA: Harvard University Press, 1998), pp. 115–157.

23. See "Liangshi liutong tizhi gaige de yuanze" ("Principles for reforming the grain circulation system"), *Neican xuanbian*, No. 22 (1998), pp. 7–11.

24. See Scott Rozelle, "Grain marketing brief," unpublished ms., 19 September 1998.

25. See, for example, Kevin O'Brien and Lianjiang Li, "Selective policy implementation in rural China," *Comparative Politics*, Vol. 31, No. 2 (January 1999), pp. 167–186.

address the economic problems of rural industry – that sector of the rural economy that has been at the core of China's economic success in the last 20 years. During the 1980s the regime pursued a strategy of local-state led development that favoured publicly owned firms at the township and village levels. But by the early 1990s, local governments, with the support of the centre, began to shift preferential treatment to private firms.[26] By the mid-1990s, local governments below the county level began a programme of state-sponsored privatization that is the prototype of the experiments now being conducted in the urban state-owned enterprises. Township and village governments are selling their enterprises for private operation, even in places like Sunan, the home of the "collectivist model of rural development."[27] Along with outright sales, there are half-way arrangements that turn collectively owned enterprises into shareholding arrangements.[28] By the end of 1997 about a third (520,000) of all collectively owned enterprises nation-wide had been reformed. Of these, the largest number changed into shareholding co-operatives (21.3 per cent).[29]

The impetus for this change was a recalculation of local interests. The need for more revenue at both the national and local levels overshadowed concern about forms of ownership. Originally local officials promoted collectively owned enterprises because it served both the interests of local governments and the officials who served in them. Township and village enterprises yielded revenue for local coffers that could then be used for administrative expenses and for individual cadre bonuses. Successful development of local industry also elicited admiration from the higher levels. But by the early 1990s collectively owned enterprises were becoming liabilities rather than assets. Local agricultural banks and savings and loan co-operatives, the major lenders to this sector, were coming under increasing pressure from the upper levels as they failed to collect their loans: there was no easily identifiable party liable for the debt. Instead of collateral, township and village enterprise loans were guaranteed by local government agencies or officials.

Local authorities could afford to shift their support because private firms were finally becoming a viable alternative source of tax revenue. By the early 1990s, private firms were beginning to grow both in number and in scale, as individual savings increased and political restrictions on private business eased. To ensure that these firms grow, county authorities provide various types of assistance and offer incentives, including changing one's household status, to individuals who start

26. For an elaboration of points made in this section see Jean Oi, *Rural China Takes Off: Institutional Foundations of Economic Reform* (Berkeley: University of California Press, 1999).

27. See James Kung, "The evolution of property rights in village enterprises: the case of Wuxi county," in Jean C. Oi and Andrew G. Walder (eds.), *Property Rights and China's Economic Reforms* (Stanford: Stanford University Press, forthcoming, 1999).

28. Eduard Vermeer, "The development of the shareholding cooperative system: a property rights analysis," in Oi and Walder, *Property Rights and China's Economic Reforms*.

29. Chen Jianguang, "Dangqian xiangzhen qiye fazhan qingkuang ji duice jianyi" ("The current development of TVEs and some suggestions"), *Jingii gongzuozhe xuexi ziliao*, No. 27 (1998), pp. 36–47.

private businesses over a certain size.[30] The symbiotic relationship that developed between the private sector and local governments lessens the threat to the local state of a rising private business class.[31]

While some township and village cadres resisted and resented this shift in support, those in the most developed villages agreed that the scale of their operations had become so large that it was no longer possible for them to continue their "hands-on" involvement. Some small firms have been sold or leased because of labour problems; some township and village enterprise managers are no longer willing to accept a subordinate role and limited pay when others with similar skills have become rich in private firms.[32] Consequently, for some villages, it is easier to sell some of the enterprises or at least sell part of the shares in them and get income without the headaches. Limited privatization is embraced to improve the overall efficiency of rural industry and increase profits.

Does this mean that privately owned firms will soon overshadow collectively owned enterprises in China's countryside; that private businessmen will replace local communist officials in economic and political power? A number of factors argue against this. Local officials still control numerous resources on which private business depends. Moreover, privatization is still limited: in some places only the smaller and more problematic are being sold while the larger and more economically profitable are being kept under local state control. Of those that have been turned into shareholding co-operatives, local governments often still retain controlling interests. Local governments are unlikely to relinquish completely the access that they currently have to non-tax revenues of publicly owned firms. Another consideration is the social and political consequences that might come with changes in ownership systems. The dislocations of transition to a market economy found in Eastern Europe and the former Soviet Union have been attenuated to an extensive degree in China by the redistributive socialism that existed at least to a limited extent under local state corporatism.[33] Local governments will have to think carefully about how a larger private sector will affect their ability to provide an economic cushion for their communities. This is yet another reason why the state may want to maintain collective ownership of land.

Reform in Village Leadership: Peasant Discontent and Democratic Elections

The spectre of peasant discontent and unrest has already appeared in parts of the countryside that remain mired in poverty. Peasants have

30. See Jean Oi, "The evolution of local state corporatism," in Walder, *Zouping in Transition*, pp. 35–62.
31. See David Wank, *Commodifying Communism: Business, Trust, and Politics in a Chinese City* (Cambridge: Cambridge University Press, 1999).
32. See Kung, "The evolution of property rights in village enterprises."
33. Jean Oi, "The fate of the collective after the commune," in Deborah Davis and Ezra Vogel (eds.), *Chinese Society on the Eve of Tiananmen: The Impact of Reform* (Cambridge, MA: Council on East Asian Studies, Harvard University, 1990), pp. 15–36.

always had the means to show their unhappiness with government policies and local officials, even during the Maoist period.[34] But unlike in the past, their resistance is now overt, protesting against high taxes, low grain prices, land requisitions, social and cultural policies, and abusive officials.[35] Some have been large, violent demonstrations, such as occurred in Renshou county, Sichuan, where 10–15,000 people were involved.[36] Others are more peaceful and use law to argue against their local officials.[37]

What is new and surprising is not the existence of such disturbances so much as the state's response. The centre strongly supports the Organic Law of Village Committees (*cunweihui zuzhi fa*), passed in draft form in 1987, which promotes village assemblies and competitive elections of village officials. But one should not jump to any conclusions about what this might mean for democratic change under communist rule. Here, the CCP has a clear underlying policy agenda. While the end result may be more democratic participation in villages, elections are being pushed by the central state, not as an end in themselves but as a means to solve the problems of economic stagnation and cadre recruitment in poor villages that are "paralysed" or "partially paralysed" after decollectivization transferred the rights to the income from the sale of the agricultural harvest from village government to the individual peasant producers.[38] The urgency of the situation has been compounded by an ageing village leadership and lack of interest among talented individuals to serve as cadres.[39]

Village elections are a pressure valve to let peasants vent their dissatisfaction, but one meant to point the responsibility for continued poverty and poor leadership in villages away from the central authorities. Elections put the burden of success and failure directly on the villagers and their popularly elected leaders. The central authorities hope the successful implementation of competitive elections and village representative assemblies will elicit more rather than less compliance. Examples suggest that after leaders are popularly elected, peasants pay their fees and obligations

34. See Jean Oi, *State and Peasant: The Political Economy of Village Government* (Berkeley: University of California Press, 1989), ch. 5.

35. For a detailed discussion and examples, see Thomas Bernstein, "Instability in rural China," in David Shambaugh (ed.), *Is China Unstable? Assessing the Factors* (Washington, D.C.: Sigur Center for Asian Studies, July 1998), pp. 93–110. Also see Kevin O'Brien and Lianjiang Li, "Villagers and popular resistance in contemporary China," *Modern China*, Vol. 22, No. 1 (January 1996), pp. 28–61.

36. See Bernstein, "Instability in rural China."

37. Kevin O'Brien and Lianjiang Li, "The politics of lodging complaints in rural China," *The China Quarterly*, No. 143 (September 1995), pp. 756–783. Also Kevin O'Brien, "Rightful resistance," *World Politics*, Vol. 49, No. 1 (October 1996), pp. 31–55.

38. See, for example, Wang Qinglin and Fan Wenke, "Jiaqiang nongcun jiceng dang zuzhi jianshe shi dangwuzhiji" ("Strengthening the construction of rural Party organization at the grass roots is a pressing task"), *Hebei nongcun gongzuo* (*Hebei Rural Work*), No. 12 (1994), pp. 7–8.

39. See, for example, Zhang Guoqing, Fan Zhiyong, and Yan Xinge, "Zhuazhu san ge huanjie, gaohao cunji ganbu guifanhua guanli" ("Seize the three links, manage the standards of village-level cadres well"), *Hebei nongcun gongzuo*, No. 5 (1994) p. 42.

more fully, but whether this will always be the case is the risk that the regime has decided to take.[40]

A Mid-term Assessment: Conflicting Goals and Directions of China's Rural Reforms

As China has been on the road between a Maoist and market system, the decision makers have driven at varying speeds and in different directions while trying to achieve diverse results in a changing rural context. In some instances the regime seems intent on clinging to earlier policies; in others it moves boldly ahead. The regime refuses to privatize land, but it supports the privatization of rural industry. Private grain traders and a grain market have been allowed to develop, but this was followed by a return to a state monopoly for the procurement of grain. Most surprisingly, a regime known for resisting political reform is promoting village self-governance and competitive village elections. While there may still be an ideological compass, the lack of consistency in rural policies suggests that other more immediate and pressing issues guide decision makers.

The establishment of village elections is an instance where the cost of not taking this action outweighs the risks. While the state may fear that allowing village elections will provoke other sectors to demand political reform, not taking such a step may entail even more serious problems, given the signs of increasing discontent in the countryside and the difficulties of finding suitable leaders for the poorest of China's villages. Potentially, the policy of village elections is the most radical of the rural reform measures. In practice, the impact of this policy is likely to be muted, at least in the short term, by problems in implementation. Preliminary evidence suggests that there may be a negative correlation between levels of industrial development and political participation in China's villages, both in interest in attending village assembly meetings and in the occurrence of contested elections.[41] It is also true that the Communist Party has only consented to go part of the way down the road of reform. Party officials, that is the village Party secretary, who may still be the most powerful decision maker in China's villages, are not subject to popular election.

In sum, the rural reforms have not moved in step and there is no reason to believe that future policies will be any different. Some policy areas are likely to be reformed more than others. Some policy decisions will move the economy closer to the market, while others at times may even go backwards. This should not be surprising. China is a country riddled with policy contradictions. While it arrests dissidents, it also promotes democratic village elections and encourages peasants to attend village

40. On village elections and their role in village politics see Jean C. Oi and Scott Rozelle, "Elections and power: the locus of decision making in Chinese villages," paper presented at the conference "Elections in Taiwan, Hong Kong, and Mainland China: Does Limited Democracy Lead to Democracy?" Hoover Institution, Stanford University, 5–6 March 1999.
    41. *Ibid.*

assembly meetings. One can explain these contradictions by pointing to divisions within the leadership or by arguing that different sectors are under the control of different levels of the system. This study has shown that policies may serve more than one set of agendas, interests and audiences.

Demolishing Partitions: Back to Beginnings in the Cities?

Dorothy J. Solinger

Using euphemisms and albeit haltingly, the leaders of the PRC in its 40s began blasting the barricades their forebears had constructed to design what they had considered a fully pristine, orthodoxly socialist, separate urban realm. The result of this recent demolition is that, as the system turns 50, its political elite – along with the markets they have licensed – is remodelling the metropolises into places less distinct socially from the rural areas outside them and much less homogeneous internally than the urban areas from which they are metamorphosing.

This transformation is occurring since decision makers in the 1990s, under the threat of economic assault, began to put squarely on to the market the two most controversial, ideologically problematical categories most persistently resistant to marketization in the 1980s: ownership and labour. Specifically, top politicians are demolishing the partitions between public and private sectors, state and other patterns of ownership, and urban and rural workers. A pivotal question emerges: is "reformist," "communist" China at two-score-and-ten returning its cities to the very socio-economic systems that the regime's founders once set out to "reform"?[1]

The urban economic policies of the late 1990s are by no means new: virtually all of them are over a decade old. But as enunciated in their most dramatic form to date – at the watershed autumn 1997 15th Party Congress – they reflect a foundational shift. At the close of the 1980s it was still possible to write that "reform of the economy – and the predominance of market-oriented institutions and behavior that this would usher in – [was not] a goal in itself."[2] But by the end of the 1990s, with stark economic threats at hand, marketization and even the dissolution of a significant amount of the state ownership of the economy had become just that, goals in themselves. And as Party and state chiefs gave the go-ahead to massive sales of state assets, bankruptcy of state firms and shedding of state employees to boost enterprise efficiency, the very essence of what socialism has meant in China came under serious challenge.

This article considers how the recent agenda of reforms pertaining to ownership, employment and citizenship measure up against the situation in these areas at three benchmarks: 1949, 1979 and 1989. In outline, this is a story of abolishing and then of allowing difference, as private entrepreneur and peasant labourer were first turned into pariahs in the

1. Martin King Whyte and William L. Parish, *Urban Life in Contemporary China* (Chicago: University of Chicago Press, 1984), p. 16 refers to the "fundamental goals of the Chinese Communist Party" in its "urban reform effort" after 1949.
   2. Dorothy J. Solinger, *China's Transition from Socialism* (Armonk, NY: M.E. Sharpe, 1993), p. 3.

municipalities and replaced by the state sphere and the permanent urban-
ite worker, but then later permitted to reappear.

The 1950s were a time of progressive homogenization, elimination of
disparity and erection of partitions. In the 1960s and 1970s that drive
became fully realized and deeply, ideologically entrenched. In the 1980s,
diversity gingerly re-emerged. But it has only been in the 1990s that the
partitions appear to be truly in the midst of demolition.

The Recent Agenda

Ownership. Party General Secretary Jiang Zemin put forward two
critical chores at the 1997 congress: to "adjust and improve the ownership
structure," and to "accelerate the reform of state-owned enterprises."[3]
Together these orders amounted to placing an authoritative imprimatur
upon "economies of diverse ownership," such as the joint-stock
system, now said to be compatible with socialism just as much as with
capitalism.[4] The non-public sector was switched from being, as it
had been since reforms began, a "supplement" to state ownership, to
serving as "an important component part of China's socialist market
economy."

Meanwhile, the "public," as opposed to "state," ownership, still hailed
as "the main component" of the economic system, now includes not just
the state and collective sectors (as at the 1992 14th Party Congress) but
also the state and collective's share in the "mixed economy." This is a
logical extension of the 1994 tax code's stipulation that all forms of
ownership would be taxed at the same rate.[5]

The Party Congress commands released smaller state entities in the
interest of invigorating them through merging, leasing, contracting or
selling them off. Meanwhile larger, potentially competitive firms would
become modern corporations, joined via shareholding in large, even
transnationally active enterprises. Not only is ownership by the state no
longer sacrosanct, the reality of bankruptcy for state firms on a large scale
is definitely sanctioned. Firms clearly sinking are encouraged to merge if
possible, to fall into bankruptcy if necessary.

The immediate response to these redefinitions was a surge of privatization, in fact if not name.[6] Indeed, privatization, dispossession and forced
bankruptcies became so widespread that by the following summer the
State Economic and Trade Commission issued a notice against selling

3. BBC, Summary of World Broadcasts (SWB) FE/3023 (13 September 1997),
S1/1-S1/10.
4. Joseph Fewsmith, "Jiang Zemin takes command," *Current History*, Vol. 97, No. 620
(1998), p. 252.
5. Barry Naughton, "China's economy: buffeted from within and without," *Current
History*, Vol. 97, No. 620 (1998), pp. 275–76.
6. Barry Naughton, "China: domestic restructuring and a new role in Asia," paper
presented to the conference on the Asian Economic Crisis, University of Washington, 30
October–1 November 1998, draft of 7 October 1998, p. 24; Shu Y. Ma, "The Chinese route
to privatization," *Asian Survey*, Vol. 38, No. 4 (April 1998), p. 380; Edward S. Steinfeld,
Forging Reform in China (Cambridge: Cambridge University Press, 1998), p. 23.

small state firms, as the top Party leadership split over the extent of permissible privatization.[7]

Labour security. For the workers whose firms could no longer accommodate them, lay-offs were to become standard practice to enhance productivity, while efforts were to be made to divert these people to other posts. The hope was that, cut off from their employers and thrown into society, dismissed workers would look to the private and tertiary sectors. Thus, what began as "enterprise restructuring" could also "readjust the industrial structure,"[8] eventually "causing the flow of labour to follow the laws of the market economy."[9] Obviously, the tie binding the worker to his or her *danwei* is in the course of being cut; labour mobility must be on its way.

Meanwhile, a 1995 Re-employment Project, geared to handle the retraining, basic livelihood and provision of new positions for those laid-off, had its charge grossly expanded.[10] If successful, the project could force a shift from allocating labour to marketizing it; from state and collectively owned enterprises' dominance to more non-governmental firms; and from contracted to flexible forms of employment.[11]

But more immediately, unemployment became so acute, with at least 13 million laid-off by the end of 1997[12] and several million more since,[13] that in May 1998 a national conference proclaimed the distribution of basic living allowances and prompt payment of pensions the top priority.[14] This signals the extent to which local officials, by rapidly divesting money-losing state property and tolerating large-scale dismissals of workers, have rushed to marketize.[15]

Residency status. Prior to the 1990s a barrier separated permanent urban workers from countryside labourers hired temporarily in the cities. In 1998, however, Shanghai scholars judged that "from the 1990s, the

7. SWB FE/3278, S1/2, from Xinhua, 11 July 1998; Lo Ping, "Wenjian toulou qigai xian pingjing" ("Document reveals enterprises in a bottleneck") *Zhengming (Contend)*, No. 12 (1997), p. 17 claims that over 9,000 firms went bankrupt in September 1997; Willy Wo-Lap Lam, "Growth rate target tops leaders' agenda" and "Dissent at top over access to markets," *South China Morning Post*, 11 August 1998 and 17 September 1998, respectively.

8. No author, "Yi bashou gongcheng zai Liaoning" ("Number one project in Liaoning"), *Zhongguo jiuye (Chinese Employment)*, No. 3 (1998), p. 13.

9. Li Zhonglu, "Zai jiuye gongcheng de diaocha yu jishi" ("An investigation and on-the-spot report of the Re-employment Project"), *Gongyun cankao ziliao (Workers' Movement Reference Materials)* No. 11 (1997), p. 17.

10. *China Daily*, 26 April 1995, p. 1 on its inauguration.

11. Liu Zhonghua, "Guanyu zaijiuye gongcheng yu laodongli shichang jianshe de sikao" ("Thoughts on the Re-employment Project and labour market construction"), *Laodong neican (Labor Internal Reference)*, No. 2 (1998), p. 42.

12. *Liaowang*, 5 January 1998, in SWB FE/3136, S1/2.

13. Mo Rong, "1998 nian woguo jiuye xingshi fenxi" ("An analysis of our country's employment situation in 1998") *Zhongguo laodong (Chinese Labour)*, No. 6 (1998), p. 42, cites a Ministry of Labour and Social Security estimate in mid-1998 of another 3.5 million lay-offs.

14. *Jingji ribao (Economic Daily)*, 18 May 1998, p. 1; *Far Eastern Economic Review*, 30 July 1998, p. 46.

15. Naughton, "China's economy," p. 276.

isolation between local and outside labour has been broken." They found three causes: enterprise reform, which enlarged managers' hiring autonomy; market competition, which presses them to use cheap labour; and lay-offs of city factory hands, which force urbanites to take low-paying jobs. The result is that the two strands of the original dual labour market may be recombining in novel ways.[16]

Moreover, in both 1997 and 1998, the seemingly unchangeable superiority of the city-born created around 1961[17] via the household registration (*hukou*) system which defined urban residency status was affected by some crucial regulatory shifts. In 1997, in 450 select, "advanced" county-level towns, peasants pursuing legal, stable occupations who had been resident for two years were granted an urban *hukou*, complete with the right to send their children to school at subsidized rates. They also became eligible for basic health and welfare benefits.[18] In 1998, children got the right to inherit the *hukou* of either parent; and "peasant" spouses already resident over a number of years in a city could adopt their urban spouse's registration, as could retirees moving in with their city offspring. Moreover, rural investors who sponsored enterprises or purchased commercial housing in cities and their immediate families could obtain urban registration so long as they had legal, stable residences and occupations.[19] So the purity of official urban existence promises to be steadily diluted.

Thus in three facets of the urban political economy – ownership, labour and residency status – in the late 1990s, the core divisions that had delimited urbanism were blurring, even threatening to disappear. Just how different a pass were these institutions from where they had been ten, 20 and 50 years before?

Past Benchmarks

Ownership. While wholesale trade was nationalized soon after takeover and 1,000 of the larger industrial companies were converted into joint public-private enterprises by 1954, some 70 per cent of retail trade and about half major capitalist industry remained in private hands up to late 1955. But with the colossal campaign to remould capitalist industry

16. Beijing daxue Zhongguo jingji yanjiu zhongxin chengshi laodongli shichang ketizu (Beijing University Chinese Economy Research Centre Urban Labour Market Task Group), "Shanghai: chengshi zhigong yu nongcun mingong de fenceng yu ronghe" ("Shanghai: urban staff and workers and rural labour's strata and fusion") *Gaige* (*Reform*), No. 4 (1998), pp. 106–107; Peng Xizhe, Zheng Guizhen and Chen Yuexin, "Chanye jiegou tiaozheng zhong de Shanghai fangzhiye wailai nüxing renkou" ("Shanghai's outside female textile workers in industrial structural readjustment") *Zhongguo renkou kexue* (*Chinese Population Science*), No. 3 (1998), pp. 38–43, 56. Thanks to Barry Naughton for these articles.

17. Kam Wing Chan, *Cities With Invisible Walls* (Hong Kong: Oxford University Press, 1994), p. 76; and Dorothy J. Solinger, *Contesting Citizenship in Urban China* (Berkeley: University of California Press, 1999), ch. 3.

18. "Gradually reform small towns' household management system," *Baokan wenzhai* (*Periodicals Digest*), 24 July 1997, p. 1; Xinhua, 30 July 1997, in SWB FE/2986, G/8. Thanks to Kam Wing Chan for the former piece.

19. *Hua sheng yuebao* (*China Voice*), October 1998, p. 78; *Xingdao ribao* (*Singdao Daily*), 11 August 1998, p. A6 and 26 September 1998, p. A5; and *Guangzhou ribao* (*Guangzhou Daily*), 28 August 1998. Thanks to Zai Liang and Kam Wing Chan for these articles.

and commerce, in the short span of just one year, 99.6 per cent of the output of private industry had fallen into state hands, and 82 per cent of the firms in the commercial sector had also been transformed.[20]

Thereafter until the state constitution of 1978 legitimated going into business on one's own (with just a short interlude in the early 1960s), private economic operations were proscribed, pitilessly censured and subject to severe punishment, so vehemently during the Cultural Revolution that the dark shadow of that castigation continued to fall across enterprising efforts throughout the 1980s. By 1978, some 77.6 per cent of industrial output was turned out by state-owned firms and the remaining 22.4 per cent by collectives, which were also virtually the state's.[21]

With the closing of the Eleventh Party Central Committee's 1978 landmark Third Plenum, cautious proposals for ownership reform were raised by economists Dong Furen (in 1979) and Li Yining (in 1985 and 1986). But State Planning Commission opposition forestalled action.[22] Once the political climate eased with the 1987 13th Party Congress's consensus that China was in the "primary stage of socialism," more plans appeared for the paid transfer of enterprise property rights.[23] The climax was Party General Secretary Zhao Ziyang's report to its Third Plenum in 1988, suggesting the public sale of small state firms and encouraging large and medium ones to issue their own stocks, much the same programme as was announced in 1997.[24]

During the 1980s ownership by the state was challenged along three different paths: enterprise reform, a set of "capitalistic practices," and the steady expansion of the private sector. In the efforts at enterprise reform, however, two flaws were outstanding: none really challenged ownership, and there were no effective governance mechanisms.[25] "Capitalistic" tactics abounded before 1990, including leasing, begun in 1984 and involving 66 per cent of the small state commercial firms by 1986,[26] mergers, under way by 1988,[27] and shareholding, initiated in Shenyang in 1982, where a securities exchange had national reach by 1986. Nearly 80

20. Dorothy J. Solinger, *Chinese Business Under Socialism* (Berkeley: University of California Press, 1984), pp. 308–309.

21. Guojia tongjiju bian (State Statistical Bureau) (ed.), *Zhongguo tongji nianjian 1989 (1989 Chinese Statistical Yearbook)* (Beijing: Zhongguo tongji chubanshe, 1989), p. 267.

22. Joseph Fewsmith, *Dilemmas of Reform in China* (Armonk, NY: M.E. Sharpe, 1994), pp. 188–89.

23. *Guangming ribao (Bright Daily)*, 19 December 1987, p. 3; *Jingji cankao (Economic Reference)*, 10 February 1988, p. 2; *Renmin ribao (People's Daily)*, 20 May 1988, p. 5; and *Shijie jingji daobao (World Economic Herald)*, 24 October 1988, p. 14.

24. *Beijing Review*, 14–20 November 1988.

25. Louis Putterman, "The role of ownership and property rights in China's economic transition," *The China Quarterly*, No. 144 (1995), pp. 1052, 1063; Shu Y. Ma, "The Chinese route to privatization," pp. 380–81; Naughton, "China," p. 17; and Steinfeld, *Forging Reform*, pp. 2–6.

26. Yue Haitao, "Leasing invigorates small businesses," *Beijing Review*, No. 27 (1987), p. 25; Lora Sabin, "New bosses in the workers' state," *The China Quarterly*, No. 140 (1994), p. 953; *Renmin ribao*, 8 May 1987, p. 5, and 24 May 1987, p. 2.

27. *Jingji ribao*, 2 May 1988 and 4 October 1988, p. 1; *Renmin ribao*, 3 February 1989, p. 5.

cities had engaged in negotiable securities transfer by late 1988;[28] as of mid-1987, over 1,000 enterprise groups were registered.[29] But, as Zhao Ziyang himself admitted (trying to cloak his true purposes?), these experiments posed no threat to the dominant role of public ownership;[30] state offices also supervised the use of the funds.[31]

Bankruptcy experimentation started with a 1983 study and Cao Siyuan's 1984 draft law. In 1988, a national law went into effect; soon a "job security panic" hit the workforce, with reformers' repeated intention to shut failing firms.[32] But though 98 cases reached the courts by 1989, the freeze on anything that smacked of capitalism after the Tiananmen incident and Zhao Ziyang's fall halted the process for several years. Though cases mounted after 1991, especially after 1994,[33] ongoing obstacles were the state's unchanging commitment to resettle and succour the unemployed, plus the scarcity of social security funds.[34] By 1997, a mere one per cent of state enterprises had initiated bankruptcy proceedings.[35]

The private sector's expansion made the biggest dent in state ownership; after the State Council's 1981 regulations on "individual" ventures, they usually received official support throughout the 1980s. The 1988 Seventh National People's Congress legitimized larger "private" firms by amending the state constitution, and, after a downturn in 1989–90, this sector grew rapidly in the approving atmosphere following Deng Xiaoping's famous 1992 Southern Tour and the 14th Party Congress.[36] Where in 1985 the state sector was producing 65 per cent of industrial output and the "individual" or private sector just 1.84 per cent, by 1996 the state's share had plummeted to 28.5 per cent and the private sector's had jumped to 15.5. In addition, the 39.4 per cent attributed to the "collective" sector was certainly largely private as well.[37] Meanwhile, a category called "other," containing foreign-invested industry – amounting to just 1.2 per cent in 1985 – had expanded to 16.6 per cent.[38]

By the 1990s competition from non-state producers and a more marketized environment combined to undermine the state sector much more

28. Solinger, *China's Transition*, p. 134.
29. *Renmin ribao*, 10 August 1987, p. 2.
30. Foreign Broadcast Information Service (FBIS), 17 November 1988, p. 27.
31. Solinger, *China's Transition*, p. 187.
32. Andrew G. Walder, "Workers, managers and the state," *The China Quarterly*, No 127 (1991), p. 479.
33. Yang Yiyong *et al.*, *Shiye chongji bo* (*The Shock Wave of Unemployment*) (Beijing: Jinri zhongguo chubanshe, n.d. (probably 1997)), p. 216.
34. FBIS, 1 January 1995, p. 47 and 19 January 1995, p. 41.
35. Neil C. Hughes, "Smashing the iron rice bowl," *Foreign Affairs*, Vol. 77, No. 4 (July/August 1998), p. 75.
36. Sabin, "New bosses," pp. 959–964; and Martin Brosseau, "The individual and entrepreneurship in the Chinese economic reforms," in Lo Chi Kin, Suzanne Pepper and Tsui Kai Yuen (eds.), *China Review 1995* (Hong Kong: The Chinese University Press, 1995), p. 25.31.
37. Sabin, "New bosses," pp. 952–53, 969–970.
38. State Statistical Bureau (ed.), *Zhongguo tongji nianjian 1997* (*1997 Chinese Statistical Yearbook*) (1997 nianjian) (Beijing: Zhongguo tongji chubanshe, 1997), p. 415.

than organizational tampering alone could do.[39] As that sector's shrinkage proceeds, the boundaries between it and other sectors are becoming far less significant than they used to be.

Labour security. Among the fundamental urban goals of the Party in 1949 were to realize full employment, job security replete with benefits, minimal income and life-style differences, and comfortable consumption standards for all residents.[40] The leadership therefore shepherded the population into state and "collectively"-owned firms. By mid-1956, 85 per cent of the personnel in commerce had been "transformed"; at the year's end, 99 per cent of the staff and workers of private industrial concerns were working in public-private joint firms.[41]

Less than a decade after taking over, the country's new leaders had replaced a world of workshops – where jobs were insecure and unemployment frequent, wages low and welfare benefits absent – with cities marked by large, modern firms that in every way fulfilled their plans.[42] A population that had been highly mobile geographically found its movement strictly controlled, as urban workers were sorted into *danwei* from which they virtually never departed.[43]

Though a hierarchy of urban industrial labour emerged, with three distinct statuses enjoying differing levels of pay, benefits and work security, urbanites as a group received adequate and roughly comparable wages, subsidized housing and other public goods.[44] Because of the ostracism of the private sector, and the near exclusion of peasants from the cities, in 1978 employment in the state and collective sectors combined totalled 100 per cent of the working population (78.4 percent in state firms, 21.6 in collectives).[45]

However the nod to private employment in 1979 – necessary, given the cessation of rustification and the immediate need for job placements for millions – meant new entrants began finding posts outside the state sector: in 1980 only 63.5 per cent of new entrants went into state firms.[46] Where the numbers of urbanites in private firms and self-employed individuals totalled just 814,000 in 1980, by 1990 the figure had grown

39. Barry Naughton, *Growing Out of the Plan* (Cambridge: Cambridge University Press, 1995), and "China's economy," p. 275.
40. Whyte and Parish, *Urban Life*, p 16.
41. Solinger, *Chinese Business*, p. 308.
42. Andrew G. Walder, "The remaking of the Chinese working class, 1949–1981," *Modern China*, Vol. 10, No. 1 (1994), pp. 4–10.
43. Barry Naughton, "*Danwei*: the economic foundations of a unique institution," in Xiaobo Lü and Elizabeth J. Perry (eds.), *Danwei: The Changing Chinese Workplace in Historical and Comparative Perspective* (Armonk, NY: M.E. Sharpe, 1997), pp. 169–182; Whyte and Parish, *Urban Life*, p. 22.
44. Walder, "The remaking," pp. 28–38; Naughton, "China," p. 25.
45. Guojia tongjiju renkou yu jiuye tongjisi, laodongbu zonghe jihua yu gongzisi, bian (Department of Population and Employment Statistics, State Statistical Bureau, Department of Overall Planning and Wages, Ministry of Labour), *Zhongguo laodong tongji nianjian 1997* (*China Labour Statistical Yearbook*) (*1997 nianjan*) (Beijing: Zhongguo tongji chubanshe, 1997), p. 15.
46. Sabin, "New bosses," pp. 945–48; Deborah Davis, "Job mobility in post-Mao cities," *The China Quarterly*, No. 132 (1992), p. 1065.

to 6.7 million and in 1996 the official count was 23.29 million.[47] The first half of the 1990s saw an average of 10.85 million new private jobs annually.[48] Among state employees, people moving into business increased quickly from the mid-1980s.

Two other trends after 1978 split workers from their prior unalterable bond to the firm: limited-term contracts and government encouragement to mobility. Though the notion of fixed-term tenure was first raised in 1982, its affront to what the Chinese considered core socialist values (full employment, job security) meant it was slow to take hold. A 1986 Regulation on Labour Contracts specified that all new labour be hired on limited-term contracts, but by mid-1988 only 8 per cent of state industrial workers were on contracts.[49] And though the 1994 Labour Law demanded contracts for all employees, its implementation was overtaken by the growing push to "downsize." But urban labour exchange centres appeared for skilled workers, and it became possible to take short-term unpaid leave. Still, despite these moves in the direction of shattering the famous "iron rice bowl," work for all with life-long tenure remained the norm at the end of the 1980s.[50]

Once the 1990s got under way, however, as official job assignments were reduced, personal connections played an increasingly dominant role in job-seeking.[51] Meanwhile the *danwei*'s control of careers diminished with an incipient labour market and new freedom to find positions.[52] In Shanghai from 1985 to 1995 the percentage of urbanites assigned jobs by labour departments dropped from 28 to 18, as those locating jobs on their own escalated from 9 to 19 per cent; meanwhile, 35 per cent of 5,800 rural migrants surveyed there in 1995 had found their posts themselves.[53] Thus, urbanites and migrants were becoming similar in searching for work.

The most crucial development in the 1990s was the huge increase in the number of those dismissed and effectively without a job, or at least without a steady, secure one. Here again, years of indecision had passed from 1979, when Xue Muqiao first suggested eliminating permanent jobs.[54] The late 1980s witnessed scattered reports of job losses for "redundant workers," but managers generally still abstained from dismissing employees openly.[55]

47. *1997 nianjian*, p. 116.
48. Barry Naughton, "China's emergence and prospects as a trading nation," *Brookings Papers on Economic Activity*, No. 2 (1996), p. 285.
49. Gordon White, *Riding the Tiger* (Stanford: Stanford University Press, 1993), pp. 138–143, 159.
50. Davis, "*Job Mobility*," pp. 1062–64, 1085; Walder, "Workers, managers," p. 477; FBIS, 8 June 1984, p. K15.
51. Yanjie Bian, "*Guanxi* and the allocation of urban jobs in China," *The China Quarterly*, No. 140 (1994), p. 979.
52. Lowell Dittmer and Xiaobo Lu, "Personal politics in the Chinese *danwei* under reform," *Asian Survey*, Vol. 36, No. 3 (1996), pp. 247–49; and Naughton, "*Danwei*," p. 184.
53. Wang Feng, "Invisible walls within cities," paper prepared for Conference on Social Consequences of Chinese Economic Reform, Harvard University, 23–24 May 1997, Table 2.
54. Richard Baum, *Burying Mao* (Princeton: Princeton University Press, 1994), pp. 94–95.
55. FBIS, 14 September 1988, p. 36, and 28 September 1988, pp. 52–53; Walder, "Workers, managers," pp. 473, 477.

It was then Vice-Premier Zhu Rongji's mid-1993 austerity programme – with its stiff curtailment of guaranteed credit and consequent
rises in firm losses – that induced serious unemployment.[56] By 1994,
when the Labour Law granted firms freedom to fire if near bankruptcy,[57]
the practice of *xiagang* (employees nominally retained ties to their
danwei but were effectively without work to do) began to gather speed.[58]
By spring 1996, urban unemployment, once strictly anathema to the
Communist Party, was being termed "inevitable in a market economy,"
which in China by that time unquestionably existed.[59] By December
1997, the National Labour Work Conference announced, apparently with
much chagrin: "Dismissing and laying off workers is a move against our
will taken when we have no way to turn for help, but also the only way
to extricate ourselves from predicament."[60]

This acquiescence in allowing market forces to play themselves out has
once again recast the subdivisions within the working class. The lines are
no longer drawn by residence (urban versus rural) and the possession of
a permanent, state-sector job, as they had been up to the early 1990s.
Instead, with wages in the state sector slipping below those outside it, and
with job security sacrificed to competition, gross disparities segregate
workers even within the state sector, in accord with firms' economic
success.[61]

The 1995 Ninth Five-Year Plan unveiled an employment policy aimed
at accelerating the development of the non-state economies and the
tertiary sector (both erased in the 1950s); giving vigorous support to
small and medium firms, the mainstay of the pre-1949 economy; obliter-
ating boundaries distinguishing different kinds of workers; encouraging
workers to transfer jobs across enterprises, trades and regions; and urging
the urban unemployed to do the work once done just by migrant peasant
workers.[62] Thus the top leadership has fully legitimated a return to an
urban labour market that its predecessors had eradicated decades ago.

Residency status. In pre-1949 China, cities and countryside formed a
continuous web, with no separation between their populaces.[63] But beginning with injunctions in 1952 discouraging rural residents from entering
municipalities – as millions did so[64] – followed by increasingly harsh and

56. Naughton, "China's emergence," p. 294, and *Growing*, pp. 274–300; and Wing Thye
Woo, "Crises and institutional evolution in China's industrial sector," in Joint Economic
Committee, Congress of the United States (ed.), *China's Economic Future* (Armonk, NY:
M.E. Sharpe, 1997), pp. 164–65; SWB FE/3358, G/3, from Xinhua, 14 October 1998.
57. FBIS, 19 July 1994, pp. 18–26, from Xinhua, 5 July 1994.
58. Niu Renliang, "Xiagang zhigong chulu sikao" ("Thoughts on the way out for the
laid-off staff and workers"), *Lingdao canyue* (*Leadership Consultations*), No. 1 (1998), p. 8.
59. FBIS, 14 June 1996, p. 52, from *Jinrong shibao* (*Financial Times*), 15 April 1996,
p. 1.
60. *Ming bao* (*Bright Daily*), 19 December 1997, in SWB FE/3107, G/7.
61. Ching Kwan Lee, "The labor politics of market socialism," *Modern China*, Vol. 24,
No. 1 (1998), pp. 3–33.
62. FBIS, 14 June 1996, p. 54 and SWB FE/3107, G/7.
63. Whyte and Parish, *Urban Life*, pp. 10, 12, quoting Frederick W. Mote.
64. Walder, "The remaking," pp. 14–15.

ultimately effective repatriations of peasants from towns in 1955, 1957 and 1961, the cities became pretty much devoid of farmers for about two decades. The borders barring outsiders from becoming residents, enforced by rigid registration checks, food rationing, and governmentally-assigned jobs and housing, forged a clear distinction between those who were of the metropolis and those who were not.

With the fall of the communes, the reactivation of commerce and services, and the stimulation to urban construction, by 1983 the regime granted the "floating population" the right to inhabit temporarily in urban areas, at first under quite restrictive conditions. Throughout the 1980s progressively more lenient regulations, plus increasingly flourishing markets, steadily undermined the barriers that had made city dwelling impossible for peasants before.[65]

Eventually "villages" of co-locals gathered together in large cities, where outsiders from the same native place shared space and occupations. Their presence lent a richness and diversity to the sizeable metropolis that had been wanting for at least 30 years. Given the booming economy, the overwhelming majority found work and a place of abode. Despite their lack of power and fundamental legitimacy, and the uncertainty over their continuing right to remain, considerable economic variation developed among them, with some remarkably wealthy by the 1990s.[66]

Is the bulwark against rural outsiders disintegrating? Has city residency status become a non-exclusive category available to all urban dwellers? As the PRC turns 50 this would be claiming too much. The Ninth Five-Year Plan's aim to co-ordinate urban and rural workers in one grand job market[67] defies realization. For the wave of unemployment washing across the country since 1997 has affected treatment of migrant workers. Major cities, though usually incapable of stemming the flow of floaters, are nevertheless bent on restricting it, clearing out some to free posts for natives and reserving certain occupations for locals. Some have achieved a fair amount of success.[68] Migrants continued also to be ineligible for unemployment insurance and the Re-employment Project, and excluded from the contract system.

Conclusion

Have Chinese urban areas now come full circle, back to the beginnings that so unsettled the early communist leaders? No, this is not yet the case.

65. Solinger, *Contesting Citizenship*, ch. 2.
66. Laurence J. C. Ma and Biao Xiang, "Native place, migration and the emergence of peasant enclaves in Beijing," *The China Quarterly*, No. 155 (1998), pp. 546–581; Yuan Yue *et al.*, *Luoren – Beijing liumin di zuzhihua zhuangkuang yanjiu baogao (The Exposed – A Research Report on the Condition of the Organization of Migrants in Beijing)* (Beijing: Beijing Horizon Market Research and Analysis Company, 1995); Li Zhang, "Strangers in the city," Ph.D. dissertation, Cornell University, 1998); Solinger, *Contesting Citizenship*.
67. See former Minister of Labour Li Boyong's speech at the 1997 National Labour Work Conference (SWB FE/3111, S1/4, from Xinhua, 17 December 1997).
68. Dorothy J. Solinger, "The impact of openness on integration and control in China," paper prepared under a grant from the Smith-Richardson Foundation to the University of California's Institute on Global Conflict and Co-operation for the study, "China and its provinces."

Yes, the partitions sustaining difference are just about demolished. But the state sector still governs over 70 per cent of industrial assets and over two-thirds of industrial employment, and contributes the same percentage of industrial income tax revenues.[69] Moreover, the marketization that undermined the state sector contained a twist that was never expected.

Markets made China prosperous, lifting the average urban family's disposable income from 343.4 *yuan* in 1978 to 5,160.3 in 1997.[70] But they also pushed the actual unemployment rate up to around 7 per cent, causing cold feet among decision makers.[71] Thus, even in the face of a threatening financial crisis that destabilized many of its neighbours, in late 1998 some laid-off state workers were rehired, and a massive stimulus programme served only state-owned firms, failing ones among which received special loans.[72] These developments do not imply that partitions, once pulled down, are being reproduced. But they do lend a caution to judgements that the PRC at the end of 50 years of socialist rule is no longer socialist at all.

69. Hughes, "Smashing the iron rice bowl," p.71.
70. Xinhua, 10 December 1998, in SWB FE/3409, G/8 (without saying if this is in constant *yuan*).
71. SWB 3155, G/13, from *Ming pao*, 18 February 1998.
72. Maggie Farley, "Building boom in China blocks market reforms," *Los Angeles Times*, 1 November 1998, pp. A1, A6; Erik Eckholm, "Not (yet) gone the way of all Asia," *New York Times*, 15 November 1998; Xinhua, 30 November 1998, in SWB FE/3399, G/9.

The Environment in the People's Republic of China 50 Years On

Richard Louis Edmonds

This article describes and analyses changes in the environment and related policy developments in the People's Republic over the past 50 years. When discussing the quality of China's environment it must be remembered that the population of the country has doubled over the past half century and the economy has grown rapidly, particularly over the last two decades.[1] Pessimists argue that the current population of over 1,200 million has exceeded the number which can be supported at a good living standard.[2] Despite such views, there has been some ground for optimism in recent years, with China's greater environmental awareness and increased openness, its realization that the environment can be a tool in international diplomacy, and the increasing importation of environmental protection techniques. Yet overall, China has not done enough to maintain environmental quality and has not chosen to make many environmentally friendly transport investments.

The Early Years

During the 1950s, the Chinese focused on reconstructing a war-torn country and devising means to promote rapid economic growth. From the mid-1950s many hillsides were cleared and wetlands filled to create new farmland. The view of the times was that humans should exploit resources and can conquer nature if armed with Mao Zedong thought and "science." The general result was increased rates of degradation and pollution. On the positive side, the first nature reserve and wildlife conservation laws did appear in 1956.

During the Great Leap Forward (1958–61) the pace of exploitation was accelerated: a large number of trees were felled to supply fuel to produce steel, and land reclamation projects destroyed wetlands and led to increased flooding. The Great Leap with its emphasis on economic growth is now considered an era of major environmental degradation. After some attempt to design policies to increase agricultural production and conserve soil after the famine of the early 1960s, Chairman Mao Zedong proclaimed the Cultural Revolution in 1966. Commentators inside and outside China see this as another period of environmental degradation and infrastructure neglect as a result of the anarchy and wanton exploitation of natural resources. Thus while there was some basic economic con-

1. Degradation of China's environment started long before 1949. For some examples see Mark Elvin and Liu Ts'ui-jung (eds.), *Sediments of Time: Environment and Society in Chinese History* (Cambridge: Cambridge University Press, 1998).
2. For example Zhongguo kexue bao she (ed.), "Shengcun yu fazhan" ("Survival and development") (Beijing: unofficial report of the Chinese Academy of Sciences, 1989), pp. 9, 17.

struction, environmental matters were largely neglected prior to the 1970s.

The Birth of Environmental Consciousness

Efforts to deal with ecological problems through international contacts began in a modest way around 1972 after the People's Republic sent a delegation to the First United Nations Conference on the Human Environment in Stockholm. In 1973, the government created a national environmental protection organ and environmental planning became included in national plans. Largely for economic rather than ecological reasons, the Chinese did have considerable success using integrated pest management and biogas in the 1970s.[3] The transformation to family farming in the late 1970s, however, weakened integrated pest management and the production of biogas, as communes had provided a better scale of operation to maintain these techniques. Moreover, the new short-term land contracts encouraged families to exploit land in ways that was not sustainable. For these reasons, it would be erroneous to see the reinstatement of Deng Xiaoping to power in 1978 as the beginning of a positive transformation of environmental management in China. Rather, it gradually improved throughout the 1970s although there were setbacks in some areas.

The environmental debate intensified during the second half of the 1970s and the 1980s as some people argued that economic growth could not continue without considering its impact upon the environment, while others argued that China must follow the "pollute first and clean up later" pattern. Amidst this debate the government promulgated the Environmental Protection Law in 1979 for "trial implementation," and the concept of harmonious development (*xietiao fazhan*), similar to the idea of sustainable development formulated by the Bruntland Commission, was adopted as official policy in the early 1980s. The implementation of these policies, however, fell short of their enactment. The full Environmental Protection Law was adopted in 1989. There has been strengthened determination to deal with environmental problems in the 1990s, but environmental policy continues to be held back by priority for economic growth. The upgrading of the National Environmental Protection Agency to the State Environmental Protection Administration in March 1998 signalled an attempt by the government to put more managerial bite into environmental plans. Yet there still is criticism of the low level of investment in environmental protection.[4]

3. According to Rudolf G. Wagner, "Agriculture and environmental protection in China," in Bernhard Glaeser (ed.), *Learning from China? Development and Environment in Third World Countries* (London: Allen & Unwin, 1987), p. 135, by 1979 China was using various combinations of plants and animals for pest control over a larger area than any country in the world. By 1978 there were 7 million biogas (methane produced by the decomposition of organic matter) reactors in use, mostly in southern China, especially Sichuan. These reactors, while important locally, produced less than 2% of China's total energy supply.
4. Projections made by the World Bank provide some optimism for the Chinese environment if appropriate investments are undertaken. See Todd M. Johnson, Feng Liu and

Resource Shortages Versus Pollution

Resource degradation. While pollution continues to pose severe problems, the most threatening environmental problem in my view is the reduction in natural resources. Cropland continues to shrink, although at slower rates in the last couple of years, and the government has admitted that it has underestimated arable area, so that per capita ratios are not as bad as believed in the early 1990s.[5]

Water shortages remain arguably a more critical issue than arable land shortages, especially in North China, with many sources shrinking or drying up during the last quarter of a century, although, as Nickum points out, the situation is not likely to lead to a major crisis in the short term.[6] Plans are under discussion to transfer large quantities of water north.[7] These controversial grand plans, however, will not happen for decades, if at all. Increased charges for irrigation water and the assignment of water quotas to industries have resulted in some savings. As incomes rise, however, domestic water consumption is likely to increase, aggravating the problem.

Vegetation cover generally has been decreasing over the last 50 years, although as with land area, data must be carefully looked at. Flooding in the Chang (Yangtse), the Nen (Nonni), and the Songhua (Sungari) River valleys during the 1990s is recognized as a partial result of vegetation loss. The need to supplement the Basic Forestry Law of 1986 with a new regulation banning tree-cutting in the upper Chang River valley in 1998 demonstrates the gap between law and practice. In the 1990s, several large forestry and grassland projects have been implemented, and China's "Agenda 21" aims to have China's forests "fully sustainable" for pro-

---

footnote continued

Richard Newfarmer, *Clear Water Blue Skies* (Washington: World Bank, 1997). In *China Urban Environmental Service Management* (World Bank Report No. 13073-CHA, 1994), p. vi, the World Bank had pointed out that between 1980 and 1992 the amount of GDP spent on pollution control increased from 0.40% to 0.67% but further argued that the future would be brighter if the government raises its investment in pollution control and monitoring to a higher proportion of GDP.

5. Robert F. Ash and Richard Louis Edmonds, "China's land resources, environment and agricultural production," *The China Quarterly*, No. 156 (December 1998), pp. 844–46 and Vaclav Smil, "China's agricultural land," *The China Quarterly*, No. 158 (June 1999), pp. 415–19). According to "Regional briefing," *Far Eastern Economic Review*, Vol. 161, No 50 (10 December 1998), p. 16, the government still plans to reclaim more than 1 million hectares of land along the coast by 2040 or 2050 for 20 to 30 million residents with possible negative ecological impacts.

6. James E. Nickum, "Is China living on the water margin," *The China Quarterly*, No. 156 (December 1998), p. 880. According to Liu Changming, "Underground water table under heavy pressure," *China Environment News*, No. 44 (1993), p. 6, the groundwater table in northern China has been dropping at a rate of 50 centimetres per annum, and in places it is 200 feet (70 metres) below where it was in the 1950s. The most pessimistic arguments about water shortages come from Lester Brown. For a recent example of Brown's views in relation to China and India see, "Feeding nine billion," *State of the World 1999: A Worldwatch Institute Report on Progress Toward a Sustainable Society* (London & New York: W. W. Norton, 1999), pp. 115–132.

7. For details see Liu Changming, "Environmental issues and the south-north water transfer scheme," *The China Quarterly*, No. 156 (December 1998), pp. 899–910.

duction by the mid 21st century.[8] Social instability, however, could easily negate these efforts.

China suffers from serious soil erosion, especially in the Loess Plateau region. Great efforts at tree-planting, terracing and check dam construction have been undertaken since the 1950s, some of which were not carefully managed. In the last decade soil conservation plans have shifted from individual plots to entire river basins which can provide for more effective control. Overall, however, soil fertility has been dropping in recent decades because farmers have been leaving fields fallow for shorter periods as they seek to maximize output. At the same time, the Chinese estimate that arid or semi-arid land is degrading into a desert-like barren landscape at a pace of 2,400 square kilometres per annum,[9] and although China has improved an estimated 4 million hectares of salinized-alkalized land since 1949, problems of salinization and alkalization are getting more serious due to inefficient drainage, excessive irrigation and salt water intrusion along the coast.

Nature conservation. After an early start, wildlife conservation stagnated until a legal framework was put in place in the late 1980s and early 1990s. While certain endangered species are recovering, many populations continue to remain low or are decreasing.[10] At the end of 1997, there were 926 nature reserves covering about 7.4 per cent of China's national territory which could be an adequate total level for a developing country. Nature reserve officials, however, are expected to maximize income from the reserve lands which compromises conservation efforts,[11] and as in many places in the world, some of these reserves exist in name only.

8. Recent projects include the "Three Norths Shelterbelt" project (*sanbei fanghulin*), the "Greening of the Plains" project, the "Greening of the Taihang Mountains" project, the 18,000-kilometre long "Coastal Protective Forest" project, the "Chang River Middle and Upper Reaches Protective Forest Construction Project," and the "Continual Production Timber Forest Base Construction Project." With these plans, China hopes to have 15 to 16% of its total area planted in trees by the year 2000, up from 13.39% in 1994. For details of some of these projects see Guojia huanjing baohuju: Guojia jihua weiyuanhui, *Zhongguo huanjing baohu xingdong jihua 1991–2000 nian* (*China's Environmental Protection Activity Plan 1991–2000*) (Beijing: Zhongguo huanjing kexue chubanshe, 1994), pp. 69–73.

9. "China seeks foreign aid to fight increasing desertification," *China News Digest*, GL98–153 (16 November 1998), p. 2(4). By 1991 the State Council felt that desertification in northern China·was damaging enough to call for the establishment of a National Sand Control Aid Group. In 1992 the Ministry of Forestry began a National Sand Control Ten-Year Plan and in 1994 China signed the United Nations Convention on Combating Desertification.

10. Reasons for disappearance of species and reduction of numbers are not unique to China: destruction of habitats for agriculture, industry and housing, government eradication policies for certain species, excessive hunting, pollution from pesticides and industry, and poor management and the small scale of many nature reserves and parks. Officially animals and plants receiving first-class protection are those which are endemic, rare, precious or threatened and those accorded second-class protection are species whose numbers are declining or whose geographical distribution is becoming more restricted.

11. Lara Dangerfield, "Growing treasures," *China Now*, No. 153 (1995), pp. 10–11.

Pollution. The state of pollution in China has been described in many sources.[12] Briefly, the seven major river systems were considered badly polluted or barely acceptable in 1997 although some, such as the Huai and Songhua, have reduced pollution levels in recent years.[13] Ground water and coastal regions are polluted to various degrees. Thus while there has been progress in water pollution control, it has been offset by new pollution sources.

Likewise, despite considerable investment in air pollution control technology, China's industrial sulphur dioxide emissions doubled between 1982 and 1997 and all major Chinese city centres have SO_2 emission levels which exceed legal limits. A study by the Washington-based World Resources Institute has concluded that nine of the ten worst air polluted cities in the world are found in China.[14] This problem is tied to the continuous dependence of China upon coal as a source of energy. Table 1 demonstrates that although the dominance of coal in China's industrial energy use has been reduced over the past 50 years, the push for industrial development has caused coal consumption to rise steadily from the 1980s.

Despite considerable environmental costs, the Chinese strategy for energy development has been more rational in recent years given the resource base. Funding constraints and organizational competition,

Table 1: Energy Consumption in China 1957–1998

	1957	1980	1990	1995
Overall consumption (1,000,000 tonnes)	96.44	602.7	987.0	1290.0
Percentage of which was:				
Coal	92.3	72.2	76.2	75.0
Oil	4.6	20.7	16.6	17.3
Natural gas	0.1	3.1	2.1	1.8
Hydropower	3.0	4.0	5.1	5.9
Nuclear power	0	0	n.d.	< 0.1
Non-biomass renewable energy	n.d	n.d	n.d	< 0.1

Notes: Percentages for coal/oil/gas/hydro exclude nuclear and renewable sources. 1995 are estimated figures.

Source: *Zhongguo tongji nianjian 1996* (*China Statistical Yearbook 1996*) (Beijing: Tongji chubanshe, 1997), p. 203.

12. For a recent study see Eduard B. Vermeer, "Industrial pollution in China and remedial policies," *The China Quarterly*, No. 156 (December 1998), pp. 952–985.
13. "1997 Report on the Environment in China" (internet version: State Environmental Protection Administration, 1998), pp. 3–5 states that the Chang, Zhu (Pearl) and Huang Rivers were barely acceptable.
14. Maggie Fox, "Chinese cities' bad air imperils children – study," Reuters new release, 25 January 1999. The study looked at total suspended particulates, sulfur dioxide and nitrogen dioxide. The ten cities listed in the report, in descending order of total suspended particulate levels were: Lanzhou, Jilin, Taiyuan, Jiaozuo, Rajkot in India, Wan Xian, Urumqi, Yichang, Hanzhong and Anyang.

however, limit the ability of the country to use the best foreign technology and management expertise. Plans are to transfer electric hydro-power from the south and west to the north and east, to establish thermal power plants at coal mining sites, and to move direct current power to areas of demand by a national grid rather than transport coal.

China's first nuclear power station became operational at Qinshan in Zhejiang province in December 1991. A station at Daya Bay in Guangdong is now running and there are several under construction. So far, the Chinese say that monitoring at Qinshan and Daya Bay has indicated no perceivable impacts on the surrounding environment. The major issue for the future of nuclear power will be whether or not an active anti-nuclear movement will develop. The current political climate suggests that it will be some time before this happens.

While renewable energy is beginning to be taken seriously, most effort in this area goes into hydro-power. Large hydro projects such as the Sanxia (Three Gorges) Dam, however, could lead to their own environmental problems and go against the general world trend to avoid large dams.[15] Other renewable sources – geothermal, tidal, wave and wind power – are receiving limited attention. There is no large-scale use of solar technology for electrical generation yet in China.

While SO_2 levels have been dropping in city centres, automobile traffic congestion has created levels of NO_x at intersections that often exceed safety levels.[16] Railways were the mainstay of China's modern transport network from the 1950s to 1980. Since 1980, under the influence of Western development strategies, there has been a move away from rail as the "key link" to road and air transport.[17] While some praise this move as a shift towards a more balanced transport network,[18] the unfortunate side-effect has been the sacrifice of air quality and more land for transport use than would have been the case had rail and inland waterways continued to receive priority.

The number of vehicles used to haul passengers surpassed the number of road freight vehicles in 1997. While private vehicle growth has been tremendous, the number of sedans in the vehicle total remains below 20 per cent whereas the world-wide ratio of passenger cars to lorries and

15. For details of the arguments surrounding the Sanxia project see Richard Louis Edmonds, "The Sānxiá (Three Gorges) Project: the environmental argument surrounding China's super dam," *Global Ecology and Biogeography Letters*, Vol. 4, No. 2 (July 1992), pp. 105–125.
16. Regulations for managing the supervision of auto emissions were formulated in 1990. For details on vehicle emissions see Michael P. Walsh, "Theme paper 2: motor vehicle pollution control in China: an urban challenge," in Stephen Stares and Liu Zhi (eds.), *China's Urban Transport Development Strategy: Proceedings of a Symposium in Beijing, November 8–10, 1995* (Washington: World Bank Discussion Paper No. 352, 1996), pp. 118–122.
17. In fact, according to Mark W. Speece and Kawahara Yukiko, "Transportation in China in the 1990s," *International Journal of Physical Distribution and Logistics Management*, Vol. 25, No. 8 (1996), pp. 56–57, to reduce short-trip passenger use, railway ticket prices were drastically increased in the mid-1980s rather than investing in further construction.
18. Joyce Y. Man, "Transportation infrastructure and regional economic development in China," *International Journal of Public Administration*, Vol. 21, No. 9 (1998), p. 1318.

buses is about 80 per cent.[19] Thus the potential for further expansion of the private car in China remains frighteningly large, with traffic and pollution implications which the Chinese are now belated trying to control.[20] One source has predicted car growth will jump from two vehicles per 1,000 people in 1995 to anywhere between 53 and 83 per 1,000 by 2020, with the number of motorcycles possibly growing even faster.[21] At the same time it is clear that road length has not kept pace with the expansion in the number of vehicles. The result is that traffic bottlenecks in large cities are endemic and ever greater numbers of vehicles are trying to travel on poor quality rural roads. Currently only five cities – Beijing, Shanghai, Tianjin, Guangzhou and Hong Kong – have metro railways. Yet the devolution of transport development to local authorities which has been occurring in the 1990s suggests that roads will be favoured as local government shows more willingness to invest in them than in other forms of transport, presumably because of the short-haul capability of local road networks which benefit local interests.[22]

Since the 1980s, intensification of agriculture and the proliferation of village and township enterprises has led to the increase of pollution outside cities. Rural non-state enterprises have expanded rapidly in a largely uncontrolled fashion. Since the mid-1980s, farmers have been encouraged to increase use of organic fertilizer and the production of organochlorine pesticides has been banned, but chemical fertilizer and pesticide usage continues to climb. China's average annual fertilizer usage per hectare is estimated to be twice the world average. Despite efforts to consolidate and shut down small highly polluting factories, the number of serious cases of untreated rural waste being discharged is growing with rural village and township industries accounting for nearly 38 per cent of China's industrial solid wastes, over 7 per cent of industrial waste water and 56 per cent of industrial dust in

19. Guojia tongjiju (ed.), *98 Zhongguo fazhan baogao (China Development Report 1998)* (Beijing: Zhongguo tongji chubanshe, 1998), p. 126.

20. In the case of Beijing, the government banned leaded petrol in Beijing from 1 June 1997 ("Leaded gas to be banned in Beijing," *China News Digest*, GL97–069 (12 May 1997), (5); began random vehicle checks in the city ("Tougher car emission measurements to be used by China," *China News Digest*, GL98-054 (17 April 1998), (3); introduced buses fuelled by liquefied petroleum gas ("News from 'China Daily'," *China News Digest*, GL98-043 (23 March 1998), (3), and announced plans for more commuter rail transport projects as the city was preparing for the 50-year celebration ("Beijing to receive major funding for city improvement," *China News Digest*, GL98-061 (1 May 1998), (3). Tougher new auto carbon filter standards were issued in 1998 ("New requirement set to cut auto emission," *China News Digest*, GL97-15 (12 November 1997), (4). However, a fuel tax which was to encourage emission reductions raised objections from taxi drivers ("Proposed fuel tax to impact auto industry and public transport," *China News Digest*, GL98-167 (18 December 1998), 1(6)) and from farmers as well as the automotive industry. According to "Concerns about fuel tax prompts hoarding of gasoline nationwide," *China News Digest*, GL98-169 (23 December 1998), (3), the tax also led to hoarding so that implementation was postponed.

21. Stephen Stares and Liu Zhi, "Theme paper 1: Motorization in Chinese cities: issues and actions," in Stares and Liu Zhi, *China's Urban Transport Development Strategy*, pp. 48, 51.

22. Speece and Kawahara, "Transportation in China," p. 67.

1997.[23] As a result of changes in the countryside, the Ministry of Agriculture now estimates that polluted cropland reduced grain production by enough to feed 65 million people, the current official number of Chinese not being adequately fed.

In the last 20 years, China's pollution problems have grown in geographical scale. Rivers have become polluted throughout their length. Acid pollution has grown from affecting a few cities to a situation where more than half the rainfall in southern China is now overly acidic.

Another major change over the last two decades has been the growth in domestic waste. Rubbish in urban areas now contains inorganic matter at levels similar to those found in developed countries. Industrial waste likewise has increased in volume. Most urban refuse is removed to farms or rural dumping sites at ever-increasing distances from cities. Considerable progress was made in urban rubbish treatment in the 1990s, with the government claiming that in 1997 over 50 per cent was "properly treated" for the first time. China only began to deal with toxic waste after the government approved a motion to adopt the Basel Convention on the Control of Transboundary Dangerous Wastes and Their Disposal in 1991 and promulgated the "Environmental Policies on the Disposal of Medium and Low-level Radioactive Wastes" in 1992. Overall, economic growth continues to outstrip environmental protection leading to increasing pollution problems.

China, the International Community and the Environment

For the Chinese government poverty is seen as the main cause of environmental degradation in developing countries, and it is not considered reasonable to expect these countries to maintain lower emission levels or install expensive equipment to control emissions. Instead, developed nations should transfer funds and technology and acknowledge that they emit the majority of pollutants including those which could be causing global warming. This latter point represents a change in policy of the last decade but also can be seen as part of a foreign policy initiative to increase influence amongst developing countries. As an example of this change of attitude during the last decade, China has been willing to ask for international disaster relief aid rather than "go it alone."

Wildlife conservation took the lead in international co-operation since it was seen by international donors as less politically controversial than other aspects of environmental co-operation. China has sites in the UNESCO "Man and the Biosphere Programme" and on its World Heritage Commission's list, and it has nature reserves on the International Important Wetlands List. At the same time, China has joined in global environmental change programmes.[24] The State Council rapidly approved

23. "1997 Report on the Environment in China" (internet version: State Environmental Protection Administration, 1998), pp. 8, 10, 14–15.

24. Lester Ross, "China: environmental protection, domestic policy trends, patterns of participation in regimes and compliance with international norms," *The China Quarterly*, No. 156 (December 1998), pp. 809–835.

China's Agenda 21 on 25 March 1994, making it one of the first developing countries to do so. Generally, the environment has been viewed as a good area for bilateral co-operation, as was witnessed by American President Clinton's and French Prime Minister Jospin's visits to China in 1998.

Prospects for China's Environment

Despite the increase in pollution over the past 50 years, the most threatening of China's environmental problems remains the degradation of resources. In particular, the western and border areas are under strain. Since the 1950s, considerable numbers of Chinese have been relocated to the west to develop poor areas, settle the frontiers and reduce population pressure in the east. This expansion led to serious degradation in semi-arid fragile ecosystems. Today, these areas are no longer seen as destinations for surplus population. If efforts at responsibility revegetation, conservation and population control begun during the 1980s and 1990s prove successful, benefits can be expected in the first quarter of the 21st century.

While resource degradation threatens most of China, an immediate problem facing the urban and township populations of the eastern and central regions is pollution. Dealing with the rural pollution problem, however, will require a tremendous investment by the Chinese government as well as stricter enforcement of regulations.

Many analysts see improved economic efficiency, largely implemented through raising the price of fuel and other industrial inputs, as the key to improving China's environment; higher pricing has indeed helped to control pollution from state-run industries. Pressure from government via the State Environmental Protection Administration and to a lesser degree other relevant ministries, however, remains the main force regulating investment in environmental control since many inputs remain artificially underpriced.

Today there is an emphasis on major infrastructure development: oil and gas, power plants, telecommunications, road, air, ports, rail, construction, and other aspects of modernization. Of the 210 major projects in the "The Compilation of Major Technology Introducing Projects of the PRC from 1993 to 2000," 137 are in energy, petroleum, coal mining, transportation, telecommunications, agriculture and general urban development. Clearly, infrastructure is high on the Chinese agenda, especially in light of the Asian financial crisis.

Continued growth of energy use for transportation – especially increased use of petroleum and coal – will prove to be both environmentally and financially unsustainable. Further dependence upon oil will place China in jeopardy as this is a dwindling resource. Once investment is made in pipelines and vehicles, however, it will be very costly to remake the transport infrastructure. China must remain dependent upon coal to some degree into the mid-term, and there will be a clear need to improve technologies related to coal use and to renewable forms of energy.

China does not seem to be seriously looking at its potential to leapfrog over current technologies used in the developed world but rather is following models used in other countries, perhaps because of a lack of confidence. For example, one American report has quoted Deputy Director of the Energy Research Institute, Zhou Dadi, as responding to a question about hydrogen energy in 1997 as follows: "There is no practical plan to develop hydrogen over the next 20 years."[25] Although the report did indicate that there is a beginning of research on hydrogen fuel cell vehicles, China has not seriously taken up this technological challenge and is simply replicating the fossil fuel energy transport pattern found in Europe, North America and North-east Asia. In addition, China's planners are still attempting to replicate a Western-style personal road transport infrastructure rather than a safer, land-saving, community-friendly public transport structure which can reduce congestion and expand personal mobility for a society's poorer citizens. To some degree that can be seen as a geographical representation of the idea that "to get rich is glorious." It is hoped that China will realize this mistake before it replicates the pattern already ubiquitous in the country's largest cities and throughout the developed world.

Thus although ministries in charge of investment often give environmental protection low priority, China needs to continue efforts at energy efficient infrastructure development as well as strict population control and extensive environmental education. At the same time it is essential that China evolve into a more open society while maintaining political stability. Without these measures, it could find itself entering into an ecological down-spin during the forthcoming 50 years.

25. James S. Cannon, *China at the Crossroads: Energy, Transportation, and the 21st Century* (New York: INFORM Special Report, June 1998), p. 13.

China's Foreign Relations: The Long March, Future Uncertain*

Michael Yahuda

As we mark the 50th anniversary of the People's Republic of China (PRC) we have the opportunity to assess China's experience over five decades in accommodating itself to the outside world. It is an opportunity to take stock and to consider in the light of this experience what is China's current international standing and what may be said to be its agenda for the future with regard to the conduct of foreign affairs.

China as a Great Power

Perhaps the most important point to make is the significance of China's standing as one of the world's great powers – or, to use the preferred term of China's current leaders, "big country" (*daguo*). It is difficult for us today to recall how abject China seemed before the establishment of the PRC. Derided as the "sick man of Asia" and described by the founder of the Republic of China at the turn of the century as a "heap of loose sand," a China that was unified under the leadership of Mao Zedong was able in the space of less than two years to inflict decisive defeats on Western armies for the first time in modern Chinese history. We now know how much China's forces had benefited from Soviet military assistance at the crucial time."[1] Nevertheless it was the Chinese performance in Korea, where at terrible cost their "volunteers" at first hurled back and then held on against armies with command of the air and employing superior fire power, that earned the PRC the great power status for which Chinese had long yearned since being humiliated by Western powers more than 100 years earlier. China's great power status was duly recognized at the Geneva Conference in 1954, much to the satisfaction of Beijing then and since.[2] From that time on the PRC's status as a great power was never again really challenged although, lacking the global reach of the Soviet Union (until its demise in 1991) and of the United States, it has remained a great power only on a regional scale.[3]

* This article has benefited from the constructive criticism of David Shambaugh and from the other contributors to the China Quarterly workshop in Aveiro, 28–31 January 1999.

1. For the enormous extent of Soviet assistance that also played a significant part in the victories of the communist armies in the decisive victories of the civil war, see Sergei N. Goncharov, John W. Lewis and Xue Litai, *Uncertain Partners: Stalin, Mao and the Korean War* (Stanford: Stanford University Press, 1993), and Michael M. Sheng, *Battling Western Imperialism: Mao, Stalin, and the United States* (Princeton: Princeton University Press, 1997.)
2. Liang Liangxing (ed.), *China's Foreign Relations: A Chronology of Events (1949–1988)* (Beijing: Foreign Languages Press, 1989), p. 17
3. For a critical assessment of China's status and achievement as a great power see Samuel S. Kim, "China as a great power," in Orville Schell and David Shambaugh (eds.), *The China Reader* (New York; Vintage Books, 1999), pp. 448–458.

Curiously, having achieved that status neither China's leaders nor their intellectual spokespeople have been able to articulate a clear vision of the purpose to which that great power will be used. To begin with they denied that China would act as great power. Asserting the equality of all states and decrying power politics as the bullying of the weak, Mao and Zhou habitually declared that their country would never act as a hegemon. Nevertheless, despite the rhetoric to the contrary, the Chinese behaved very much in the traditional role of great powers. Thus even at Geneva the PRC joined hands with the Soviet Union in the pursuit of a wider international settlement in pressing their smaller ally, the Vietminh, against its will to withdraw from areas where it exercised effective control south of what was to become the DMZ. Thereafter Chinese spokesmen expected to be heard on every international issue of the day. In due course the PRC became a nuclear power, a donor of foreign aid, entered into conflict with the Soviet Union and reached "a political settlement with the United States on the basis of equality, and in disregard of the interests of its smaller associates" all of which, as Hedley Bull pointed out in 1977, were indicative of the "behaviour of a member of the great power club, not of a spokesman of the international proletariat" – or, he may have added, of the self-styled leader of the Third World.[4]

China has also experienced difficulty in establishing consistently good workable relations with others. With the exception of Pakistan, all China's alliances have ended in acrimony, and yet the relationship with Pakistan is habitually presented as if it were the model. For a country whose conduct of foreign policy is characterized by an extraordinarily heavy dose of realism and by a relative lack of transparency and openness to others, it is striking how much the rhetoric of its diplomacy is shaped by the concepts of friendship and principle. It is as if the calculations of power and interest were alien to Chinese foreign policy makers.

Successive Chinese governments have experienced particular difficulty in dealing with countries that are deemed stronger or potentially challenging to China. Yet paradoxically, Chinese international power and influence may be said to have been greatest when it was aligned with first the USSR in the 1950s and then with the United States in the 1970s and 1980s.[5] At the same time China has experienced difficulties with smaller powers largely because it perceives itself as benign and does not quite understand why smaller neighbours do not necessarily see it in that light.

One of the key characteristics of China as a great power has been the demand by its leaders that others should it treat it as their equal. Perhaps only Russia has been as insistent as China upon being treated as the equal of other great powers. One of the underlying causes of the break-up of the Sino-Soviet alliance was Mao's perception that he personally and China itself were regarded in Moscow as ultimately subordinate to Soviet interests. Similarly, many of the problems inherent in Sino-American

4. Hedley Bull, *The Anarchical Society* (London: Macmillan, 1977), p. 205.
5. I am indebted to Lucian Pye for this point.

relations stem from Chinese fears of American superiority and their feelings of vulnerability. Interestingly, much of this was disguised during the period of tripolarity (1971–89) when despite its lack of military comparability China was treated with respect by both the superpowers; indeed for most of the 1980s it was in the enviable position of being cultivated by both.

Two reasons may be advanced for Chinese difficulties in coming to terms with the identity of their country as a great power. The first is the burden of the historical legacy of what is described as a mythical golden age of the imperial past that lasted for 5,000 years until the advent of the West in the 19th century when Chinese civilization stood alone in magnificent splendour and virtue and when the holder of the Chinese throne ruled over "all that was below Heaven." Contemporary Chinese cannot begin to match the relative achievements of their forebears in the realms of science, technological prowess, economic performance, military prowess and, even more damagingly, cultural distinction. Even as they point to earlier Chinese discoveries of the four necessary foundations of the modern age (paper, printing, gunpowder, the magnetic compass) they implicitly draw attention to the paucity of their contemporary contribution. It would be difficult for contemporary Chinese to define their place in the world in any way that would not seem to fall short of past achievements. This may be seen as the external dimension of Lucian Pye's observation that "China is a civilization pretending to be a state."[6]

The second reason stems from the collapse of Chinese power and civilization in the 19th century and the first half of the 20th century in the face of the onslaught of Western power and modernity. That experience gave rise to the myth of the "century of shame and humilation" in which China is portrayed as the victim with a series of entitlements to the restitution of lost sovereign territory and the restoration of injured pride and dignity. Yet many of these territorial claims are arbitrary as they rest on dubious treatments of the historical record where contemporary concepts are read into past relationships which were based on principles and practices alien to the modern world.[7] Since modernization in China is indissolubly associated with Westernization there is a tendency of contemporary communist reformers to repeat the intellectual fallacy of the Confucian reformers of the late 19th century who sought to use Western technology to buttress Confucian rule and the values on which it rested. Thus the Deng Xiaoping concept of "socialism with Chinese characteristics" suggests that China's identity once again is seen as turning on values and principles that differ fundamentally from those of the modern (that is Western) world with whose capitalist international economy he sought to link the Chinese economy.

6. Lucian W. Pye, "China: erratic state, frustrated society," *Foreign Affairs* (Fall 1990), p. 58.
7. For further elaboration see Michael Yahuda, "The changing faces of Chinese nationalism: dimensions of statehood," in Michael Leifer (ed.), *Nationalism in Asia* (London: Routledge, forthcoming, 1999).

Towards a New Approach

After the Tiananmen killings and especially following the demise of the Soviet Union, several Chinese leaders claimed that the West tried to make use of China's increasing linkages with the outside world in order to undermine and transform their system – a policy they called "peaceful evolution." In view of that it is striking how much China's leaders have sought to integrate their country into the international system in the era of reform, especially in the last ten years since the end of the Cold War. There is little doubt that it was Deng Xiaoping personally who encouraged these developments as a necessary element in his campaign to speed up China's economic development, as expressed in the talks he gave in the course of his famous Southern Tour (*nanxun*) in 1992.[8] The remarkable economic growth that saw the country's total output quadruple between 1978 and 1995 was driven in no small part by external economic relations. During the same period the sum of imports and exports as a percentage of gross national product grew from less than 10 per cent to more than 56 per cent and foreign trade as a whole grew more than 13 times, from US$21 billion to $280 billion.[9] Meanwhile Western influence and popular culture as mediated through Hong Kong and Taiwan became pervasive as the effects of globalization made themselves felt in terms of information flows, design, technology, management and even political ideas.[10]

In this process China has developed from first seeking unilateral advantage from the public goods provided by international institutions towards playing an increasing participatory role in multilateral international organizations and in the promotion of its own ideas for international norms and regimes. Thus in the 1980s China became a member of the World Bank and the International Monetary Fund, and began to adapt some of its bureaucratic *modus operandi* in accordance with their practices. It began draw immense benefits as the country rapidly became the Bank's largest and favourite customer.[11] But in the 1990s China began to participate more actively in multilateral diplomatic settings even to the extent of embracing new forms of diplomacy. In specific terms, China has joined the key regional organizations the Asia Pacific Economic Co-operation (APEC) forum in 1991 and the ASEAN Regional Forum (ARF) in 1993. Although both institutions operate by co-operation and consensus and are not rule-making bodies that bind members, they nevertheless involve China in a continual process of multilateral diplomacy. The

8. For further discussion see Michael Yahuda "Deng Xiaoping: the statesman," *The China Quarterly*, No. 135 (September 1993), pp. 563–65.

9. Kim, "China as a great power," pp. 450–51.

10. See for example, the excerpts cited in "Education, media, and culture," in Schell and Shambaugh, *The China Reader*, pp. 215–296. See also Thomas Gold, "Go with your feelings: Hong Kong and Taiwan popular culture in Greater China," *The China Quarterly*, No 136 (December 1993), pp. 907–925.

11. Harold K. Jacobson and Michel Oksenberg, *China's Participation in the IMF, the World Bank and the GATT: Toward Global Economic Order* (Ann Arbor: University of Michigan Press, 1990).

former is concerned primarily with trade and investment and is committed to the principles of free trade and open regionalism. Along with the
other developing countries, China is pledged on a voluntary basis to
abolish tariffs by the year 2020, ten years after the developed countries
should have completed the process. The ARF is concerned with security,
and also operates on a co-operative basis through which it seeks to
promote security by the building of trust, the developing of confidence-
building measures, the exercise of preventive diplomacy, the discourage-
ment of the use of force in the course of disputes and so on.[12] China
participates in its various groups and although it has agreed as a matter
of form to discuss the disputed claims to the Spratly Islands on a
multilateral basis, little direct progress has been registered so far in
tackling security issues involving China. The only multilateral approach
of a practical kind in which China is involved is concerned with biodiver-
sity in the South China Sea. In 1996 China joined the academic-driven
Council for Security Co-operation in the Asia-Pacific (CSCAP). This had
been established three years earlier to institutionalize the large numbers
of regional security seminars and conferences that began in the late
1980s. It was technically unofficial and was dubbed "second track" to the
ARF's "first track" diplomacy. CSCAP is designed to discuss a broad
range of proposals and ideas to further the work of the ARF. The Chinese
contribution so far, according to many participants, is to hold back much
of the work through a series of procedural points.

Beyond the region China has become a participant in a wide range of
international regimes and committed itself to observe a large number of
international conventions that have the effect of constraining the government's freedom of action in ways that previously would have been
deemed intrusive infringements of China's sovereignty. Thus reversing
previous "principled" positions, China signed the Non-Proliferation
Treaty in 1992, and the Comprehensive Nuclear Test Ban Treaty in 1996,
over-riding elements in the military who objected that because of its
technology deficiencies the country was handing an advantage to the
Americans in particular. In fact the Chinese government has agreed to
join a number of different kinds of regimes with varying degrees of
readiness to observe those rules that limit its freedom of action. These
include arms control, trade, the environment, intellectual property rights
and even human rights. China has signed the two UN conventions on
cultural, social and economic rights and that on civic and political rights,
but it has yet to ratify them.

However the depth of the Chinese commitment to this more interna-
tionalist approach is still unclear. China is still ruled by a communist
party which has shown itself to be absolutely determined to hold on to
power and to have been ruthlessly successful in eliminating political
opposition. Its decision-making processes at the highest levels are still
clouded in secrecy, where rumour takes the place of transparency.

12. For a full account, see Michael Leifer, *The ASEAN Regional Forum* (Adelphi Paper
302, London: IISS/Oxford University Press, 1996).

Formally the Party is still committed to a communist ideology to which it has attached a strong nationalistic design. Indeed the Party leaders encourage and benefit from the inculcation of patriotic sentiments. China's leaders still tend to treat interdependency with suspicion.

Continental Ease and Maritime Difficulties

Historically China has been a continental country and much of its security concern was focused on Inner Asia. It is only with the advent of the West that the maritime dimension has come to the fore. And of course one of the contrasts between Maoist and Dengist China has been the former's emphasis on the interior and on self-strengthening and the latter's emphasis on the coastal regions and on engagement with the outside world. It is argued here that this historical experience is reflected in the greater ease with which China's leaders have handled their continentalist as compared with their maritime relations.

Since the end of the Cold War China has experienced an unprecedented period of relative peace in modern history when it has been free from the threat of attack by more powerful countries. Indeed since the demise of the Soviet Union in 1991 the PRC has enjoyed a degree of strategic latitude in dealing with maritime East Asia. This has been reinforced as a result of a series of agreements with Russia and the Central Asian states, beginning in April and December 1996, that have not only settled nearly all the outstanding border problems, but have also established new forms of relations based on mutual troop reductions and various confidence-building measures. Chinese spokesmen have hailed the April 1996 agreement as China's first multilateral treaty. More significantly perhaps, these new arrangements have transformed the once contentious region in which Chinese and Soviet forces confronted each other in huge numbers into what a Chinese official scholar has called "a region of peace, friendship and co-operation."[13]

The Chinese side has not sought to take advantage of the immense shift in the regional balance of power in its favour. Nowhere is this more evident than in Chinese treatment of the Republic of Mongolia. Immediately upon the demise of the Soviet Union, the long-term protector of Mongolia, China's leaders signed agreements with the Republic and recognized its borders. No mention was made of Mao's claims upon the former province of Outer Mongolia nor of Chinese patriotic history teachings that Mongolia gained its independence illegitimately.

The relationship with Russia has gone from strength to strength, until in April 1996, apparently at the initiative of the Russian side, it reached the level of a "strategic partnership." Since then the Chinese side has established partnerships with the other permanent members of the Security Council as well as Japan and Germany. Interestingly, only the one with the United States has been called "strategic," even if restricted to the

13. Xia Yishan, "Sino-Russian partnership marching into 21st century," *Beijing Review*, 5–11 May 1997, p. 9.

sense of building towards it – the others being called variously "comprehensive" or "constructive." These are seen collectively in Beijing as being appropriate for what is described as the growing trend towards multipolarization. They all involve agreements to treat each other equally and affirmations that they are not directed against third parties.

What Beijing has in mind is a series of measures designed to hold at bay aspects of globalization and growing American influence. Multipolarity, coexistence between states with different systems, religions and so on are seen as leading to a "democratic" stable world order devoid of confrontation. Interdependence should not undermine the "economic security of sovereign states," nor should there be discrimination in international trade, nor attempts to "use currency and financial levers to impose political and economic conditions which violate the legitimate national interests of any particular country." There should be no unilateralism, no attempts by to "bypass the UN Security Council." Major powers should also "refrain from efforts aimed at expanding existing, or setting up new, military and political alliances." Additionally the two sides stressed "the exceptional importance of preserving and strengthening the Treaty on the Limitation of Antiballistic Missile Systems, which was and remains, one of the cornerstones in maintaining strategic stability throughout the world.[14]

But the trouble with the Chinese vision is that it questions the core of what other resident states in the region see as the basis for order. Regional stability is seen by them to rest on the series of formal security alliances that the United States has with several states on the maritime periphery of East Asia. They are seen as complementary to the attempts within the region to establish looser forms of security through their intramural consultative processes or in the broader parameters of the ASEAN Regional Forum, that also includes China.[15] More generally, the American military presence has been seen as a stabilizing influence that has served the general interest of all the major parties including the PRC despite its opposition to American arms sales to Taiwan. In this view it is as much in China's interests as Japan's and other regional states that the American–Japanese alliance should remain viable lest Japan and its neighbours should have to confront the problems inherent in it assuming responsibility for its own strategic defence.

Yet Chinese leaders have begun to sketch out an alternative vision of how to maintain strategic stability. General Chi Haotian, the Minister of Defence of the PRC, in a speech in Singapore in late November indicated that he saw the American alliance system as an attempt to weaken and contain China. Yet four days earlier the American Defense Secretary

14. This version of the statement issued by ITAR-TASS news agency in *BBC Monitoring Service: Asia-Pacific*, 25 November 1998, differs slightly in wording from that issued by the Chinese side in *Beijing Review*, 14–20 December 1998, pp. 6–8. But as far as I can tell the differences are insignificant.
15. See Allen S. Whiting, "ASEAN eyes China: the security dimension," *Asian Survey*, Vol. 37, No. 4 (April 1997), pp. 299–322; and Renato Cruz De Castro, "The controversy in the Spratlys: exploring the limits to ASEAN's engagement policy," *Issues and Studies*, Vol. 34, No. 9 (September 1998), pp. 95–123.

released a report affirming that America would strengthen its alliances and that despite economic difficulties and uncertainties about Korea "it's important to stress that the continuity of America's commitment remains unchanged."[16]

The Chinese approach lacks credibility as the PRC has continued its practice of what has been called "creeping assertiveness" in thickening its presence in the disputed islands in the South China Sea.[17] Moreover the Chinese have yet to respond to South-east Asian concerns that by establishing structures on Mischief Reef they have suddenly and surreptitiously established a military presence in the heart of maritime South-east Asia less than 200 miles from the coast of the Philippines and when the nearest inhabited Chinese territory is Hainan Island more than 1,000 miles away to the north. Not surprisingly, rather than forsaking the United States, the Philippines is actively considering enhancing the alliance that had lost much of its significance after the American withdrawal from its bases there in 1991.[18] What South-east Asians have also found disturbing is that Chinese pressure about American alliances is directed towards them rather than the United States. Perhaps the Chinese new approach is still evolving, but what is striking is the difference between the treatment of its continental and maritime peripheries.

The most serious illustration of China's difficulties in developing a credible policy to deal with its maritime neighbours centres on the question of Japan. China's concern to elicit an appropriate apology for wartime aggression and atrocities does not absolve its leaders from recognizing that Japan may have legitimate security needs. Unfortunately there is no sign of any such acknowledgement. As we have seen, Chinese leaders appear to oppose as a matter of principle the long-term continuity of the American provision of security for Japan as agreed by their alliance. At the same time they object whenever senior Japanese leaders contemplate transforming Japan into a "normal country" capable of providing for its own security. Moreover, China's leaders joined with their Russian counterparts in denouncing as unacceptably provocative any move by Japan to participate in research towards the development of Theatre Ballistic Missile Defence. Yet both sets of leaders maintained the right to retain a variety of missiles equipped with a range of warheads,

16. The idea that American alliances were a relic of the Cold War that should be set aside in favour of consultative processes was first formally put forward by officials of the PRC's Ministry of Foreign Affairs at an ARF meeting in Beijing in March 1997. For a report of Chi Haotian's speech see Michael Richardson, "Gently, China flexes strategic muscles in Asia," *International Herald Tribune*, 28 November 1998. The American report dated 23 November 1998 is entitled *The United States Security Strategy for the East Asia-Pacific Region*.

17. The phrase is drawn from Michael Leifer, "Chinese economic reform: the impact on policy in the South China Sea," in Gerald Segal and Richard Yang (eds.), *Chinese Economic Reform: The Impact on Security* (London: Routledge, 1996), p. 147.

18. Following evidence in October 1998 of construction activity by the Chinese on Mischief Reef (an islet within what the Philippines considers to be its territorial waters) Manila found that Beijing reacted coolly to its offer to develop the reef jointly, even though the PRC has long advocated that as a temporary way of handling the dispute. Meanwhile the ASEAN summit meeting in Hanoi, 15–16 December 1998, largely averted the issue. See "South China Sea: a weakened Asean is no match for China," *Far Eastern Economic Review*, 24 December 1998, pp. 18–20.

including nuclear ones, that in effect constitute a real threat to Japan. For good measure the Chinese claim there is no reason to object to the development by North Korea of longer-range missiles that clearly would also reach Japan.[19] As long as China's leaders fail to take account of Japan's security needs their approaches to questions of regional security will remain badly flawed.

Relations with the United States

This is undoubtedly the key relationship for China. As the sole surviving superpower, the United States is the dominant power in the world and in the Asia-Pacific region. Unlike the former Soviet Union, the United States excels in all the dimensions of what the Chinese define as "comprehensive national strength" (zonghe guoli). Notwithstanding the expectation that China's aggregate economic and military capabilities will grow significantly relative to most other countries, a carefully compiled study by RAND has concluded that the United States will maintain its "military prominence" in the region well into the second decade of the next century.[20]

Although Chinese publications have been discussing the alleged relative decline of the United States for many years, Chinese actions speak louder than their words, and even these have changed as America asserted its pre-eminence in the wake of the Asian economic crisis. America has become China's main export market and hence source of foreign exchange. It is by America above all that China's leaders crave to be treated as equals. Whenever China's leaders and officials seek to identify the ultimate levels of performance which they seek to emulate it is to America that they turn. Most of China's international problems sooner or later seem to end up with an American flavour. The United States is seen as the principal source of pressure on China to adhere to a range of international obligations that it has undertaken, from issues to do with nuclear and other forms of the proliferation of weapons of mass destruction to matters of human rights, intellectual property rights, a raft of trade issues and China's admission to the World Trade Organization. America is China's most important "neighbour" by far in the sense that it is American deployments and policies that are decisive in shaping security issues involving Korea, Japan, Taiwan, aspects of the South China Sea and South Asia. Moreover it is America above all which has an interventionist agenda to bring about political change in China.[21]

Given China's relatively weak hand, it may be said to have conducted relations with the United States with great diplomatic skill. Nevertheless the Chinese government needs foreign investment and access to Western

19. *International Herald Tribune*, 16–17 January 1999.
20. Charles Wolf Jr., K.C. Yeh, Anil Bannezai, Donald P. Henry and Michael Kennedy, *Long Term Economic and Military Trends 1994–2015: The US & Asia* (Santa Monica: Rand, 1995), pp. xvi–xvii.
21. See for example the argument of David Shambaugh in "The United States and China: cooperation or confrontation?" in Schell and Shambaugh, *The China Reader*, especially pp. 471–72.

markets to continue to generate the kind of economic growth that it needs to maintain itself in power – or, as it puts it, to maintain "stability." To these ends it needs a stable peaceful international environment especially within its own region. The United States is the key element in ensuring that both conditions are available to China. Perhaps it is concern about the underlying dependency inherent in such an asymmetrical relationship that makes Chinese leaders especially sensitive to American policy. Whenever problems arise, as they necessarily will, given the divergence of interests between the two sides and their very different histories, cultures and political systems, the typical Chinese response is to argue that that would lead to a "step backwards" or to a downturn in the relationship. The consequences are rarely if ever spelt out. But the concern in Washington is that bad relations with China could lead once again to conflict in East Asia, the only place since the Second World War where the Americans have fought two major wars – both of which involved China directly or indirectly. Interestingly, another argument for American engagement that remains largely tacit is the fear of the consequences of the disintegration of China to itself, the region and the world as a whole.

Conclusion

The PRC has made great strides to join the modern world in the 20 years since beginning the process of reform and opening-up and, as we have seen, these have accelerated since the end of the Cold War. Moreover, the Chinese leaders have gone a long way to establish a peaceful international environment within the region which is conducive to China's main task of developing its economy. But China's approach to its maritime neighbours and to the management of disputed maritime territories is still unnerving to the extent that the neighbours seek the assurance of support from the United States. China has not yet reached the point of sufficient transparency at home to allow it to be truly integrated into the international community. In addition China is still in the middle of a vast transformation that has a long way to go before it can be said to have run its course. Hence in its foreign relations, as well as in its domestic affairs, it is true to say that despite the enormous progress that has been registered, many deep-seated problems remain and for the time being the region and the wider world have more to fear from a China that can act as a "spoiler" than from any leadership that a still relatively weak China could possibly hope to provide.

The People's Liberation Army and the People's Republic at 50: Reform at Last

David Shambaugh

The People's Republic of China (PRC) may not have had the opportunity to celebrate 50 years of statehood had it not been for the People's Liberation Army (PLA) – nor, for that matter, is it likely that the PRC would have come into existence in the first place were it not for the PLA (as is evident in Mao's often-cited observation that, "Political power grows out of the barrel of a gun!").[1] As the Chinese Communist Party (CCP) rode the military to power in 1949, the army also subsequently acted on several occasions to rescue the regime, maintain the Party in power and *ergo* sustain the People's Republic. The PLA has also been the designated protector of "state sovereignty" and "unifier" of China – acting to incorporate Tibet, Inner Mongolia, Manchuria and border regions in the south-west and north-west during the early 1950s, and fighting several border wars against China's neighbours thereafter – and it is the PLA that is ultimately charged with ensuring both that Taiwan does not seek "independence" and that China's territorial claims in the East and South China Seas are protected.

These mandates – to maintain domestic order, safeguard national security and maintain the Communist Party in power – have been constant roles over time. Yet in 50 years the PLA has also evolved and changed substantially as an institution. Some qualitative departures have been taken in several core dimensions, affecting not only PLA capabilities and organization but also its institutional identity.

In 1949, the Red Army, as it was then called, propelled the CCP to power after 28 years of battling Kuomintang, Japanese and warlord forces. During this long period the armed forces grew from rag-tag guerrilla units into a disciplined (if poorly equipped) force of nearly two million soldiers. Having ridden the army to power, the Party still needed to rely on it to unify and govern the country. The PLA was instrumental in establishing the General Administrative Regions and governing large portions of China prior to 1954, and the armed forces were also instrumental in the "mopping up" campaigns against residual "bandits" and "splittists" in the early 1950s. Just as the PLA was consolidating power, however, it was severely tested on the battlefield in Korea. Despite sustaining huge losses (an estimated three million), Mao's "volunteers" held their own against United Nations forces. But the experience

---

1. Some revisionist histories question the degree to which the CCP came to power as the result of a "revolution." It may be more appropriate to consider the CCP's ascension to power and the establishment of the PRC as the result of a combination of the collapsing Kuomintang state and the military victory won by the PLA (then Red Army) over KMT forces on the battlefield. The revisionist view is expressed, for example, in my "The building of the civil-military state in China, 1949–1965: bringing the soldier back in," in Timothy Cheek and Tony Saich (eds.), *The Construction of State Socialism in China, 1949–1965* (Armonk, NY: M.E. Sharpe, 1996).

convinced Chinese commanders of their backwardness and the pressing need for modernization.

This is a quest that has bedeviled the PLA ever since. Lack of sustained commitment, inadequate financial resources, technological constraints, unreliable access to international assistance and the vagaries of politics have all served to restrict the PLA's pursuit of professionalization and modernization. It has been able to field some modern weapons which give it the attributes of a major power,[2] as well as evolving its doctrine, tactics and organizational structure,[3] but, generally speaking, military reforms have been slow to come, reflecting their lowest priority among the Four Modernizations. Reform of the military began after the landmark Central Military Commission meeting of December 1985, when significant reductions in the force structure ensued, but it has really only been since the mid-1990s (particularly after the Gulf War) that serious and sweeping reforms have been undertaken. These have involved complex changes, but the most important departures can be encapsulated in four categories: defence doctrine and training; force structure, command and control; military leadership and Party–army relations; and weaponry. Several important elements will necessarily slip between the cracks of this schema, but these factors will highlight the principal parameters of reform as the PRC turns 50.

Defence Doctrine and Training

Defence doctrine evolves and responds to several factors, including a nation's social and political culture, its military and strategic traditions, contemporary global military doctrines and the nature of warfare, and a nation's strategic environment. The latter two are exogenous to a nation, while the first two tend to serve as mediating prisms through which external stimuli are filtered. Together they provide a nexus out of which emerges a nation's defence doctrine.

In the case of the contemporary PLA, these factors interact in uncertain ways. We know much more about the exogenous variables than the indigenous ones. For example, it is amply evident that the PLA has intensively studied the nature of contemporary warfare over the last decade – particularly the Iran–Iraq war of the 1980s, the 1991 Gulf War and the Yugoslav conflict of 1999. This has especially been the case with the study of high-technology warfare and the Revolution in Military Affairs.[4] Many lessons have been learned in terms of training and tactics, but there have also been lessons of doctrine and derived strategy. Half of

2. Particularly nuclear weapons and air, sea and ground-based ballistic missiles delivery systems.

3. These are traced in Harlan W. Jencks, *From Muskets to Missiles: Politics and Professionalism in the Chinese Army, 1945–1981* (Boulder: Westview Press, 1982); Harvey W. Nelsen, *The Chinese Military System* (Boulder: Westview Press, 1997 and 1981); Ellis Joffe, *The Chinese Army After Mao* (Cambridge, MA: Harvard University Press, 1987).

4. For a sampling of this study see Michael Pillsbury (ed.), *Chinese Views of Future Warfare* (Washington, D.C.: National Defense University Press, 1997).

these are what the PLA describes as its current operative military doctrine: "limited war under high-technology conditions" (*gaoji jishu tiaojian xia jubu zhanzheng*). The other half is so-called "active defence" (*jiji fangyu*) which can be traced back at least to Peng Dehuai and the 1950s, although it has evolved considerably in recent years from a continental land-based doctrine to one that is more oriented to China's periphery and emphasizes air, naval and space-based systems.[5] This doctrinal evolution has been analysed in some detail by Paul Godwin and others in recent years,[6] and includes an awareness by the PLA of at least the following elements:

- conflicts tend to be short rather than protracted;
- they are characterized by intense application of firepower rather than manpower;
- long-range "stand-off" precision guided munitions (PGMs) are the weapon of choice, and supplement strategic air power;
- mobile "rapid reaction" forces are more important than positional warfare;
- the "electronic battlefield" and over-the-horizon location and targeting capability requires total "battlespace awareness" at all times of day and night and in all weather conditions;
- satellites and airborne command posts and early-warning provide critical intelligence;
- information warfare and electronic countermeasures can confuse and disrupt enemy communications, command and control;
- battlespace penetration (force insertion), the element of surprise and stealth are critical to the initial phase of combat and disrupting an enemy's capability to respond effectively;
- combined arms and joint force operations are important and require close co-ordination and repetitive training.

These are some of the principal lessons drawn by PLA analysts and strategists in recent years, and they have been intensively studied by the Academy of Military Sciences and the PLA's many staff colleges. Few militaries in the world have devoted as many resources, in such a sustained and concentrated fashion, to studying the nature of contem-

---

5. China has over 12,000 miles of land frontiers, over 11,000 miles of coastline, 1.86 million square miles of claimed territorial waters, and 30,000 square kilometres of naval air space to protect. Interview, PLA General Staff, 6 December 1998.

6. See Paul H.B. Godwin, "From continent to periphery: PLA doctrine, strategy and capabilities toward 2000," in David Shambaugh and Richard H. Yang (eds.), *China's Military in Transition* (Oxford: Clarendon Press, 1997); Godwin, "Chinese military strategy revised: local and limited war," *The Annals of the American Academy of Political and Social Science*, Vol. 519 (January 1992); Godwin, "Changing concepts of doctrine, strategy, and operations in the Chinese People's Liberation Army, 1979–1987," *The China Quarterly*, No. 112 (December 1987); Nan Li, "The PLA's evolving warfighting doctrine, strategy, and tactics, 1985–1995: a Chinese perspective," in Shambaugh and Yang, *China's Military in Transition*; David Shambaugh, "The insecurity of security: the PLA's evolving doctrine and threat perceptions towards 2000," *Journal of Northeast Asian Studies*, Vol. XIII, No. 1 (Spring 1994); and Alastair I. Johnston, "China's new 'old thinking': the concept of limited deterrence, *International Security*, Vol. 20, No. 3 (Winter 1995).

porary warfare. At the same time, in many of these areas PLA study has not been translated into application or development. In analysing the PLA today, ambition must not be confused with capability. Understanding these elements of warfare and the necessity of adapting the associated doctrine, training, command and tactics is the first step to assimilating and implementing them, but the PLA remains a long way from fielding a military force that can fight this kind of modern war. It has taken some of the first important steps – organizing rapid reaction units, undertaking much more night training, working on electronic countermeasures and information warfare, combined arms operations, and so on – but remains extremely backward in terms of equipment and weaponry, the educational level of its forces, and many other critical features needed to field a modern military.

Force Structure, Command and Control

Reform of the PLA's force structure began in the mid-1980s with the first round of streamlining. Between 1985 and 1987 one million service personnel (including civilians, *wenzhi ganbu*) were demobilized.[7] About 70 per cent of the cuts came from the ground forces, while the air force was reduced by 25 per cent. More than 30 units at or above the corps level were eliminated, as well as 4,054 divisional and regimental units.[8] Over 300,000 officers were demobilized, retired or transferred to civilian posts. The PLA Capital Construction Corps were transferred to civilian control and the PLA Railway Corps put under the authority of the Ministry of Railroads. But elements of both – along with border and special guard units, fire-fighting brigades, and a large number of ground force personnel – were transferred to the newly created paramilitary People's Armed Police (PAP). By 1987 the PLA had been reduced from 4.2 million to 3.2 million (including over 300,000 officers), but Deng Xiaoping still thought it too large a force. Further rounds of demobilization in 1989, 1992, 1994 and 1998–99 further reduced the number under arms to approximately 2.5 million. The majority of the recent cuts have come from the ground forces (19 per cent), while the Air Force and Navy have each been reduced by approximately 11 per cent. These reductions have largely come from north-eastern China (primarily the Liaoning Military District of the Shenyang Military Region) and from the least combat-ready infantry divisions.

Simultaneously, the PAP has grown to 900,000, a reserve force of 1.2 million has been reconstituted, while the militia has been reactivated and linked to PAP and local public security units. The reserves, which largely comprise demobilized officers and servicemen, now undergo regular training and are fairly well-equipped. Thus, while the PLA has shrunk by

7. The best study of PLA demobilization is Yitzhak Shichor, "Demobilization: the dialectics of PLA troop reduction," in Shambaugh and Yang, *China's Military in Transition.*
8. Arthur S. Ding, "The streamlining of the PLA," *Issues & Studies* (November 1992), pp. 92–93.

nearly 1.5 million over 15 years, this figure is misleading as one must consider the 900,000-strong PAP and 1.2 million reserves as part of the armed forces: they certainly are in command terms, as each is responsible to the General Staff Department (GSD) line of control. If these forces are added together, the total forces-under-arms still remain nearly 4.6 million!

Other key organizational reforms have changed the force structure. In the late 1980s the eleven military regions were amalgamated into seven in order to improve the centralization of command and control from the General Staff Department in Beijing. In 1989–90 this recentralization went a step further when the Central Military Commission (CMC) ordered all main and regional force units placed under GSD control (the latter had previously been controlled by military regional commanders). As a result, the movement of any forces of brigade size or larger must be authorized specifically by the GSD, and in no case can troops be moved across military region boundaries without CMC approval. Access to weapons and supplies was similarly tightened under the control of the General Logistics Department. Some of this recentralization was motivated by what the PLA learned from studying the Soviet military structure,[9] but it was also partially stimulated by the post-Tiananmen fear of disloyal regional commanders. Concomitantly, another key reform of the late 1980s was to restructure the PLA's 36 army corps into 24 Group Armies (*jituanjun*) that combined units previously commanded separately. Each Group Army is composed of 50,000–60,000 personnel supported by armoured, artillery, engineering, anti-chemical and logistics support units.[10] These initiatives grew out of the PLA's study of U.S. "Air-Land Battle" doctrine and combined arms operations. For example, the PLA no longer fields tank divisions as such, but rather integrated mechanized armoured divisions. It is moving towards the mechanization and mobility of all units, and will soon no longer have any infantry "foot soldiers" as such.[11] The overall emphasis to make "joint" what had previously been a highly compartmentalized command and deployment structure, but it has only really been applied to the ground forces and still begs true joint service operations. In recent years the GSD has contemplated a radical reorganization and further streamlining along the lines of the U.S. Joint Chiefs and regional commands, but this was apparently postponed in 1998 by the CMC as "too destabilizing" given the order for the PLA to withdraw from business and other initiatives at the time.[12]

Another key reform that will affect training was that given by the CMC in 1998 for the military and PAP to divest themselves of all commercial assets and activity. While the PLA's decade-long commercial involvement earned various units, officers, soldiers and their dependents important supplementary income during a time when defence budgets remained

9. Ironically, the U.S. military gives its field commanders far greater individual authority.
10. A Special Arms Department (*Te bing bu*) was formed under the General Staff Department and combines and fulfils procurement needs for these units.
11. Interview with former General Staff Department official, 8 December 1998.
12. Interview, National Defence University, 16 July 1998.

low, there is little doubt that it was highly deleterious to professionalism, readiness and training regimen.[13] The military's deep involvement in corruption, smuggling, prostitution and criminal triad activity also caused problems for a government trying to crack down on such activities. In addition, the PLA's influence over certain business sectors, such as telecommunications and aircraft production, skewed the corporate arena, making it difficult for domestic or foreign companies to complete effectively. For all these reasons, the PLA, PAP, Public and State Security Ministries were ordered out of business at the end of 1998. The directive is not being fully complied with: military units are finding ingenious ways to circumvent it, and more questions than answers remain concerning the disposition and fate of these enterprises, but it is nevertheless clear that many units have complied. By the end of 1998, approximately one-third of the estimated 15,000 PLA enterprises had their assets transferred to the State Economic and Trade Commission, were undergoing audits of their accounts, and were in the process of being "civilianized." It remains to be seen if the audits will result in arrests or court martials. As a result of the divestiture directive, General Logistic Department sources claim that the military will lose an estimated 5.1 billion *renminbi* ($600 million) of income per annum.[14] This department, which is responsible for military finance, had hoped to be compensated for this amount, and to fix the PLA budget as a defined percentage of total state expenditure and gross domestic product in future defence budgets, but was rebuffed in the 1999–2000 budget.

Increasing the educational level of troops is another recent reform intended to turn the PLA into a more technology-intensive force. At present only 50 per cent of officers have education beyond senior middle school, while the goal is that all junior-level officers will hold a B.A. or equivalent by 2010.[15] To do this, the PLA is just beginning to introduce a Reserve Officer Training Corps (ROTC) system into universities and vocational schools, and has sent delegations to the United States to study the American ROTC system. Of course, one of the most important reforms of recent years was the reintroduction of ranks in 1988 (after a 25-year hiatus). Also, beginning in 1999, conscription service periods were reduced to two years across all services. This reform will reduce the number of conscripts in the PLA from 82 per cent of its total strength to less than 65 per cent by 2000.[16] While the aim of this is to develop a more permanent force that relies on career personnel, it will also have the negative effect of not permitting rank-and-file soldiers enough time to master expertise in high-technology weaponry. Resource constraints also limit "live fire" training, although simulation training has increased in all three services.

13. See James Mulvenon, "Military corruption in China," *Problems of Post-Communism* (March/April 1998), pp. 12–21.

14. Interview, General Logistics Department, 9 December 1998.

15. *Ibid.* This figure rises considerably at and above the group army level, and among those who graduate from the National Defence University.

16. "Army seeks mobility in force cuts," *Janes Defense Weekly*, 16 December 1998.

Taken together, these reforms of the force structure and command and control dovetail with the doctrinal "lessons" of modern warfare noted above, and they put into operation some of the lessons learned. These are important changes, and they represent recognition of what the modern battlefield environment entails, but old habits, norms and systems die hard. The PLA still remains heavily compartmentalized, under-resourced and ill-equipped, lacking in direct exposure to more modern methods, and with relatively poorly educated and paid soldiers.

The PLA Leadership and Party–Army Relations

Another stalwart element of PLA command and control that appears to show signs of incremental reform is the composition of military leadership and the nature of Party–army relations. Following the passing of patriarch Deng Xiaoping, the High Command of the PLA is almost entirely new. There has been near total turnover of the top 20 to 30 military officers in China during the last three years. This includes all the commanders, deputy commanders and political commissars in all seven military region commands; the directors and deputies of the General Staff, Logistics and Political Departments; the commanders of air, naval and ground forces; the commandants of the National Defence University and Academy of Military Sciences; the chairmen of the Commission on Science, Technology and Industry for National Defence and the new General Armaments Department, and other bodies. The Central Military Commission itself has seen more than half its membership turn over in the last few years. Only the top echelon of the Second Artillery, China's ballistic missile forces, has gone relatively untouched. Much more personnel turnover and organizational reform is anticipated in the next few years, as the PLA proceeds with downsizing, upgrading and streamlining its force structure.

Personal allegiances in the High Command no longer reflect pre-1949 Field Army loyalties. Rather, career paths to the top have much more to do with field service and commands, training in military academies and battlefield experience. While merit now counts for more, patronage politics are not dead in the PLA: many of today's most senior military have ties to retired General Zhang Zhen, and it is evident that current CMC Vice-Chairman General Zhang Wannian has also worked to install a number of his former subordinates in key command positions.

Significantly, the new High Command also largely comprises officers with battlefield, command and lengthy service experience. These are officers who commanded troops in the 1979 Sino-Vietnamese border war, the 1988 Nansha conflict, the 1969 Sino-Soviet border clashes, 1962 Sino-Indian conflict and the Korean War. With one or two exceptions, they are not individuals who have spent their careers as political commissars. Relatedly, the new High Command no longer comprises soldier-politicians, active in the rough-and-tumble world of Chinese elite politics. This signals a potentially very significant development in the Chinese political system: the breaking of the "interlocking directorate" and long-standing symbiotic tie between the Communist Party and PLA.[17] We are now witnessing, for the first time in 70 years, a growing bifurcation of the two institutions. The PLA today is much more prepared to resist Party encroachment into military development, and attempts to pull the PLA into domestic politics or domestic security.

This also raises the issue of accountability of the armed forces, that is, the relationship of the army to the Party and state. The issue of putting the PLA under the command of the state, instead of the Communist Party, was first floated and debated during the Zhao Ziyang era of the late 1980s, and cropped up again in 1997. After Zhao's purge in 1989, he and his advisors were sharply criticized for propagating this "bourgeois" concept. But the debate resurfaced in the wake of the 1997 National People's Congress, when the National Defence Law was passed. This law clearly states a number of times that the armed forces are subordinate to the state (*guojia*), the National People's Congress and its Standing Committee, the President of the republic, and the State Council. Only in Chapter III, Article 19, is mention made that "the armed forces of the People's Republic of China are subject to the leadership of the Chinese Communist Party."

We will have to wait for a crisis to see how such constitutional stipulations play out. Historical experience, including 1989, is not encouraging in this regard. Nevertheless, the National Defence Law is a very significant document, and may signal important changes in the identity and accountability of the PLA.[18] It is too early to conclude that a "national army" is emerging in China, but a debate about the issue has clearly simmered inside the armed forces and among politically reformist intellectuals.

Establishing such accountability is one of the central components of the process of democratization. This has now been accomplished in Taiwan – where the armed forces had a long history of subservience to the ruling Kuomintang – and it has also now occurred in South Korea, Indonesia, Thailand, the Philippines, Bangladesh, Pakistan, and some countries in Africa and Latin America. The decline of the praetorian guard has been a key feature of post-authoritarian politics in Asia. In recent years regime change has taken place across the region without military intervention, amid extreme financial hardship and social instability. This is testimony to the new strength of democratic institutions and more professional identities of armed forces across Asia. Taken together with other recent developments in Chinese politics, such as village-level elections and more open demands for structural political reform, the

17. For an explication of this thesis see my "The soldier and the state in China: the political work system in the People's Liberation Army," *The China Quarterly*, No. 127 (September 1991), pp. 527–568.
18. The National Defence Law must also be seen as part of a larger and important process to govern military procedures through law and regulations. In the last decade nearly 120 military-related regulations have been adopted by the CMC, State Council and National People's Congress, as well as more than 1,000 rules and regulations adopted by individual PLA service arms and Military region commands. Source: *China's National Defense* (Beijing: Information Office of the State Council, 1998), pp. 18–19.

changing nature of the army–Party relationship may portend the further dismantling of the Leninist system and preliminary movement towards nascent democratic reform in China. These indicators should clearly not be overstated, but they are potentially significant.

Another characteristic of the new High Command is that, with few exceptions, they have largely spent their careers in regional field commands deep in the interior of China. They have generally not travelled abroad and do not speak foreign languages. Accordingly, many display a distinctly insular and non-cosmopolitan world view. Some are highly xenophobic, suspicious of the West, hostile towards Japan, condescending towards China's neighbours and anti-American in particular. They have been trained in a world that prizes secrecy, and thus do not appreciate the importance of defence transparency. Their backgrounds as field commanders make them more comfortable with battlefield tactics than global security issues or political-military issues. Further, they all come from ground force backgrounds; only the commanders of the Navy and Air Force, appropriately, hail from these services. Given the direction the PLA is moving – trying to become a high-tech military capable of peripheral defence that emphasizes air and naval power projection, nuclear weapons modernization, ballistic and cruise missiles, electronic countermeasures, information warfare, anti-satellite weapons, laser and precision-guided munitions, and so on – one is struck by the fact that today it is a military led by soldiers with minimal exposure to these kinds of weapons, technologies and doctrine. These are individuals with little exposure to modernity, much less modern warfare. Beneath them, however, there is a whole layer of major generals and senior colonels who are completely opposite. It is this cohort who will manage the PLA in the early 21st century, as the current High Command retires.

Weaponry

Concomitant with the doctrinal reforms outlined above, the PLA Air Force and Second Artillery have become favoured sectors for research and development in the post-Cold War era. Following lessons from the Gulf War and Yugoslav conflict combined with the PLA's new operational doctrine of "limited war under high technology conditions," air and missile power have become the weapons systems of choice in building the PLA arsenal for the 21st century. New generations of intercontinental, medium and short-range ballistic missiles are being developed, and priority has been placed on acquiring MIRV and cruise missile capabilities. Two new indigenous fighters are under development. The F-10, a fourth-generation multi-role fighter, has been plagued with problems but may be ready for serial production in 2001–02. It uses a delta wing canard configuration, incorporates stealth-like design features, avionics (from Israel) and is far advanced over the current top-of-the-line F-8II.[19] The JH-7 (FBC-1) is a twin-engine strike fighter designed for long-range air cover missions, and is also in the flight-testing stage. As

19. "Air Force frontliners to see new fighter breed," *Janes Defense Weekly*, p. 26.

noted above, the PLA Air Force has also bought 48 Su-27 fighters, with a contract for production of 200 more (designated the F-11). The 1997 contract calls for the first 50 to be assembled from kits at the Shenyang Aircraft Corporation factory (the first two were flight-tested in late 1998), and licensed production will commence thereafter. The Air Force is also negotiating to acquire 20–60 Su-30 multi-role strike fighters from Russia, as well as AWAC early-warning and control aircraft from Russia and Israel. Once all these aircraft are in operation, and phased retirements of antiquated aircraft are completed, China will possess a diversified and 1980s-quality air force – but this will not be until about 2005–2007, even assuming all goes well in production and testing. One cannot be too optimistic on this score given the chronic problems that have plagued the civilian and military aircraft industry in China. Further, pilot training for combat situations in all-weather conditions and regular maintenance will be necessary, and the PLA Air Force's record on both scores has not been commendable to date.

The new doctrine of peripheral defence has, of course, also included increased attention to developing a blue-water naval capability (*yuanyang haijun*), although this ambition has been severely hampered by lack of funds, an inadequate indigenous production base (to produce, for example, heavy cruisers, aircraft carriers and nuclear submarines), and lack of access to Western sources of supply for key technologies and armaments. China's top-of-the-line destroyer, the *Luhu* (of which the PLA Navy possesses two in active service), is outfitted with German and American engines, French and American radars and sonars, a French helicopter, Italian torpedo launchers, and French surface-to-air and ship-to-ship missiles. Since 1989 China has been prohibited from purchasing Western military equipment and there is little sign of a significant relaxation on this ban any time soon, despite loosening in European Union restrictions on some electronics. Even with restricted access to Western naval technologies and platforms, the Navy has upgraded electronic countermeasures, radar and sonar, fire control systems, and onboard armament on refitted *Luda* destroyers and *Jianghu* frigates. These are being supplemented by new generation *Luda III* destroyers, *Jiangwei*-class frigates, *Houjian* and *Houxian* missile patrol craft, and *Dayun* class resupply vessels. It is unclear to what extent the new 7,000 ton *Luhai* class destroyer incorporates foreign equipment and technologies. In all, the Navy has added nearly 20 surface combatants to its fleet over the last decade. The most important addition will be the two *Sovremenny* destroyers being built in Russia's St Petersburg shipyards. These vessels are armed with Moskit (SS-N-22 "Sunburn") anti-ship missiles and Uragan (SA-N-7 "Gadfly") surface-to-air missiles. Russia has also sold four Kilo diesel electric submarines in recent years, although the PLA Navy has experienced maintenance and operation difficulties with them. Also under development are Chinese-built Song class Type 093 and 094 (SSN and SSBN respectively) submarines.[20] Submarine construction and

20. "New PLAN to train, purchase vessel mix," *Janes Defense Weekly*, 16 December 1998, p. 25.

operation is extremely complex, and the Chinese record in each has been very poor to date.

Without access to equipment and technology from the West, the PLA will never be able to close the weaponry and defence technology gaps appreciably vis-à-vis Japan and the West. Transfers from Russia are meeting certain needs, but they are far from sufficient to provide the PLA with a power projection capability. Most Western analysts place the PLA's conventional capabilities 20 to 30 years behind the state-of-the-art, with the gap widening. Today, China's best conventional military capabilities resemble early 1980s European equipment. In many areas the technologies and hardware are of 1960s or 1970s vintage. For example, of the PLA's 8,500 main battle tanks 6,000 are T-59 vintage (so identified as it was 1959 when they came into operation). The remainder are T-69, T-79, T-80, T-85 and T-90 models. China's main tank factory at Baotou has produced more heavy trucks (in a joint venture with Mercedes Benz) than tanks, and the Shenyang Aircraft Corporation has produced more buses than planes, over the last decade. The situation for the PLA Air Force is similar. Fully 2,000 of its 2,748 fighter-interceptors are the J-6, a modified version of the 1960s vintage MiG-19. The PLA Navy remains a coastal green-water force with few real ocean-going warships. The PLA is attempting to plug some of its most glaring gaps through purchases of select equipment from Russia and Israel, but its overall order-of-battle remains extremely antiquated.

In the area of ballistic missiles, however, China's capabilities are considerably better – and improving. Great emphasis is being placed on achieving long-range precision strike capability, and also on mastering new information warfare techniques associated with the revolution in military affairs.[21] There is no doubt that China is actively studying these technologies (including laser-guided munitions, electronic countermeasures, computer viruses, anti-satellite weapons, high-powered microwave weapons, satellite photo reconnaissance, over-the-horizon sensors, phased array radars and high-speed telecommunications),[22] but one must not confuse ambition with capability. These are extremely complicated technologies to master, test, produce, deploy, assimilate and maintain. There exist numerous impediments – financial, human, technological – to China's ability to acquire and deploy such high-tech systems.

From the desire to develop these latter technologies and weapons systems, one could infer that China is preparing for asymmetrical military contingencies against opponents possessing state-of-the-art militaries (such as Japan or the United States), particularly in potential conflict over Taiwan. The purchase of aircraft, submarines and destroyers from Russia all appear to be "contingency-driven." They seem to indicate preparations to present a credible threat to Taiwan in the first decade of the next century (probably around 2007). Moreover, these purchases and the

21. Major Mark A. Stokes, "China's strategic modernization: implications for U.S. national security," unpublished manuscript, 1997; and Pillsbury, *Chinese Views of Future Warfare*.
22. Stokes, "China's strategic modernization."

emphasis on improving electronic counter-measures and Information Warfare capabilities further suggest a readiness to engage and disrupt U.S. aircraft carrier battle groups in a Taiwan conflict. The persistent attempts to acquire in-flight refuelling capability, and the development of the F-10 and FBC-1 fighters, perhaps indicate a desire to project air power into the South China Sea and beyond.

These acquisitions aside, there appears to be little evidence that PLA procurement patterns, indigenously or exogenously, are driven by specific threat perceptions or military contingency planning. On the contrary, China seems to be building on its few strengths, consolidating "pockets of excellence," while trying to "leapfrog" certain technology gaps and acquire a military capability in the first quarter of the 21st century that is of world-class standards. In other words, apart from Taiwan, PLA procurement seems driven by status factors more than specific contingency planning. Either way, the PLA finds itself far behind in research and development, and will find it very hard to catch up. Despite recent reforms that will begin the long and cumbersome process of overhauling China's laggard defence industries (including the creation of a central General Armament Department to oversee the process), the military-industrial establishment in China has to date proven almost wholly unable to meet the needs of the PLA services and move the military into the era of modern warfare.

Conclusion

In the five areas examined in this article, it is clear that the PLA is undergoing substantial organizational reform and incremental modernization. While recognizing that new departures and progress have been made, it would be premature to conclude that the PLA has crossed the threshold of modernity. It knows where it has to go, but it cannot seem to get there – and the chances of reaching this goal are severely constrained by a series of financial, resource, technological, organizational, cultural, creative and external constraints. This general prognostication does not, however, mean that in certain sectors and in certain contingencies the PLA will not be able to attain its desired goals. Much of the art of warfare is the ability to concentrate capabilities and bring to bear one's best resources to achieve specific, and often narrow, ends. Given that China's national security and defence needs are really quite limited, and geographically defined close to home, the PLA's ability to bring substantial force to bear against an adversary in its neighbourhood is not insubstantial. This point should especially not be lost on Taiwan, nor on Japan and the United States.

The PLA has been in transition most of this decade,[23] but the scope and pace of change is broadening and quickening. New training regimens are being undertaken, new tactics are being tried in accordance with new defence doctrine, new organizational hierarchies are being created, a new

23. See the articles in Shambaugh and Yang, *The Chinese Military in Transition*.

force structure is being put in place, new commanders are being appointed, and new weapons are being produced and fielded. The key operational and research questions for the next decade will therefore have much to do with the assimilation of these new innovations. Many militaries, including the Taiwanese at present, have encountered great difficulties in absorbing and assimilating new technologies and methods. The PLA will quickly learn the lessons that "software" is more important than "hardware," and it is not so much what you have that counts, but how you use it.

The Chinese Legal System: Continuing Commitment to the Primacy of State Power

Pitman B. Potter

The development of the PRC legal system reflects the commitment of the Chinese Communist Party to maintaining its monopoly on political power. In 1949, the Chinese Communists were committed to the notion that political power depended on control of political (and legal) institutions. By 1959, in the wake of the Anti-Rightist Campaign and ongoing campaigns against counter-revolutionaries, the Party's unfettered control over legal institutions and personnel was well entrenched. A decade later, the ideological and political themes of the Cultural Revolution left the role of formal law and legal institutions further marginalized.

By 1979, the Party leadership had embarked on a legal reform programme aimed at building legitimacy and furthering economic reforms. As discussed by Anthony Dicks in *The China Quarterly*'s 1989 review of the PRC at 40, the first decade of legal reform saw significant albeit qualified achievements.[1] The China Spring of 1989 revealed the extent to which the ideals of legal reform had taken root. The pro-democracy demonstrations were replete with legal symbolism, while the regime itself attempted to portray its martial law activities and the violence that followed as being in accordance with law and regulation. But the Tiananmen crisis also saw traditionalists in the Party leadership signal their continuing commitment to maintaining a monopoly on political power.

The achievements and limitations of the first decade of reform set the tone for developments in the years that followed. By 1999, law-making and institution-building have reached impressive levels. At the same time, however, the imperative of maintaining political supremacy for the party-state remains a salient feature in this process. Rejecting suggestions that maintaining its political monopoly is incompatible with pursuit of the rule of law, the party-state has pursued a process of selective reform aimed at preserving political power while promoting economic development.

Influences on the Legal System: Borrowed Norms and Local Context

At the very outset of legal reform, legal specialists were admonished to learn from China's past and from the experience of foreign countries.[2] These two sources of law were conflated, however, as the law-making record of the Republican and early PRC period was based largely on imported foreign models. Thus, the enactment in 1979 of a Criminal Law,

---

1. Anthony Dicks, "The Chinese legal system: reforms in the balance," *The China Quarterly*, No. 119 (September 1989), p. 540.
2. "Zhongguo faxuehui zai jing zhengshi chengli" ("The China Law Society is formally established in Beijing"), *Faxue yanjiu (Studies in Law)*, No. 5 (1982), p. 8.

Criminal Procedure Law and organizational laws for the People's Courts and the People's Procuracies drew on enactments from the 1950s, which in turn were based on Soviet experience and on Republican statutes borrowed from German models. The 1981 Economic Contract Law also stemmed from prior regulations and drafts derived from Soviet and European codes, as did the 1986 General Principles of Civil Law (GPCL). During the 1980s, legislation on such matters as environmental protection, regulation of foreign and domestic business, intellectual property, and civil procedure and arbitration drew increasingly on European and North American models. This borrowing process accelerated during the second decade of legal reform to include a range of economic measures. In addition, foreign pressures created an impetus for legislation in the areas of human rights, criminal law and procedure, and administrative law.

The borrowing of foreign forms of law and legal institutions has been limited, however, by the general ambivalence towards liberal norms supporting individual rights and the restraint on state power which inform the legal systems of Europe and North America. Law is not a limit on the party-state, but rather is a mechanism by which political power is exercised and protected. Examples can be seen from the role of law in the 1980s to achieve policy goals of economic development and social stability.[3] The issue in autumn 1998 of internal regulations restricting foreign exchange transactions and the response in early 1999 to the decision by the Hong Kong Court of Final Appeal on the right of abode expressed the Chinese government's prioritizing of policy outcomes over legal processes. The resilience of this instrumentalism was reinforced most recently by the incorporation into the 1999 Constitution of the term *yifa zhiguo* to denote the concept of "rule of law," when in fact the phrase connotes "rule through law" when compared to the alternate *fazhi grojia* formulation proposed by certain intellectuals to convey the rule of law ideal. The *yifa zhiguo* terminology still met resistance, however, because of its implications for the potential autonomy of law.

The local context for legal reform also depends on the identity and outlook of the individuals who influence the content and operation of law. Particularly important is the expanding range of bureaucratic officials associated with various legal institutions. The Party's political-legal committee system (*zhengfa xitong*) continues to dominate the process of legal reform, although its senior leadership contains few if any trained lawyers. Other legal bureaucracies such as the State Council's Legal Affairs Bureau, the National People's Congress (NPC) Legislative Work Committee, the Ministry of Justice, and the law departments in the various State Council ministries and commissions are dominated by senior officials with little formal legal training. While their influence is significant, legal bureaucrats remain essentially

---

3. See generally, Pitman B. Potter, "Riding the tiger: legitimacy and legal culture in post-Mao China," *The China Quarterly*, No. 138 (June 1994), p. 325.

bureaucratic-political actors who tend to reinforce the subordination of law to state power.

The discourse of law and legal institutions is also influenced by a cadre of intellectuals engaged in legal research and teaching. However, their effectiveness is coloured significantly by several factors. First, the initial cadre of legal specialists involved in the law reform effort largely comprised survivors from the persecutions of the Anti-Rightist Campaign and the Cultural Revolution, whose experiences had a chilling influence on their willingness to challenge the orthodoxy of Party supremacy.[4] Many of those who were newly recruited into the law reform effort were selected on the basis of their knowledge of English, and had little if any formal legal training. As the reforms progressed, such legal training as was made available tended to emphasize rote learning of the content of rules, rather than legal analysis of rules and their application based on varying fact situations.[5] And, as is the case with other elite sectors, selection for legal research and teaching posts, as well as judicial positions, continues to give significant weight to Party membership. Thus, despite their potential to act as a community promoting reliance on legal knowledge, China's legal intellectuals often lack the academic training, career exposure and intellectual commitment to the liberal ideals that are embodied in the foreign legal norms they are charged with selecting and interpreting.

Institutions

Informed by the interaction of legal norms and local context, the Chinese legal system has seen significant changes in its institutional framework. Of particular importance are institutions of law-making, administration and dispute resolution.

Legislative reform: strengthening the National People's Congress. Through the first 30 years of the PRC, the NPC was little more than a "rubber stamp" charged with giving legislative form to CCP policy directives. The 1980s saw it play an increasingly important role in the legislative process.[6] Under the 1982 Constitution, the NPC's legislative duties extended to enacting basic statutes of national application, as well as passing amendments to the Constitution and reviewing decisions by the State Council and the NPC's Standing Committee (NPC-SC). The 1982 Constitution also expanded the powers of the Standing Committee

4. For a representative example, see Zhang Xinxin and Sang Ye, "Lawyer," in W.J.F. Jenner and Delia Davin (eds.), *Chinese Lives: An Oral History of Contemporary China* (New York: Pantheon, 1987), pp. 189–194.
5. See generally, William P. Alford and Fang Liufang, "Legal training and education in the 1990s: an overview and assessment of China's needs," manuscript, 1994.
6. Murray Scot Tanner, "Organizations and politics in China's post-Mao law-making system," in Pitman B. Potter (ed.), *Domestic Law Reforms in Post-Mao China* (Armonk, NY: M.E. Sharpe, 1994); Kevin O'Brien, *Reform Without Liberalization: The National People's Congress and the Politics of Institutional Change* (New York: Cambridge University Press, 1990).

to include not just enactment of law but also supervision of the work of the State Council and other administrative bodies. Efforts to strengthen the role of the NPC-SC were continued in the 1990s by Qiao Shi, who supported the supremacy of law over CCP members, and the authority of the NPC and its Standing Committee to supervise enforcement of the Constitution, legislation and the work of state organs.

However, the NPC remains heavily influenced by the Party. The legislative process itself is generally initiated by decisions from the Party's *zhengfa xitong*, and draft laws undergo review and approval in principle by the Politburo, its Standing Committee and selected Party elders. The membership of the NPC-SC must be approved by the Party Politburo. The NPC's dependency on the Party was evident in the removal of Qiao Shi in the wake of disagreements with Jiang Zemin over Party leadership of law-making and law enforcement.[7] Recent examples of legislative debates in the areas of contract and administrative law and even in the process of debating a law on legislation suggest that law-making continues to be initiated and directed from above.[8] After discussions are completed among selected experts and in various NPC and State Council committees, few opportunities are provided for meaningful input from the citizenry who are the subjects of law.

Administrative reform: restraining the bureaucracy. Administrative bureaucracies in China have long dominated the process of governance. With policies of legal and economic reform came a growing consensus recognizing the need for restraints on bureaucratic power. Courts were granted power to hear complaints against administrative decisions pursuant to the Civil Procedure Law (1991, draft 1982). The Administrative Litigation Law (ALL) formalized the courts' authority to review administrative agency decisions, while the State Compensation Law (SCL) permitted monetary redress to individuals and organizations harmed by unlawful bureaucratic action.

The ALL and the SCL are not without their limitations, however. The SCL excludes the possibility of compensation for harm by officials acting outside the scope of their duties, where the complainant has caused harm through its own acts, or "under other circumstances prescribed by law." The ALL does not permit review of discretionary decisions, which are commonplace in light of the textual ambiguities of Chinese laws and regulations. In addition, ALL review does not extend to the lawfulness of the underlying regulations upon which administrative decisions are based, which in effect permits administrative agencies to legislate their own immunities from ALL review. Furthermore, the ALL's provisions on exhaustion of administrative remedies, which are strengthened by the "Regulations of the PRC on Administrative Reconsideration," further

7. "Qiao Shi's words on democracy in China," in *China News Digest* (electronic media), 2 June 1997; "The 15th CCP National Congress closed, Qiao Shi is out," *China News Digest* (electronic media), 19 September 1997.

8. See papers presented to the Conference on Lawmaking in the PRC, Leiden University Law Faculty, 26–28 October 1998.

shield administrative decisions from judicial review. Finally, the ALL does not extend to Party decisions, thus prohibiting judicial scrutiny of the most fundamental sources of state power. As a result, despite initial enthusiasm, popular willingness to use the ALL to challenge bureaucratic abuses has waned.[9]

Efforts to restrain bureaucratic power have extended as well to administrative rule-making, although the emphasis remains on compliance with higher-level directives rather than accountability to the subjects of rule. During the first decade of reform, measures were taken to bring agency rule-making powers under greater supervision from higher-level departments.[10] The Administrative Supervision Law (1997) authorized the amending or annulment of regulations deemed inconsistent with laws and regulations issued at higher levels. However, the statute offers little support for the subjects of administrative action to challenge bureaucratic rule-making. The Administrative Procedure Law enacted at the end of 1998 may help to address this question, although here too there are significant limits. The Legislation Law remains in the drafting stage, held up by bureaucratic conflicts over rule-making authority.

Developing institutions for civil dispute resolution. The first decade of legal reform saw a revitalization of judicial institutions. The Civil Procedure Law signalled an effort to give the courts greater authority to resolve an increasingly large and complex array of private disputes. In addition, the People's Courts are responsible for compliance with the New York Convention on the Recognition and Enforcement of Foreign Arbitral Awards, to which China acceded in 1987. Increased attention has also been paid to training judges, first under the Supreme Court's Senior Judges Training Centre and later at the PRC Judicial Institute.

Unfortunately, the effectiveness of the Chinese court system remains weak. Courts are often unable to compel production of evidence and enforce awards.[11] Corruption and poor training remain significant problems. Court processes of internal and informal fact-finding and decision-making often leave disputants vulnerable to abuses of power and political connections by their adversaries. Furthermore, the Party continues to play a dominant role through "adjudication committees," which review and approve judicial decisions.

Arbitration of disputes has emerged as a workable compromise between the overly informal procedures of traditional mediation and the problems of the judicial system. Under the Arbitration Law of the PRC (1994), arbitration committees are being established under the provincial

9. Minxin Pei, "Citizens vs. mandarins: administrative litigation in China," *The China Quarterly*, No. 152 (December 1997), pp. 832–862.
10. "Tentative Regulations on the Procedure for Enacting Administrative Laws and Regulations" (Xingzheng fagui zhiding chengxu zanxing tiaoli) (State Council, 21 April 1987).
11. See generally, Anthony Dicks, "Compartmentalized law and judicial restraint: an inductive view of some jurisdictional barriers to reform," and Donald C. Clarke, "The execution of civil judgments in China," both in *The China Quarterly*, No. 141 (March 1995).

governments to handle a wide array of economic disputes. Maritime disputes are subject to the China Maritime Arbitration Commission, while labour disputes are handled by the local Labour Administration. Arbitration and conciliation of disputes involving foreigners are most often handled by the China International Economic and Trade Arbitration Commission (CIETAC), although the local provincial government arbitration bodies also have jurisdiction to handle these types of cases.

While arbitration proceedings are often perceived as reasonably fair and effective, problems remain. Requests to other administrative units for co-operation in the collection of evidence, protection and sequestration of assets, production of witnesses, and other matters often go unheeded. Arbitrators are known to engage in what are essentially *ex parte* contacts with the disputants, either during the course of the mediation process that was previously intertwined with arbitration or during the course of preparing the matter for hearing.[12] Bureaucratic politics have also played a role, as Chinese courts often insist on subjecting arbitral decisions to extensive review prior to enforcement.

Law and Regulation: The Application of Legal Norms in Local Context

The instrumentalist approach to law in the PRC privileges the party-state and permits significant variation in the content and performance of specific legal and regulatory regimes depending on policy priorities. The contrast between the regime's apparent commitment to strengthening the role of law in economic transactions and its refusal to be bound by legal restraints in the management of political order reveal the extent to which law remains contingent on political priorities.

Law in the service of economic growth. The post-Mao legal reform programme was linked expressly to the economic reforms. Laws on contract, property rights and foreign business relations revealed the willingness of the Chinese state to implement formal law in pursuit of its policy goals.

The post-Mao economic reforms required a legal system for protecting property and contract relations. Private property rights received formal recognition under the post-Mao legal reforms. Echoing provisions dating to the 1950s, the 1978 and 1982 Constitutions formally recognized rights to personal property. These were entrenched yet further in the 1986 General Principles of Civil Law. Property rights were later extended through legal protections for patents, trademarks, copyright and other intellectual property rights. Property rights in corporate assets have also been strengthened through a securities regulatory regime, and through the enactment of a Company Law (1993) and the Securities Law (1998).

The recognition of private property rights is particularly important in

12. For examples, see Huang Yanming, "The stylization and regularization of the management and operation of the Chinese arbitration institute," *Journal of International Arbitration*, Vol. 11, No. 2 (1994), p. 77.

the area of land use. While the PRC Constitution and the GPCL held that land ownership was the exclusive province of the state and the collective, land use rights were granted for private farming and business operations.[13] In 1990, China enacted regulations permitting businesses to take long-term interests in land for the purpose of sub-division and development. The Law of the PRC on Urban Real Estate (1994) expanded the possibilities of private land use rights, but also tightened state control over the granting and exercise of these rights.

The expanded recognition of property rights remains conditional upon deference to state interests. The Constitution extends protection to property, but only to the extent that it is "lawful property," the definition of which remains the exclusive province of the state.[14] Constitutional requirements that the exercise of citizens' rights, including the right to own property, do not conflict with state or social interests grant the state a monopoly to interpret those interests and thus to determine the extent to which private property rights will be recognized and enforced.[15] A constitutional amendment in early 1999 recognized private property rights for the first time since the end of the Mao period, although the state will retain significant discretion to determine the conditions under which these rights may be exercised.

China's contract law system also emerged during the 1980s, driven by the needs of economic reform. The Economic Contract Law (1981) served as a basis for domestic transactions, while the Foreign Economic Contract Law (1985) was aimed at transactions involving foreigners. The Technology Contracts Law (1987) covered domestic agreements for the sale and licensing of technology. In addition, the 1986 GPCL contained a number of general principles applicable to contract relations. The legislation on contracts in the PRC reflected efforts to balance imperatives of state control with the need to promote autonomy in contract relations. The original 1981 Economic Contract Law went to significant lengths to retain state approval authority even while recognizing increased autonomy for contracting parties. The 1986 GPCL characterized contracts as civil law obligations, suggesting greater autonomy for contracting parties and their transactions. The 1993 revisions to the Economic Contract Law of the PRC reduced the influence of state planning on contract relations, but still made contracts subject to state policies, and retained general restrictions against contracts deemed contrary to state and public interests.

Efforts to draft a unified contract law began nearly simultaneously with the enactment of the 1993 Economic Contract Law revisions, and reflected an ongoing effort to harmonize norms of freedom of contract with the requirements of the state-managed economy. A draft of the

13. Pitman B. Potter, "China's new land development regulations," *China Business Review*, March–April 1991, pp. 12–14; Donald C. Clarke and Nicholas C. Howson, "Developing PRC property and real estate law: revised land registration rules," *East Asian Executive Reports*, 15 April 1996, pp. 9–17.
14. Constitution of the PRC 1982, Art. 13.
15. *Ibid.*, Art. 51.

statute released in August 1998 and the final text enacted in March 1999 emphasized principles of fairness, good faith and the protection of social and economic well-being as limits to contract autonomy.[16] Thus, the imperative of state control remains in evidence, even as the government has shown a willingness to permit expanded autonomy in contract relations.

The use of legal reform in support of the economic reforms extended to foreign economic relations – particularly foreign investment and trade.[17] Apprehensive about the potentially deleterious effects of direct foreign investment, the Chinese government initially imposed significant controls. Direct foreign investment in equity joint ventures, co-operative enterprises and wholly foreign owned enterprises faced limits on size, duration and scope of business. Representative sales offices were permitted but were accorded generally less favourable treatment than foreign investment enterprises. In the 1990s, foreign investors were encouraged to participate in portfolio investments in Chinese securities, and also allowed to establish holding companies as vehicles for co-ordinating investment networks. Despite these efforts, in many cases the content of particular laws and regulations lagged behind actual business and regulatory practices, and the implementation of the regulatory regime has been uneven.

Reform also extended to the foreign trade area, with reorganization of the administrative apparatus; enactment of laws and regulations on trade licensing, customs procedures and the like; and an application to resume a seat at the GATT and to join the WTO. The Foreign Trade Law (1994) clarified the decentralization in China's foreign trade companies, while also affirming China's right to restrict imports and exports in pursuit of national policy goals. Yet, as indicated by the WTO Working Party's Draft Protocol on China (1997), China still has not conformed to GATT requirements on transparency and enforcement of trade regulations.

In the regulation of foreign economic relations, the state retains a prominent role. State control over foreign investment projects is exercised through the processes for approval and supervision, targeting economic sectors for foreign investment, and finance and tax supervision. In foreign trade, licensing and customs requirements, import substitution rules, formal and informal quotas, and other measures enable the state to direct transactions. Law remains dependent upon policy, but the state's apparent commitment to policies of economic reform has lent relative stability and effectiveness to the legal system governing foreign economic relations.

The use of law for political control. Drawing on a legacy of public and punitive typologies of law from both the Republican and Imperial periods, the PRC has long emphasized law as an instrument of social

16. "Zhonghua renmin gongheguo hetong fa (caoan)" ("Contract Law of the PRC – draft") (Legal Affairs Committee of NPC Standing Committee, 20 August 1998).
17. See generally, Pitman B. Potter, *Foreign Business Law in China: Past Progress, Future Challenges* (San Francisco: The 1990 Institute, 1995). Also see *Doing Business in China* (looseleaf, Interjura).

control. Recurring references to the legal system as a tripartite network of *Gong-Jian-Fa* organs, comprising in descending order of importance the Public Security Bureaus (*Gongan*), Procuracy (*Jiancha*) and Courts (*Fayuan*), suggest a viewpoint that the legal system is primarily about criminal law enforcement in pursuit of social control.

During the first three decades of the PRC, social control and public security were achieved primarily through administrative regulation and political campaigns.[18] Driven in part by the need to protect itself, and also by the need to build legitimacy, the post-Mao regime enacted a Criminal Law Code and a Code of Criminal Procedure in 1980, which followed closely the 1979 Regulations on Arrest and Detention (replacing measures enacted in 1954). With broadly worded provisions of flexible application, these measures had little to do with protecting the rights of criminal defendants, but instead were aimed primarily at re-establishing the state's monopoly on legitimate use of coercive force in the aftermath of the Cultural Revolution.[19]

Supplementing these efforts, administrative detention remained the dominant mechanism for social control, under the Regulations of the PRC on Security Administration and Punishment (1957, rev. 1986, rev. 1994).[20] The 1980 Criminal Law of the PRC permitted administrative detention to be imposed in lieu of criminal sanctions where the circumstances of a person's crimes were deemed to be minor and not requiring criminal punishment. The more severe administrative systems for reform and re-education through labour, which had been established pursuant to regulations issued by the State Council in 1957, were continued under new rules enacted in 1979.

In addition, the process of "shelter for investigation" (*shourong shencha*) authorized discretionary arrest and detention of suspicious individuals with little if any legal restriction imposed.[21] A legacy from the early 1960s, "shelter and investigation," was used to round up unemployed migrants and other perceived ne're-do-wells, who might be detained for a few months but who might also be sent to re-education through labour facilities. Repeated attempts have been made to formalize the process, most notably in a set of regulations issued in 1985 by the Public Security Ministry regulations which conferred oversight authority on the People's Procuracy. Although separate notices issued in 1990 by the Procuracy and the Public Security Ministry attempted to curtain abuses of *shourong shencha* procedures, there was still little if any meaningful external

18. See generally, Shao-chuan Leng and Hungdah Chiu, *Criminal Justice in Post-Mao China* (Albany, NY: State University of NY Press, 1985); Victor H. Li, "The evolution and development of the Chinese legal system," in John M. H. Lindbeck (ed.), *China: Management of a Revolutionary Society* (Seattle & London: University of Washington Press, 1971).
19. For general discussion of criminal justice in China under the 1980 legislation, see Donald C. Clarke and James V. Feinerman, "Antagonistic contradictions: criminal law and human rights," *The China Quarterly*, No. 141 (March 1995), p. 135.
20. Amnesty International, "China – punishment without trial: administrative detention," 1981.
21. Tao-tai Hsia and Wendy I. Zeldin, "Sheltering for examination (*shourong shencha*) in the legal system of the People's Republic of China," *China Law Reporter*, Vol. 7 (1992), p. 97.

scrutiny, and abuses multiplied.[22] With the revisions to the Criminal Procedure Law in 1996, "shelter and investigation" was to be eliminated, although many of the flexible provisions of the process were incorporated into the revised statute.

Revisions made in 1996 to the Criminal Procedure Law, and the subsequent amendment of the Criminal Law in 1997, were part of a broad effort to reform the criminal justice system in response both to international criticisms and to domestic pressures. Revisions to the Criminal Procedure Law purported to eliminate unregulated administrative detention and to curtail the prosecutory powers of the Procuracy. Criminal defence counsel were granted earlier access to prosecution evidence. The determination of criminal liability was reserved exclusively for the courts, thus doing away with the Procuracy's previous powers to determine guilt or innocence. The revisions also imposed on prosecutors the burden to produce reliable and ample (*queshi, chongfen*) evidence of the guilt of the accused – a far cry from the "presumption of innocence" trumpeted by some optimistic observers, but a significant step nevertheless.

The revisions to the Criminal Law also reflect an effort to reduce the potential for arbitrary punishment. They provide that an act is not criminal unless specifically stated in the law – thus eliminating the "rule of analogy," which under the 1980 law had permitted criminal conviction for acts not expressly identified as criminal, by reference to the most closely analogous provision of the law. However, despite these reforms a criminal conviction may still be had for acts for which the defendant is not charged, but which are punishable under other provisions of the Criminal Law.[23] While eliminating the crime of counter-revolution, the revised law uses instead the crime of endangering state security, which is not limited by the intent requirement that informed the counter-revolution provisions of the past.

While efforts to reform the criminal justice system may improve the treatment of common criminal defendants, they appear to have little effect in the area of political offences. The regime's recent responses to efforts to establish a China Democratic Party suggest that legal requirements will bow to the needs of political supremacy. The arrest, prosecution and sentencing of activists Xu Wenli, Yao Wencai and Qin Yongmin appeared contrary to the requirements of the newly revised Criminal Law and Criminal Procedure Law.[24] The right of the defendants to hire their own attorneys was nullified through political pressure, and in at least one case active obstruction prevented the retained attorneys from acting effectively. The defendants were allegedly denied the right to

22. Lawyer's Committee on Human Rights, "Opening to reform? An analysis of China's revised Criminal Procedure Law," 1996, pp. 22 *et seq.*

23. "Zuigao renmin fayuan guanyu zhixing 'Zhonghua renmin gongheguo xingshi susong fa' ruogan wenti de jieshi" ("Interpretation by the Supreme People's Court on certain issues related to the implementation of the 'Criminal Procedure Law of the PRC' "), *Zhongguo fazhi bao (China Legal System Gazette)*, 9 September 1998, p. 2.

24. See e.g. Amnesty International, "Heavy prison sentences on Chinese dissidents," *Presswire*, 22 December 1998; Michael Laris, "Retreating from reform: China tries two dissidents," *Washington Post*, 18 December 1998.

speak in their own defence. The evidence upon which they were convicted appeared not to satisfy the requirements of law, and the sentences were widely viewed as excessive. Thus, the regime appears quite ready to ignore the requirements of its own laws when confronting challenges to its political monopoly.

The comparisons between the roles law plays in regulating the economy and in protecting the political supremacy of the party-state suggest that despite important achievements in law-making and institution-building, law remains politically contingent. Where state policies of economic development support reliance of formal rules and procedures, the legal system governing contracts, property and foreign economic relations has been relatively effective. By contrast, the criminal justice system, despite undergoing many changes of content and structure, appears still unable to constrain the exercise of political power by the party-state.

Summary

On the 50th anniversary of the founding of the PRC, the legal system plays an increasingly significant role in social, economic and even political relationships. Legal norms drawn largely from foreign experiences have been selected and applied through a plethora of newly established institutions. The role of law as a basis for government authority has become a legitimate and significant issue in the broader political discourse. Despite these achievements, law in China remains dependent on the regime's policy goals. Particularly where political prerogatives are at stake, legal requirements appear to pose little restraint on state power. In this sense, the ten years that have passed since Tiananmen appear to have had little impact on the willingness of the party-state to dispense with legal requirements in pursuit of political expediency. If we are to rely upon Dicey's dictum on the rule of law being in effect when the state becomes just another actor, the rule of law in China still seems a distant prospect indeed.

Social Welfare Reform: Trends and Tensions*

Elisabeth J. Croll

The acceleration of economic reform in the early and late 1990s has highlighted repeatedly the importance of social welfare for maintaining economic growth, social stability and political authority. Indeed each of these decade-long goals of China's government can be seen to rest on either establishing or maintaining an accessible social welfare package. Economic growth requires further enterprise reform which in turn requires alternative forms and funding of worker social welfare. Sporadic reports of urban unrest resulting from lay-offs and loss of welfare benefits and of rural discontent resulting from the continued absence of welfare benefits suggests that social stability and political authority are dependent on the government's ability to reform social welfare provisioning. Simultaneously the process of economic reform itself has altered urban and rural socio-economic and political environments and had far-reaching consequences for welfare demand, service supply and notions of security.

For the past 50 years China's multi-faceted welfare package (*shehui fuli*) has been referred to as "social security" (*shehui baozhang*) which is itself composed of three broad constituent categories: social insurance or protection, social provisioning or services, and social assistance or relief.[1] Social insurance (*shehui baoxian*) includes protection arrangements for retirement pensions and medical treatment; unemployment, maternity, sickness and work-related injury or disability benefits; and subsidies for widows and orphans. Social services (*shehui fuwu*) refers to specialized support for the elderly, disabled and abandoned as well as public services such as education, health and housing. Social relief (*shehui jiuji*) involves assistance in cash and kind to the old and disabled without income or other forms of familial support. Within this multi-dimensional package most policy and practical attention in the past has focused on the elderly and on social and public services.[2] Although in practice welfare benefits were limited in coverage and confined to certain privileged and vulnerable categories of the population, there also existed an all-inclusive contextual notion of residual cradle-to-grave security expected of the state.

* This paper is dedicated to the memory of colleague and dear friend, Professor Gordon White, in appreciation of his own research and field studies which constitute a major contribution to understanding social welfare reform.
    1. J. Dixon, *The Chinese Welfare System* (New York: Praeger, 1981); Deborah Davis "China social welfare: policies and outcomes," *The China Quarterly*, No. 119 (September 1989), pp. 577–597.
    2. See Gordon White, *Institutional Change and Social Welfare Provision in China's Transition to the Market*, Research Report to ESCOR, R6123 (1998), p. 11; Sheying Chen, *Social Policy of the Economic State and Community Care in Chinese Culture* (London: Avebury, 1996), pp. 44–45, 101; Joe C.B. Leung, "Social welfare reforms," in Bob Benewick and Paul Wingrove (eds.), *China in the 1990s* (London: Macmillan, 1995), pp. 216–223.

Entitlement

One of the clearest findings of rural and urban fieldwork conducted during the 1990s is that most respondents believe that either the central or the local state should be responsible for providing the social security provisioning to which they believe they are entitled.[3] This notion of entitlement is rooted in a rhetorical and practical legacy of state socialism and such expectations of welfare support by the state have been fostered by an increasing sense of insecurity as a result of the rapid pace of market reforms and recession, a decline in benefit coverage, the rising costs of welfare services and a new sense of inequity. Even in the lesser-developed interior villages it is sometimes said of the economy that the "only thing certain is uncertainty and change"[4] and this mood of uncertainty and vulnerability is widely echoed in the cities as markets have fluctuated, fees escalated and enterprise reform proceeded amid first inflation and then recession. For state-owned enterprise workers there have been signs of growing discontent at the prospect of losing privileged insurance benefits and services, and reports of sporadic strikes, disturbances and violence suggest that urban workers will resist any erosion of their social welfare entitlements. Indeed it is the fear of widespread social unrest that hampers the government in its current pursuit of further enterprise reform. In villages with few or no benefits or services there are constant complaints that the government is not fulfilling its ruling functions, and a heightened sense of inequity has been fostered by the media and people's increased mobility which have made available new sources of outside knowledge about insurance, services and support available elsewhere. As a result, comparative types and costs of insurance, education, health and old age assistance both within and outside China have become common topics of conversation and one of the most popular yardsticks deployed to define good governance.[5]

China's citizens continue to have a very sure sense of their entitlement to social security and services and also an equally sure sense of the government's matching obligation to supply these. Indeed, in the 1990s, social welfare has emerged as one of the most important issues underlying a new and explicit social contract between persons and the party-state: support for its legitimacy or mandate to rule in return for social security, welfare and services. Throughout the 1990s there have been some very fine studies of the role of *guanxi* or dyadic inter-personal

3. Gordon White and Xiaoyuan Shang, "Social security reforms in urban China: a preliminary research report," in Gordon White and Xiaoyuan Shang (eds.), *Issues and Answers: Reforming the Chinese Social Security System*, papers from an international workshop, Beijing, October 1995 (Brighton: Institute of Development Studies, University of Sussex, 1996), p. 4.

4. See Liu Xin, "Zhao villagers – everyday practices in a post-reform Chinese village," Ph.D. thesis, Department of Anthropology, School of Oriental and African Studies, University of London, June 1995; Elisabeth Croll, *From Heaven to Earth: Images and Experiences of Development in China* (London: Routledge, 1994); White and Shang, *Issues and Answers*, pp. 43–44.

5. Hok-Bun Ku, "Defining Zeren: cultural politics in a Chinese village," Ph.D. thesis, University of London, 1998, pp. 120–214, 327.

exchange relations based on mutual expectation and obligation,[6] and this concept of reciprocity can be extended to include relations between individual and state. Recent fieldwork in one village with only minimal local government welfare provisioning suggests that in such a case there is a three-staged village response. The first is a refusal to co-operate with the local government by resisting the imposition of certain local fees and taxes; the second is the sidelining of the local government by setting up an alternative kinship-based council; and the third is the wider questioning of the political legitimacy of the party-state on the grounds that if there is no benevolent government, there will be no righteous citizens. Such testimony suggests that this contractual relationship, based on the state's obligation to provide welfare, has become one of the main measures rating cadre performance, and by extension political legitimacy or mandate to rule.[7] While this sequence of popular responses may not be representative, it may be suggestive of a new and increasing trend. The dual challenge for China's government during the 1990s has been to continue to meet the obligation and expectations created by the previous but now outmoded welfare package and at the same time establish a new system appropriate both to a new and mounting demand for social welfare and to the changing economic and demographic conditions of both city and countryside.

Urban Demand

Urban workers, long privileged by welfare policies, were the only category of the population for whom social insurance and a wide range of benefits and services were available. Urban enterprises, almost entirely in the public sector, were functionally part of a state-sponsored and financed welfare system in which funds were almost entirely guaranteed and managed by enterprises. Indeed welfare outlays only showed up as a very minor proportion of formal government expenditure.[8] Until the 1980s these public sector city and collective work units employed most of the urban work force and provided, to varying degrees, an impressive array of benefits ranging from pensions, health, work-injury, maternity and sick leave to services such as creches, schools, clinics and collective subsidies including housing. During the 1990s this cellular provision based on permanent job security or an "iron rice bowl" and on enterprise welfare funding and management was increasingly outmoded by two socio-economic trends. First, a rising proportion of the urban population was employed outside state and collective work units and thus excluded

6. Yang Mayfair, *Gifts, Favors and Banquets: The Art of Social Relationships in China* (Ithaca: Cornell University Press, 1994; Yan Yanxiang, *The Flow of Gifts: Reciprocity and Social Networks in a Chinese Village* (Stanford: Stanford University Press, 1996); Andrew B, Kipnis, *Producing Guanxi* (Durham: Duke University Press 1997).
7. Hok-Bun Ku, "Defining Zeren," pp. 173–214; Elisabeth Croll and Ben Ku, "Social security: rights and contracts in a Chinese village," in Robert Ash (ed.), *China's Economic and Social Security* (London: Curzon, forthcoming).
8. State Statistical Bureau, *China Statistical Yearbook 1996* (Beijing: China Statistical Publishing House, 1996), pp. 229–250.

from social insurance or benefits. Secondly, the benefit funds generated and managed by state and collective enterprises declined, eroding both job security and welfare services for public-sector employees.

In the cities non-public sectors of the economy have developed at a rapid speed, creating a proliferation of new-style private and foreign-invested enterprises and small co-operative and household units with new conditions of employment. By mid-decade these non-state units produced 66 per cent of the gross output value of industry compared to 22.4 per cent in 1978,[9] and it is estimated that as many as 70 per cent of the urban population are not covered by any form of social insurance and are employed outside state-owned enterprises.[10] This trend has led to an increasing number of urban residents, including workers and managers, independent professionals, self-employed entrepreneurs, unemployed and migrants, who are now excluded, partially or completely, from the previous unit-based welfare system and for whom there are no alternative forms of social security.

For those who do continue to work in state-owned enterprises and government agencies there has been a gradual erosion of benefits over the past ten years as a result of marketization, structural reform and poor financial performance. In an increasingly competitive market, state-owned enterprises have been hampered in their development by their responsibilities for social welfare payments, which have limited new and necessary production investment and tied workers to enterprises at the same time as the state has attempted to reduce or withdraw subsidies and place enterprises on a profit-loss basis. Moreover, the financial burden imposed by the costs of social welfare to enterprises has itself increased because of the ageing of the workforce and the higher costs of medical and other services. Overall the costs of social insurance and welfare funds as a proportion of the total wage bill rose from 13.7 per cent in 1978 to around 30 per cent in the early 1990s.[11] The total number of pensioners increased from 3.14 to 30.94 million between 1978 and 1995 with the ratio of current employees to pensioners declining from 26.2 in 1978 to 4.6 in 1995.[12] In some of the older state-owned enterprises the number of retirees has increased rapidly, with the ratio of personnel supported to workers reaching 50 per cent.[13] There has been some attempt to spread or average out the burden of retirement costs across enterprises by establishing a social pooling system to which each enterprise contributes and, since the mid-1980s, this system has extended to city, municipality and provincial administrative levels.[14] Nevertheless the rising costs of pen-

9. *Ibid.* p. 403.
10. Ge Man, "China's social insurance: reflections on predicaments and directions," in White and Shang, *Issues and Answers*, p. 1.
11. *China Statistical Yearbook 1996*, p. 733.
12. *Ibid.* p. 737.
13. Zhou Daming, "On rural urbanization in China," in G.E. Guldin, *Farewell to Peasant China: Rural Urbanisation and Social Change in Late Twentieth Century China* (Armonk, NY: M.E. Sharpe, 1997), p. 17.
14. See White and Shang "Social security reforms in urban China," pp. 25–28.

sions and health care have become important factors in increasing the number of loss-making enterprises.

Even before the latest set of reforms of the 15th Party Congress and the National People's Congress (1997–98) it was evident that state-owned enterprises were having difficulties in funding enterprise-based pensions, medical or other benefits, and in continuing to provide or subsidize extensive social services for both workers and their dependants. By the end of this decade the late, partial or even non-payment of both wages and benefits has become frequent in both state and collective sectors. It is now common for workers in such enterprises to be retained on a semi-employed or "benefits only" basis to reduce both unemployment and benefit loss. In 1996 it was estimated that one-fifth to one-third of the public sector work force fell into this category[15] and, to reduce the proportion of public sector work force eligible for benefits in the future, employees are increasingly placed on short-term contracts which carry fewer benefits. The consequent erosion of the unit-based welfare system has caused financial hardship for a growing number of urban workers and increasing numbers of loss-making state-owned enterprises have had little choice but to make employees redundant. At the end of 1996 the number of unemployed was estimated officially to be six million, rising to eight million in October 1997,[16] but unofficial estimates suggest that by spring 1998 at least 12 million had been laid off and that by the end of that year another ten million workers would be made redundant.[17] In theory many such redundant workers are covered by unemployment insurance, but in practice such protection remained untested while unemployment was denied or disguised. Although many of those laid off have been re-employed in other sectors, there are expanding numbers of male and even more female unemployed workers in the cities with no benefit support. In addition there are more than 60 or 70 million migrant workers in the cities who, without urban *hukou* or residence rights, lie outside any unit-based welfare system and are not eligible for social security, welfare services or service assistance. Together the unemployed, migrants and pensioners whose incomes have failed to keep pace with inflation constitute the "urban poor" which has become a newly visible social category in China over the past decade. As early as 1993 official estimates put the urban poor at 12 million or 3.6 per cent of the total urban population and their number has been rising steadily.[18]

The increasing exclusion of substantial categories of the urban population from the unit-based welfare system, the erosion of pre-existing social insurance and welfare benefits, and the rise in the numbers of urban poor have placed increasing demands on family and local community services for assistance or relief. The age-old family support system based

---

15. White, *Institutional Change and Social Welfare Provision*, p. 4.
16. UNDP, *China Human Development Report* (Beijing: UNDP, 1998), p. 63.
17. Liu Binyan and Perry Link, "A great leap backward," *New York Review of Books*, 8 October 1998.
18. White, *Institutional Change and Social Welfare Provision*, p. 5.

on reciprocated inter-generational care has continued to play a central role in the financial and personal support of the elderly whether or not they are eligible for other forms of security and services.[19] Urban fieldwork suggests that the family unit still plays an important and central role in inter-generational care,[20] but that increasingly it is being overloaded with such responsibilities at a time when both socio-economic and demographic trends point to a dimunition in family size and role.[21] Long-term demographic trends show that the urban household now averages 3.31 persons with increasingly unfavourable dependency ratios as a result of the ageing structure of urban populations and the one-child policy.[22] Urban family incomes are themselves newly fragile as a result of inflation, unemployment and rising service costs for housing, education and health. As a result of reduced familial sources of immediate support and longer-term security there has been an escalation of demand for social assistance.

The increasing number of urban residents without any form of income or welfare support has increased the pressures on the already small assistance sector of urban social welfare.[23] Rigorously means-tested, urban social assistance has been mainly confined to the *san wu* or "three nos" category of orphans, aged and disabled who have no other means of support and temporary – or permanent – hardship households. Implementing this residual system is mainly the responsibility of the Ministry of Civil Affairs via its ancillary street and residents' committees, with assistance taking the form of either centralized provision in welfare, children's or old-age homes or dispersed home help with income maintenance, health care and welfare employment where appropriate. During the 1990s increased demand, the rising costs of real estate and services, and the absence of any additional government funding have stretched further the resources and services of urban street and residents' committees.[24] To mediate both mounting demand and fiscal constraint, local residents' committees have charged fees for their services or sought alternative commercial funding to subsidize such services. However the development of commercial industries or welfare enterprises has meant that a wide range of community services have become entirely reliant on extra-

19. See Deborah Davis and Steven Harrell (eds.), *Chinese Families in the Post-Mao Era*, (Berkeley: University of California Press, 1993).
20. White, *Institutional Change and Social Welfare Provision*, p. 25.
21. Guo Zhenglin and Zhou Daming, "Rural development and social security," in Guldin, *Farewell to Peasant China*, p. 257.
22. Sheying Chen, *Social Policy*, p. 90; A. Hussain and Liu Hong, *Compendium of Literature on the Chinese Social Security System* (London: London School of Economics, China Programme, No. 3, July 1989), p. 5; A. Hussain and Liwei Zhu, "National and regional patterns of ageing and their implication for the support of the elderly population," in White and Shang, *Issues and Answers*, pp. 59–69.
23. White, *Institutional Change and Social Welfare Provision*, p. 24.
24. Sheying Chen, *Social Policy*, p. 57, 104, 121; Gordon White and Xiaoyuan Shang, *Reforms in Chinese Social Assistance and Community Services in Comparative Perspective*, papers presented at a workshop on Chinese social welfare system reforms, Beijing, September 1996 (Brighton: Institute of Development Studies, University of Sussex, 1997), p. 7.

budgetary sources of finance with access increasingly resting on ability to pay. Overall the effect of the erosion of pre-existing systems of social welfare during the 1990s has been to reduce previous divisions between the once privileged state-sector employees and other urban residents, while the exclusion of greater numbers of urban workers from the welfare system has gone some way towards reducing previous inequalities between urban and rural populations.

Rural Demand

For the past 50 years the social welfare package in the countryside has been a quite separate and much more restricted system with no social insurance, few subsidized services available to farmers and their families, and little more than a minimal safety net guaranteed for the childless elderly and other vulnerable categories of lone persons.[25] There are some state subsidies for certain very poor categories of persons and for poor and remote communities but these are limited to social assistance for the elderly, the disabled or veterans with no ability to work, no income and no family support. They are eligible for the "five guarantees" of clothing, shelter, medical care and burial expenses, subsidies for social services, and aid for establishing income-generating activities. The most common services available in villages are schools, clinics and homes for the elderly, which in all but the poorest and most remote regions are locally established and supported. In officially designated "poor counties," primarily located in the interior provincial-level units, government funds have been made available to subsidize local services but, with the exception of education, there has been a decade-long shift in the use of poverty alleviation funds to support self-help income-generating activities rather than assisted welfare, services and relief.[26] With these exceptions the near absence of central government allocations has meant that rural townships and villages are almost entirely reliant on funds generated by local enterprises. Indeed there has been a direct correlation between township and village funds based on township and village enterprises and local provisioning of welfare services and assistance.

During the past 20 years coastal township and village governments with profitable enterprises have emulated city state-owned enterprises by allocating extensive funds to collective welfare and setting up local social security systems with similar levels of protection, service and assistance. In China's prosperous regions, township and village leaders proudly use such phrases as "rural urbanization" or "urban villages" and in some of the wealthiest coastal, suburban and delta locations, townships and

25. Guo Zhenglin and Zhou Daming, "Rural development and social security," pp. 71–122; Liu Weimeng "Reflections on some questions concerning the establishment of a social security in the rural areas," in White and Shang, *Reforms*, pp. 67–77; Stephan Feuchtwang, "Changes in the system of basic social security in the countryside since 1979," in Ashwani Saith (ed.), *The Re-emergence of the Chinese Peasantry* (London: Croom Helm, 1987), pp. 173–210.
26. Croll, *From Heaven to Earth*, pp. 135–159.

village governments have not only established a wide range of community services but also introduced social security systems offering retirement and disability pensions or maternity benefits, all of which were previously and exclusively urban.[27] Away from coast and suburb, villages may maintain a lesser range of services, perhaps establishing and subsidizing education, health facilities and care for the elderly. By the end of 1995 it was estimated that there were more than three million people receiving the five guarantees and 4,100 homes for the aged accounting for 63.2 per cent of the total number of townships in China. There was a total of 600,000 people in homes for the aged, thus making provision for 20 per cent or so of those in the five guarantee category in the whole country.[28] Inland townships and villages without enterprises seldom have local revenues to add to minimal levels of state welfare assistance. In the absence of enterprise funding any welfare services are almost certain to be financed by the imposition of local government levies or by charging substantial user fees, both of which can make heavy demands on the small cash components of farming incomes. As the costs of education, health and other services have risen, so fees for these facilities may take as much as half of average disposable incomes and, in impoverished townships and villages, greater numbers of children are withdrawn from school, there is little preventative medicine and many do not enter hospital or leave before the completion of treatment.[29] Indeed for most rural families access to services, care and assistance continues to be heavily reliant on the age-old inter-generational resource flows and mutual obligations which still lie at the centre of family support and care, while local kin networks, either informally or more formally in lineage-based groups, provide material assistance and support derived from any common resources and revenues.[30] Throughout China's townships and villages, whether or not they have enterprises, rural demand for social welfare has risen as both old and new sources of social welfare are increasingly at risk.

As in the cities the pattern of rural welfare provisioning is also cellular, confined as it is to privileged enclaves where welfare funding, almost entirely reliant on local enterprise growth and good management, is at risk. Even before the Asian crisis, which has affected township and village enterprise markets and profits, the continuing growth of such enterprises was not assured. Nation-wide figures show that by the end of 1997 one third of the 500,000 township-run enterprises had been sold off or turned into share-holding co-operatives while many open and close with some speed as a result of the vagaries of the market or of local

27. *Ibid.* pp 26–115; Zhou Daming and Zhang Yingqiang, "Rural urbanisation in Guangdong's Pearl River Delta," in Guldin, *Farewell to Peasant China*, pp. 71–122; Sheying Chen, *Social Policy*, pp. 205–257. Guo Zhenglin and Zhou Daming, "Rural development and social security," pp. 248–261.

28. Zhu Yong "A research report on the reform of China's social welfare system," in White and Shang, *Reforms*, p. 23.

29. Croll, *From Heaven to Earth*, pp. 87–94.

30. Xiang Chang and Stephan Feuchtwang, *Social Support in Rural China (1979–1991)* (London: China Research Unit, City University, 1996).

official mismanagement and enrichment resulting in the periodic lay-off of hundreds of thousands of workers at the same time.[31] Field studies in a variety of rural venues suggest that social security, services and assistance are now of mounting and widespread concern because of the erosion of these new local enterprise-funded subsidies and benefits in richer locations, the continuing absence of local community services in poorer regions and a widespread fear of reduction in guaranteed family support.

In the countryside too, demographic trends contribute to adverse dependency ratios although the two-child family still characterizes most rural households. Fieldwork in a wide range of rural villages shows that it is the risk to inter-generational resource flows which is most responsible for rural opposition to birth control policies. It is still a truism that only the birth and survival of a son can guarantee old-age support, with resistance to birth control policies defended in simple terms: no support or security for old age, no support for birth control policies.[32] Such opposition has been responsible for the continuing modification of the rules to permit the birth of at least one son in much of the countryside. Even so, with fewer sons, an ageing population, the migration of younger generations and the rising costs of services, familial support in times of need is no longer assumed. In the face of mounting urban and rural demand and continuing expectations, the government has attempted to establish a new welfare system which is appropriate to the country's new socio-economic and demographic circumstances.

Policy Reform

From the mid-1990s welfare reform has constituted one of the priority areas on the national reform agenda, not merely because of the necessity for a new welfare system to meet the changing requirements of an emerging market economy, but because its very absence was impeding the emergence of a market economy and raising the spectre of economic stagnation and social unrest. The central challenge facing the government was how to accommodate both the increasing needs of a growing proportion of the population and the financial constraints deriving from its reduced institutional and fiscal capacities. The Programme for the Ninth Five-Year Plan of National Economy and Social Development (1996–2000) and the Long Range Goals in 2010 passed at the Fourth Session of the Eighth National People's Congress set a comprehensive agenda:

To quicken the reform of the system of provision for the aged, unemployment and medical insurance and form a multi-layered social security system combining social

---

31. A. Saich, "China party/state and society relations in transition," paper presented at Conference on China in Transition, Utah, 11–13 September 1998, p. 24.
32. Hok-Bun Ku, "Defining Zeren," pp. 249–285.

insurance, social assistance, social welfare, favourable treatment and compensation, social mutual aid and individual savings.[33]

Within this broad framework, policy deliberations focused first on retirement support and then on welfare assistance and community care.

The focus on pension reform, aiming at evolving a society-wide system to replace the enterprise-based system, is not surprising given the continuing economic importance of the state-owned sector, the sensitivity of urban workers to the loss of benefits, and the central importance of reducing the welfare costs of enterprises as a pre-requisite for further enterprise reform and growth. From the mid-1990s new pension reforms have had three key objectives: to establish a society-wide system of pension-fund mobilization and management which takes over from the enterprises; to share the costs of pension insurance between individuals as well as enterprises and the state; and to move from a "pay as you go" system to some form of partial accumulation.[34] Much of the policy debate has centred around the respective roles and balance of state-organized and market-operated schemes and the degree of redistribution necessary or desirable to incorporate both economic efficiency and social equity. With the help of the World Bank,[35] a growing consensus has emerged around a shift to a three-tiered system which includes compulsory pensions organized by the state which are both basic and earnings-related, supplementary occupational pensions which may be optional or semi-compulsory, and individual pension schemes which are entirely voluntary. The most important changes mooted are the establishment of the principle that individual employees should share in insurance payments, and the shift in administration or management of pensions from the enterprise to specialized or commercialized social insurance agencies. There is a new commitment to widening the pension system to include employees in private firms, migrants and rural inhabitants, and to other forms of social insurance for employment and health. The latter is perhaps the most intractable item on the welfare reform agenda given the complementary need for reforms in health funding and delivery.[36]

During the latter years of the decade, policy attention has turned to social relief or assistance and the need to fund residual safety nets for increasing numbers of needy or poor. Given the apparent inability and/or reluctance of the government to increase funding, the main direction of national policy has been to continue to encourage localized enterprise-support for community and family care. In the early 1990s the govern-

33. Liu Weiming, "Reflections," p. 71.

34. Man Ge, "China's social insurance: reflections on predicaments and directions," in White and Shang, *Reforms*, pp. 1–17.

35. World Bank, *China: Reforming Social Security in Socialist Economy* (Washington, D.C.: World Bank, 1990), *Averting the Old Age Crisis* (Oxford: Oxford University Press, 1994), *China: Pension System Reform*, Report No. 15121-CHA, Beijing World Bank Office, 1996; *Far Eastern Economic Review*, 16 October 1997, pp. 64–66.

36. White and Shang, "Social security reforms in urban China," p. 29–31; Min Qi, "Reform of the Public Health Medical Care System and Labour Insurance Medical Care System in China," in White and Shang, *Issues and Answers*, pp. 121–154.

ment, in its Suggestions for Speeding Up the Development of Community Services, confirmed its support for developing community industries as the foundation for funding and supporting local services which were to be made available to urban residents at market prices and to the elderly, disabled and weak at little or no cost.[37] The government has also provided favourable tax reductions or exemptions to encourage the development of community and welfare enterprises on the grounds that a portion of their income subsidizes welfare.

In addition to enterprise-funded welfare at the community level there has been some government promotion of welfare activities supported and managed by non-government organizations, foundations or charities in an attempt to diversify support for community services and care. However, although market and non-government initiatives are an important part of social service and assistance reform they are by no means meant to be a substitute for home-based complementary family care which continues to underpin urban and rural welfare support. Indeed there have been several policy initiatives to strengthen family support. During the 1990s the inter-generational contract obligating mutual support and care, already enshrined in the constitution, has been re-emphasized in new legislation and explicitly incorporated within the marriage contract; while my own fieldwork in 1998 suggests that inter-generational support presently constitutes the focus of much legal and family education in communities and schools. Despite the new importance attached to social welfare reform by the central government and the number of innovations and strategies implemented by local governments, developing a policy framework which can meet the government's own three-pronged goals of providing comprehensive security, services and assistance has proved difficult and the pace of welfare reform has proceeded relatively slowly. Nevertheless in practical terms several identifiable and important new trends have emerged during the past decade.

New Welfare Trends

One of the most important trends of the reform programmes of the 1990s has been the growing separation of social welfare from its previous enterprise base. The overriding aim of "socializing" social welfare and the tentative establishment of separate social security, service and assistance systems which are not employee-exclusive and enterprise-based or managed is a major new dimension of both government reform and local initiatives. A second trend has been the decentralization of social welfare provisioning so that local governments have become key actors in accumulating funds, redistributing resources and establishing new welfare systems, with central state funds continuing to comprise only a small fraction of welfare expenditures. Additionally there has been a diversification in delivery systems, shifting responsibilities for social welfare services and activities to market services and to non-government

37. Zhu Yong, "Research report," p. 26.

organizations. The market has become an important channel for providing services with access increasingly determined via a fee structure. Although education, health and other services may have some government funding, an increasing proportion of their material resources and personnel costs are fee-based and they too are entering the market and developing entrepreneurial activities to help support their costs. Hence schools, clinics and homes for the elderly frequently have their own attached profit-making businesses based on either an entrepreneurial wing which charges fees or quite unrelated activities. As welfare services have entered the market, extra-budgetary sources of finance have increasingly compensated for budgetary constraints and in turn subsidized services and assistance for those unable to purchase them.

The establishment of non-profit organizations for supplementing funds, cushioning hardship or providing volunteer assistance is a recent innovation but nevertheless constitutes a potentially important additional channel in the delivery of social welfare services and assistance. The new non-government organizations, referred to by the government as *shehui tuanti*, have been established to fill gaps in vital welfare functions and respond to economic or physical hardship and natural disasters. Many have links with charities in Hong Kong or Taiwan and are based on mutual help, volunteer work and fund-raising. By the summer of 1996, some 200,000 such social organizations were registered with the Ministry of Civil Affairs, of which over 1,800 were at a national level with non- or quasi-government status.[38] The Ministry of Civil Affairs itself has set a pattern by establishing the China Charities Foundation to receive donations and take over some of its social responsibilities for welfare,[39] and at local levels there are cases where social welfare foundations have been set up to replace the civil administration in administering social security and raising and managing funds derived from township and village enterprise profits and donations.[40]

Finally a major welfare trend is the strengthening of informal community and family self-provisioning which has been re-emphasized as an additional means of mobilizing urban and rural community labour and resources in immediate response to local needs for support and care. In the cities the number of grass-root scattered, diversified and practical community services and facilities has increased rapidly during the past decade, and official encouragement of such informal neighbourhood services or care is an important attempt to bridge the gap between welfare demand and supply. Some of the most interesting experiments in urban self-provisioning have taken place among migrants in Beijing who, without formal residence rights to welfare support, have informally developed their own self-generating and operating community services including schools and clinics which are largely based on origins or native

38. Saich, "China party/state and society relations," p. 44.
39. *Ibid.* p. 45.
40. Guo Zhenglin and Zhou Daming, "Rural development and social security," p. 251.

place.[41] In villages too, fieldwork reveals that extended families, lineages and clans have re-appropriated their roles as local organizers of services and social assistance, with ancestral and village temples once again becoming hubs in an intricate welfare network, and that it is still the immediate family which is expected to provide the main support and care for individuals. In the cities parents of single children invest heavily in their children's education and recreation to inculcate explicit notions of inter-generational indebtedness,[42] and in the countryside parents, determined to have a son, defy birth control policies. Additionally, and on their own initiative, both rural and urban families have adopted new forms of individual and private security. In cities and suburbs wealthier families have purchased their own insurance for old age and against ill-health or loss of income,[43] while immediate and extended families maintain extensive and expensive inter-personal networks of relations which can provide access to goods and services in times of need. Mayfair Yang in her path-breaking study of guanxi suggests that one of the reasons why such networks are getting more and more complicated is because guanxi increasingly has to carry the burden of social welfare and access to services – even those to which individuals are entitled.[44] Finally the very recent and observable diminution in consumer spending and upturn in family savings is a telling sign that families newly worry about their welfare responsibilities in uncertain times.

What has emerged, then, as a result of these decade-long trends is a decentralized welfare system made up of a plurality of cellular and incremental coping strategies centrally encouraged but initiated practically by local institutions, communities and families or kin groups. As distinctive local and short-term coping strategies have arisen to meet old and new needs, local welfare packages have emerged displaying a diversity of multi-level, multi-channel and multi-means approaches to welfare provisioning. While this diversity has certain advantages given the variations in regional socio-economic profiles, there are a number of common tensions which may well affect the long-term viability of the strategies presently initiated by local governments, communities and families.

Long-term Viability

In assessing the efficacy of longer-term outcomes of welfare reform at the end of a decade of experiment, innovation and deliberation, it is

41. Xiang Biao, "How to create a visible 'non-state space' through migration and marketized traditional networks: an account of a migrant community in China," paper delivered to International Conference on China's Rural Labour Force Migration, Beijing, June 1996.
42. Cecilia Millwertz, *Accepting Population Control: Urban Chinese Women and the One-Child Family Policy* (London: Curzon Press, 1997), pp. 121–149.
43. Elisabeth Croll, "Family strategies: securing the future," in Benewick and Wingrove, *China in the 1990s*, pp. 204–215; *Business Beijing*, April 1998, p. 23; Liu Weimeng, "Reflections," p. 71.
44. Yang Mayfair, *Gifts, Favors and Banquets*, pp. 3–4.

apparent that there are certain tensions surrounding the role of the state in social welfare. Although there is a consensus that the importance assigned to state support should be reduced and a system of welfare pluralism based on a greater role of market and the family developed, it is well to remember that the direct participation of the state in China's welfare delivery has been and is still very marginal and that there is as yet no coherent and consistent nation-wide blueprint to redistribute resources and establish a more equitable nation-wide strategy. There is a clear policy commitment to the establishment of at least a minimal degree of unity and consistency at the general policy level,[45] but without a comprehensive attempt to stabilize resources and unify delivery, the present decentralized collage of frameworks and funding with their limited coverage, exclusiveness, and increasing inequity in provisioning and access is likely to continue. What this means is that a cellular, exclusive and privileged enterprise-based system based on urban work-unit has been supplemented by enclaves of equally exclusive privileged delivery but based on rural residence or share-holding. Without a unified resource base or reformed tax system, there is likely to be no redistributive mechanism for reducing inequality between populations and regions, and even the privileged enclaves are likely to be at the mercy of the market and uncertain growth. It can be argued that if these tensions remain unresolved by the central state then further decentralization and diversification of welfare support could lead to a policy and resource vacuum at the centre. Either way the government has a dilemma: if it attempts to impose and fund a new nation-wide system of social welfare it requires both resources and political authority which it now lacks; yet if it withdraws from welfare provisioning it negates the social contract and risks losing popular support and political authority.

A number of unresolved tensions also characterize the evolving partnerships between the state and new welfare delivery systems inclusive of the market, non-government organizations and individual contributions. With the growth of market services, not only does ability to pay becomes a new or more important selection criterion determining access to services and assistance, but it is much more difficult for welfare services to be responsive to needs when services are dependent on cost-recovery or on extra-budgetary funds. Where welfare entrepreneurship rests on the latter or an uneasy amalgam of commercial and welfare activities, it is also much more difficult to guarantee the level and quality of welfare services as income-generation then becomes a major activity competing for resources including space and skills. Similarly, state-sponsored partnerships with new charitable non-government organizations are uneasy and under-developed largely because there are no reliable ground rules to guide autonomous non-government organizations in establishing relationships with central and local governments. Indeed their assumption of new and expanded roles in social welfare is hampered by the fact that

45. See State Council Report quoted in Zhou Hong, "Three pillars of social security under market conditions," in White and Shang, *Reforms*, p. 81.

their very existence may be inconsistently encouraged and discouraged by central and local governments. Likewise tension characterizes the social contract between individual and state, affecting individual contributions to social welfare funding. While the notion of entitlement is well developed it is based on a one-sided expectation that central and local governments will take primary responsibility for welfare with little or no matching sense of responsibility or obligation on the part of the individual. Although this is beginning to change informally as individuals make alternative provision via the market, formal notions of individual obligation or responsibility to pay taxes or furnish voluntary or involuntary contributions do not yet equal the well-developed notions of welfare rights. Although people's reluctance to enter such schemes may well reflect the lack of confidence in political will or professional skills to maintain the value of accumulated funds and savings, evolving a new social contract will involve a shift in the perception of individual, society and state towards welfare rights and obligations.

Finally, there is the overall tension between continuing economic development and maintaining or increasing levels of welfare support. In the short term even the economic foundations of local welfare innovations and experiments are inherently unstable in that most extra-budgetary sources of funding are in one way or another based on enterprise funding, be it that of state-owned enterprises, urban community or welfare service industries, or rural township, village or welfare enterprises. Just as rapid economic growth at the beginning of the 1990s permitted enterprise-generated development of local community welfare systems, so a significant downturn in economic growth at the end of the decade has placed local government, market, community and family welfare support at greater risk than at any time during recent years. In the longer term the establishment of a nation-wide welfare framework incorporating the best of local innovations and expectations remains dependent on continuing economic reform which is itself constrained by continuing enterprise responsibilities for welfare support. How this impasse will be resolved given the interdependence of economic and social welfare reforms remains to be seen.

As the pivotal importance of social welfare has been acknowledged, social welfare reform has steadily risen to the top of national and local reform agendas. In the first years of the 1990s the central objective of the government was to separate welfare provisioning from enterprises and accord priority to economic reform. With the growing awareness that economic reform is at once social welfare reform and vice versa, so the implementation of interdependent political, economic and social reforms has become the central challenge at the top of the end-of-decade reform agenda. However, combining and prioritizing the necessary interdependent social and economic reforms is not only the next step but also increases the complexity and magnitude of the task. In this respect it is perhaps appropriate to end with a quotation from Gordon White's decade-long studies of social welfare. He concluded that "welfare reform has proven not only technically complex and economically constrained but also institutionally tangled, socially sensitive and politically charged."[46] To reform social welfare into the next century will require a combination of sustained economic growth, continued institutional reform and skilful political leadership to integrate contributions from the central and local state, the market, the community, the family and the individual into a nation-wide system which is also accessible to all China's citizens.

46. White, *Institutional Change and Social Welfare Provision*, p. 6.

Politically-Engaged Intellectuals in the 1990s

Merle Goldman

Although dissident intellectuals and students continued to be persecuted in the post-Mao Zedong regimes of Deng Xiaoping and Jiang Zemin, China's intellectuals were no longer denigrated as a class, harassed, suppressed, imprisoned and persecuted to death as they had been during the Mao era. Like the 19th-century self-strengtheners, Deng and his appointed successors regarded intellectuals as essential to achieve their goal of economic modernization and make China once again "rich and powerful."[1] Those intellectuals involved in the sciences, technology and economics in particular enjoyed elite status as advisers to the government, similar to that which intellectuals had enjoyed throughout most of Chinese history until the 1949 revolution.

Beginning in the late 1970s, Deng and his then purported successor, Hu Yaobang, rehabilitated virtually all the intellectuals purged by Mao and released them from the prisons, labour reform camps and "stinking ninth hell" into which Mao had sent them. Intellectuals were appointed to high-level positions in government, academia and the media. Deng and his reformist allies repudiated the ideology and programmes of the Mao era that had politicized intellectual activity. Because of China's opening to the outside world and the move to the market in the last two decades of the 20th century, intellectuals worked in an increasingly pluralistic cultural and intellectual environment comparable to that which existed in the early decades of the century.

Nevertheless, an influential but small number of intellectuals on either side of the political spectrum, liberal and leftist, expressed increasingly dissident views as China's economic reforms took off. On the liberal side, intellectuals associated with reformist Party leaders Hu Yaobang and Zhao Ziyang found themselves by the late 1980s in conflict with the political establishment they had joined and advised. Prominent among them were members of Hu's intellectual network, who were put in charge of revising ideology, so important for unifying China's huge population and maintaining a hold on power. As former Marxist theorists, editors and writers, they sought to fill the void left by the bankruptcy of Marxism-Leninism-Mao Zedong Thought as a result of the Cultural Revolution. They turned first to a "humanist" version of Marxism similar to that of their East European brethren at the time, in which they dispensed with much of the Leninism that still remained the abiding belief of the leadership.[2] By the mid-1980s, as they became more acquainted with Western democratic ideas, they began to propose democratic reforms.

1. Deng Xiaoping, "Respect knowledge, respect trained personnel," 24 May 1977, in *Selected Works of Deng Xiaoping, Vol. 2: 1975–1982* (Beijing: Foreign Languages Press, 1984) pp. 58–84.
2. Merle Goldman, *Sowing the Seeds of Democracy in China: Political Reform in the Deng Xiaoping Era* (Cambridge, MA: Harvard University Press, 1994), pp. 25–61.

In late 1986, proposals for political reform culminated in student demonstrations for political rights.[3] Beginning at the University of Science and Technology in Hefei, Anhui, the demonstrations moved up the coast and to Tiananmen Square, the symbolic centre of China's government. In January 1987, the veteran Long Marchers, still a powerful political force in the Deng era, put pressure on Deng to purge Hu Yaobang from his position as Party general secretary for refusing to take action against the students, and to dismiss the intellectuals in his network.

In the late 1980s, a new school of thought emerged, called "neo-authoritarianism," formulated by a younger group of more technocratic intellectuals who were associated with Deng's next appointed successor, Zhao Ziyang. As advisers on economic policies, they were attracted to the authoritarian political model of their ethnic and post-Confucian East Asian neighbours, the "four little dragons." They called for several decades of economic reform under a strong centralized leader until a large educated middle-class emerged that could lead the country toward democratization.[4] Despite their neo-authoritarian viewpoint, together with the former members of Hu Yaobang's intellectual network, they supported the student demonstrators in Tiananmen Square in spring 1989 in their demands for political reform and more freedom of speech. When Deng purged Zhao for refusing to support the imposition of martial law on 20 May and ordered the troops to disperse the demonstrators on 4 June, these highly placed intellectuals were imprisoned, sent to labour reform camps, exiled abroad or purged from the establishment. Thus, those on the liberal side of the political spectrum were silenced in the aftermath of 4 June. They and the student leaders were imprisoned for relatively short periods of time, whereas the workers who had joined the 1989 demonstrations received stiffer sentences.

Although initially there was a return of Maoists to the Propaganda Department and the media, and a revival of the politicalization of academia as in the Mao era, it also was relatively brief. Moreover, unlike the Mao period, the intellectuals as a class, their families and colleagues did not suffer for the supposed "crimes" of their associates. Therefore, while disillusioned with the regime, most intellectuals and students were not alienated from it. Most continued to work in the party-state bureaucracies, academia and the media. Those thrown out or unable to gain a position in the official establishment turned to business. The creation of a market economy and opening to the outside world offered alternatives to government employment, especially in non-state enterprises, foreign-joint ventures or private businesses. Unlike the bureaucracy or academia, where they might lose their jobs or salaries for expressing dissident views, these alternatives provided a degree of economic independence that offered some protection from political retaliation.

Even the intellectuals' access to the outside world was not interrupted.

3. Benedict Stavis, *China's Political Reforms: An Interim Report* (New York: Praeger, 1988), pp. 89–110.
4. Stanley Rosen and Gary Zou (eds.), "The Chinese debate on the new authoritarianism," *Chinese Sociology and Anthropology*, Winter 1990–91, Spring 1991, Summer 1991.

Although campaigns in the early 1990s against "all-out Westernization" and peaceful evolution were similar to the campaigns against "spiritual pollution" and bourgeois liberalization in the 1980s, they did not stop the inflow of Western ideas and products. China's growing economic and technological international interdependence made it virtually impossible to keep out influences from abroad. Furthermore, the political leadership was reluctant to back up these campaigns with threats of violence, mass mobilization and ideological zeal that had been so destabilizing during the Mao years.

Equally important, unlike the Mao era, intellectuals were able to cut themselves off from political mobilization, if they wished. They were no longer forced or willing to participate in political movements. China's large cities, universities and institutes became gathering places for foreign experts, academics, artists, writers, entertainers, audiences and visitors involved in a wide variety of cultural, intellectual and artistic endeavours that had no ostensible political content. The ideological homogenity of the Mao era gave way to a broad range of intellectual and cultural activities.[5]

While the kind of intellectual engagement in public political debates of the 1980s was suppressed through most of the 1990s, the party-state's further retreat from the cultural and intellectual realm in terms of censorship, financial support and tolerance of diversity and foreign influences sparked an explosion of artistic experimentation, a vibrant popular culture and non-political intellectual discourse. As long as the content and style of one's intellectual, cultural and professional work stayed away from politics, the party-state tolerated and at times even encouraged an apolitical culture as a diversion from political engagement.

The Jiang Zemin Era

The revival of Maoism in the aftermath of 4 June was also facilitated by the inexperience and cautiousness of Jiang Zemin, whom Deng hastily chose to replace Zhao Ziyang as Party general secretary. A number of neo-Maoists, led by conservative elder Deng Liqun, took advantage of Jiang's tentativeness to assume positions in propaganda, academic, journalistic and cultural spheres. They attempted to revitalize Mao worship and reindoctrinate the population in Marxism-Leninism. "Mao fever" (*Mao re*) spread in the early 1990s to China's major cities with the reappearance of Mao's "Little Red Book," Mao souvenirs and Mao medallions hanging in taxicabs. While some of this kitsch poked fun at Mao, the fever was also fired by nostalgia for the supposed order and honest officials of the Mao years in contrast to the succeeding disorder and corruption.[6]

---

5. Jianying Zha, *China Pop: How the Soap Operas. Tabloids and Bestsellers Are Transforming a Culture* (New York: The New Press, 1995).
6. Geremie Barmé, *Shades of Mao: The Posthumous Cult of the Great Leader* (Armonk, NY: M.E. Sharpe, 1996).

However, when Deng took his famous Southern Tour to the special economic zones in 1992 in an effort to revive the economic reforms and beat back the Maoist upsurge, he attacked the "left" as a greater danger than the right. Soon after, Mao fever subsided. Nevertheless, a group of intellectuals associated with Deng Liqun circulated four successive "ten-thousand word" statements that persisted in taking a Maoist approach, specifically in their call for the continued dominance of the state-controlled economy.[7] Their statements warned that the decline of state industries would help capitalism prevail over socialism and would impoverish state workers. In opposition to Deng's non-ideological approach, they touted socialism. Though criticized and pushed to the margins once again, as the post-Deng leadership moved in the late 1990s to reform state industries, the neo-Maoists continued to warn publicly against the evils of capitalism through several journals that they controlled.[8]

At the same time, the more open political atmosphere following Deng's trip south emboldened some of the liberal intellectuals of the 1980s and participants in past demonstrations to call publicly, in a series of petitions in 1993–94, for political reform and the release of political prisoners gaoled after 4 June. This political thaw, however, was short-lived. Some of the activists were rearrested or put under surveillance. By the mid-1990s, all public political dissent was suppressed once again. Nevertheless, although both the neo-Maoists and the advocates of Western liberal ideas were marginalized, sensitive discourse continued on both sides of the political spectrum in intellectual circles.

The collapse of the Soviet Union and the disorder accompanying Russia's move to democracy was another factor shifting the intellectual discussion in the 1990s away from the humanist and liberal tone of the previous decade.[9] In addition, a growing number of younger intellectuals reacted against the pro-Western, anti-traditional viewpoint of the 1980s, when disillusionment with Maoism had instilled an unreasoned idealism about Western societies and political life. As these intellectuals and returned students came in closer contact with the realities of Western countries through travel and study, their idealism waned.

Consequently, in the mid-1990s, a younger generation of intellectuals who came of age in the post-Mao era, some of whom were close to the "princelings," children of the Party elders, moved to another extreme. Like the neo-authoritarians of the late 1980s, they did not refer to Marxism-Leninism, but unlike them, they did not endorse a full-scale move to the market and the development of a middle class that would eventually lead China towards democracy. Rather, some of their neo-conservative views overlapped with those of the neo-Maoists in that they decried the decentralization that had accompanied China's

7. Shi Liuzi (ed.), *Beijing dixia "wanyanshu"* (*The Ten-Thousand Word and Other Underground Writings in China*) (Hong Kong: Mingjing chubanshe, 1997).

8. For representative articles, see Zhong Liu zazhi she (eds.), *Zhong Liu bai qi wencui* (*Collection of 100 Issues of Zhong Liu*) (Beijing: Jincheng chubanshe, 1998).

9. David Kelly, "Realistic responses and strategic options: an alternative CCP ideology and its critics," *Chinese Law and Government*, Vol. 29, No. 2 (March–April 1996).

move to the market and urged a retightening of centralized controls over the regions and over cultural life. They were particularly upset about the destabilizing impact of millions of migrants into the cities in the 1990s in search of economic opportunities, and called for their return to their villages.

Whereas the neo-Maoists had argued for a reassertion of a centralized economy in ideological terms, the neo-conservatives argued for it in practical terms: a strong central state was necessary to ensure stability and continuing tax revenues.[10] Without a restrengthening of party-state controls, they asserted, the Party would be unable to handle the social instabilities caused by the growing economic regionalism and internal migrants unleashed by the economic reforms. Unless the erosion of the party-state's authority was stopped, they warned that chaos (*luan*), the traditional Chinese nightmare, would result.[11] They implicitly criticized Deng's reforms for weakening the central government.

Another important intellectual current in the mid-1990s was a revival of neo-Confucianism. Although its proponents did not refer to Marxism-Leninism, the Jiang leadership found their views more in tune with its goals than the views of either the neo-Maoists or the liberals. The neo-Confucianists asserted that modernization need not mean Westernization. In fact, the seeds of modernization, they argued, could be found in Chinese history and values, specifically in Confucianism. Instead of China's deeply-embedded traditional culture being an obstacle to its modernization, as preached by the May Fourth intellectuals and Party reformers in the 1980s, they insisted that Confucianism was conducive to modernization. Citing the dynamic economies of the post-Confucian-shaped societies of their East Asian neighbours, they asserted that a revived neo-Confucianism, with its emphasis on the group, authority and education, could provide the intellectual and cultural underpinnings for China's rapid economic development while helping it avoid the immorality and individualism of Western capitalism.[12]

Counter to China's growing involvement with the outside world and growing internal regionalism due to the move to the market, the post-4 June leaders and their intellectual spokespersons not only re-emphasized ideological unity but also re-energized a spirit of nationalism, as leaders earlier in the century had done to promote political unity. Generally, the younger generation of intellectuals and urban youth readily embraced the leadership's reinvigorated nationalism. They needed little prodding. In 1993, they spontaneously protested against the rejection of China's bid to host the International Olympics in the year 2000, blaming the United States. China's apparent economic success had also awakened nationalist

10. Wang Shaoguang and Hu Angang, *Zhongguo guojia nengli baogao* (*A Study of China's State Capacity*) (Shenyang: Liaoning renmin chubanshe, 1993).

11. Luo Yi Ning Ge, *Di-san zhi yanjing kan Zhongguo* (*Looking at China through a Third Eye*) (Taiyuan: Shanxi renmin chubanshe, 1994), translated in FBIS-CHI-95-075-S, 14 April 1995.

12. See the collection of articles translated in *Chinese Studies in Philosophy*, Vol. 24, No. 3 (Spring 1993).

pride among the youth as well as among some intellectuals. They echoed their leaders' charge that the United States was attempting to contain China's rising power. Their indignation was expressed in such books as *Zhongguo keyi shuo bu* (*China Can Say No*) and the numerous variations on that theme, which became bestsellers in the mid-1990s.

Moreover, in the mid-1990s the rising tide of nationalism cut across all schools of thought – neo-Maoist, neo-conservative and neo-Confucian – with the exception of the virtually silenced liberal school.[13] Despite Deng Liqun and his allies' efforts, Jiang Zemin merely paid lip service to reviving Marxism-Leninism-Mao Zedong Thought. He stressed building "socialist spiritual civilization," but this concept had little to do with socialism and ideology. Though concerned with polite behaviour in public places, its major concern was with the revival of China as a great civilization. The leadership agreed with the neo-Confucians that Confucianism was rele-vant to the present, but stressed its authoritarian, hierarchal values rather than other Confucian teachings, such as the intellectuals' obligation to criticize officials who abused power or engaged in unfair treatment of the population.

Nevertheless, like other intellectual currents in post-Mao China, nationalist discourse was contradictory. Its stridency was challenged in articles in the still relatively liberal journals *Dushu* (*Reading*) and *Dongfang* (*The Orient*) which was suspended in May 1996.[14] Moreover, by the late 1990s the leadership tried to rein in the nationalist fervour lest it turn into xenophobia sparking demonstrations that could undermine the party-state and antagonize countries with which China sought trade and investment. Thus it discouraged writings specifically directed against the United States and Japan and stopped protestors from demanding reparations from Japan, fearing that they would ignite large-scale protests as well as frighten off Japanese investors. With the improvement of relations with the United States, inaugurated by the visits of Jiang to the United States in 1997 and President Clinton to China in 1998, the rise in nationalist sentiment that had permeated the intellectual and student circles in the mid-1990s gradually subsided.

In the late 1990s, another form of protest against the market reforms was expressed by a group of intellectuals, some of whom had been sent down to the countryside and to factories in the Cultural Revolution and so claimed to be in closer touch with ordinary working people. They expressed a moral leftist view. Though sharing some of the social ideals of the Maoists, they criticized, without reference to ideology, the increasing inequalities and rampant corruption that had accompanied China's economic reforms and involvement in the global economy. They expressed a populist dismay at the lay-offs of workers because of reform of

13. Stanley Rosen, "Nationalism and neoconservatism in China in the 1990s," *Chinese Law and Government*, Vol. 30, No. 6 (November–December 1997); Jonathan Unger (ed.), *Chinese Nationalism* (Armonk, NY: M.E. Sharpe, 1996).

14. For translations, see "Chinese intellectuals: selections from *Dongfang*," *Contemporary Chinese Thought*, Vol. 29, No. 2 (Winter 1997–98).

state industries, the lagging incomes of peasants and the plunder of state wealth by officials.[15]

As the post-Deng leadership continued to tolerate a number of different intellectual currents, a new political springtime slowly reappeared in late summer and early autumn 1998.[16] Seemingly with the tacit support of the Jiang leadership, a disparate group of intellectuals was emboldened to become more public in calls for greater freedom of expression and political reforms. Liu Ji, a vice-president of CASS and an adviser to Jiang, sponsored the publication of a series of books which gave Jiang a reformist image and criticized the nationalist, neo-Maoist discourse of the mid-1990s.[17] Following the 15th Party Congress in September 1997 where Jiang also called for political reforms, but without spelling out what he meant, several highly placed intellectuals provided the rationale.

The economist Dong Fureng, an adviser on state industry reform, publicly pointed out, as did several of his colleagues, the need for political reforms to deal with the rising unemployment, widening income gaps, environmental pollution and rampant corruption precipitated by the market reforms.[18] A provincial reform official turned businessman, Fang Jue, distributed a proposal for democratic reforms based on the Western system of checks and balances and direct elections.[19] Li Shenzhi, the retired head of the American Studies Institute at CASS, explained that contrary to the leadership's past emphasis on economic rights, one could not act as a "citizen" unless one also had political and civil rights. Since China had already made headway in providing basic economic livelihood, he urged that it now provide political and civil rights. Counter to the views of the neo-conservatives and some of China's leaders, who insisted that civil and political rights were alien to Asia, Li pointed out that the idea of such rights had been introduced and discussed in China in the early decades of the 20th century. Therefore, the concept of universal human rights, he asserted, had already become a part of China's history and culture.[20] The fact that Jiang allowed President Clinton's discussion of the indivisibility of economic rights and political rights to be aired on national television and at public gatherings when Clinton visited China in

15. He Qinglian, *Xiandaihua de xianjing: dangdai Zhongguo de jingji shehui wenti* (*The Pitfalls of Modernization: Contemporary Economic and Social Problems*) (Beijing: Jinri Zhongguo chubanshe, 1998); and the review, Liu Binyan and Perry Link, "China: the Great Leap backward?" *New York Review of Books*, 8 October 1998.

16. Joseph Fewsmith, "Jiang Zemin takes command," *Current History* (September 1998).

17. At least a dozen books were published under the auspices of Liu Ji. See, for example, Xu Ming (ed.), *Guanjian shike: dangdai Zhongguo jindai jiejue de 27 wenti* (*A Critical Time: 27 Problems to be Solved in Contemporary China*) (Beijing: Jinri Zhongguo chubanshe, 1997); or, more recently, Ling Zhijun and Ma Licheng, *Huhan: dangjin Zhongguo de 5 zhong shengyin* (*Call Out: Five Voices in Present China*) (Guangzhou: Guangzhou chubanshe, 1999).

18. "China: economist says market economy calls for political reform," *Zhongguo xinwen she* (Beijing), 15 February 1998, FBIS-CHI-98-056, 3 March 1998.

19. Fang Jue, "Zhongguo xuyao xin de zhuanbian" ("China needs new changes"), *Beijing zhichun* (*Beijing Spring*), No. 57 (February 1998), pp. 24–28.

20. Li Shenzhi, "Ye yao tuidong zhengzhi gaige" ("We must also promote political reform"), *Gaige* (*Reform*), No. 1 (1998), pp. 13–14.

Politically-Engaged Intellectuals 145

June 1998 indicated a tolerance and perhaps tacit approval of public discussion of political reforms.

In the midst of this discussion, a controversial book, *Jiaofeng* (*Cross Swords*), by two journalists from the *People's Daily* became a best-seller.[21] The book attacked the neo-Maoists and especially the "ten-thousand-word" statements not only for opposing the reform of state industry, but also for criticizing China's involvement with the Western capitalist world. But the book provoked a counterattack in the neo-Maoist journal *Dangdai sichao* (*Contemporary Trends in Ideology*), which sued the authors for quoting from one of the "ten-thousand-word" articles without authorization and distorting its contents.[22]

By late 1998, however, the atmosphere changed precipitously. A cold wind in late autumn froze some of the buds that had started to blossom. A number of different forces were pushing the cold wind, among them the effects of the Asian economic crisis, slowing economic growth, unemployed workers protesting against the reform of state industry and unpaid wages, and rising peasant discontent. These forces led not only to a slowing of state industry reform but also to a retreat from more public political discussion. Jiang's liberal adviser, Liu Ji, was "retired" as a vice-president of CASS, while the older Maoist propagandist Wang Renzhi stayed on as an active vice-president at the academy. A compilation of articles calling for political reform, *Zhengzhi Zhongguo* (*Governing China*)[23] was not allowed to be reprinted and one of its editors was put under house arrest. Fang Jue, who had proposed a system of a Western-style democracy, was also arrested.

Another indication of a retreat was reflected in the 20th anniversary celebrations of the "practice criterion" in May 1998[24] and the more restrained 20th anniversary of the launching of Deng's reforms at the Third Plenum of the 11th Central Committee in December 1998. A speech by Jiang Zemin set the parameters of what could be discussed on this anniversary and reasserted Deng's Four Cardinal Principles, in which obedience to the Party was paramount.[25] Such restraint in marking this watershed event revealed the wariness of the Jiang leadership about moving forward with further reforms, economic as well as political, for fear of provoking unrest.

---

21. Ma Licheng and Ling Zhijun, *Jiaofeng: dangdai Zhongguo san ci sixiang jiefang shilu* (*Cross Swords: A Record of Three Episodes of Liberated Thought in Contemporary China*) (Beijing: Jinri Zhongguo chubanshe, 1998).

22. Yeh Hung-yen, "Authors of the book 'Crossing Swords' sued over copyright infringement, Beijing intermediate court opens trial," *Dagong bao* (Hong Kong), 27 November 1998, p. 3, FBIS-CHI-98-331, 1 December 1998.

23. Dong Yuyu and Shi Binhai (eds), *Zhengzhi Zhongguo: mianlin xin tizhi xuance* (*Governing China: Choices We Face in the New System*) (Beijing: Jinri Zhongguo chubanshe, 1998).

24. Sun Changjiang, "Zhenli zhizheng ershi nian" ("Twenty years after the conflict over truth criterion"), *Ershiyi shiji* (*Twenty-first Century*), No. 50 (December 1998), pp. 24–28.

25. "China: Jiang addresses plenum anniversary meeting," Xinhua, 21 December 1998, FBIS-CHI-98-355, 22 December 1998.

Non-establishment Political Activists

Other forces cooling the reform atmosphere were the actions of democratic activists emboldened by President Clinton's visit to China and China's October 1998 signing of the UN Covenant on Civil and Political Rights. A number of non-establishment intellectuals tested the leadership's commitment to the covenant by attempting to set up political organizations. Among them were ex-Red Guards, survivors of the 1978–79 Democracy Wall movement, and participants in the spring 1989 demonstrations, who sought to establish the first opposition party in the PRC, the China Democracy Party. By late 1998 several of their leaders were charged with seeking to overthrow the government and given long prison sentences, ranging from 11 to 13 years.[26]

Another association, the China Development Union, established ostensibly to deal with environmental problems and hold seminars on political issues, was also disbanded, officially because it was registered in Hong Kong rather than in Beijing, but primarily because of the Party's fear that such an organization would take political actions. Although by 1998 over one million non-governmental organizations were apparently established in China, a large number of which dealt with intellectual, social and cultural issues, none was allowed to engage in political activities and none came close to the relatively independent political think-tanks of the 1980s.[27]

Nevertheless, the effort to establish the China Democracy Party was unprecedented in that it was the first attempt to set up a public political opposition party in the PRC. Moreover, its efforts were not confined just to Beijing and Shanghai but spread from the north-east to the south-east. Another new approach used by political dissidents in the 1990s was revealed when the Party arrested its leaders, at which time they confiscated their computers. Computers, fax machines, cell phones and the Internet have transformed the means of political communication in China in the 1990s. They have the potential to become China's equivalent to the Soviet *samizdat*, the underground typewritten literature that ultimately helped to bring down the Soviet Union and the Soviet Communist Party. In autumn 1998, the Party also arrested and later sentenced to two years in prison the owner of a computer software company who had supplied thousands of email addresses to Chinese dissident publications in the United States, thus enabling them to communicate through the Internet with thousands back in China. Whereas the Party had no trouble closing down the Democracy Wall in Beijing in 1979, it remains to be seen whether it can similarly control the Internet, which has been called China's "virtual Democracy Wall."[28]

26. Erik Eckholm, "Beijing sends potential dissidents a message: don't," *New York Times*, 25 December 1998.
27. Tony Saich, "Changing state–society relations: some inferences from the NGO sector," ms., January 1999.
28. He Xintong, wife of Xu Wenli (who has since been sentenced to 13 years), speaking at Fairbank Center, Harvard University, August 1998.

Another group that the Jiang government repressed was the families of those students and citizens who were killed or imprisoned on 4 June 1989. The families have doggedly sought a reversal of the negative verdict on the Tiananmen Square demonstration. Ding Zilin, a professor at the Chinese People's University whose only son was killed, has led the effort to compile a list of those killed on 4 June and to distribute funds sent by overseas Chinese dissidents to the families of the victims. Also among those asking for a re-evaluation were former officials, such as Zhao Ziyang who was placed under house arrest in 1989, and Zhao's personal secretary, Bao Tong, who had been imprisoned for defending the students. On each 4 June anniversary or on the occasion of a visit of a prominent foreign leader, members of this group have been detained by the government for fear that they might stir up a protest which would gain popular support.

The leadership, however, is most concerned with those who have joined with disaffected workers in attempts to set up independent labour unions. The Party regards this relatively small number of marginal intellectuals as having the potential to spark widespread social unrest. Some of these people are ex-Red Guards, who would have been intellectuals had it not been for the suspension of their education in the Cultural Revolution; others wrote the journals of the 1978–79 Democracy Wall movement and still others participated in the 1989 demonstrations.

With the bankruptcy and reform of state industries leading to spreading workers' demonstrations in the late 1990s, the Party's fear of an alliance between disaffected workers and intellectuals became palpable. Jiang instructed local authorities to guard against intellectuals colluding with unemployed workers. News of various intellectuals being arrested for helping or joining with workers to set up independent unions in different urban areas has leaked out to the press in Hong Kong and the West. So far, however, there is a lack of concrete evidence and detail on these underground unions. It is difficult to estimate the number and size of such alliances. All that is known is that those engaged in such activities are being arrested all over the country from Heilongjiang to Shenzhen.

Whereas the party-state moves swiftly and harshly against such intellectual organizers, it was more cautious in the 1990s towards demonstrating workers and pensioners in China's rust belts – Sichuan, Shaanxi, the north-east and Hubei. In many cases, local officials have paid the back wages and pensions in order to stop the demonstrations.[29] The greater caution towards the workers reflects the party-state's fear that a violent crackdown could ignite social unrest into a conflagration that would spread quickly and be difficult to contain. Ever since the Polish Solidarity labour union developed into a political movement in 1980 with the help of Poland's intellectuals and overthrew the Polish Communist Party, China's leaders have feared a similar development in China. They have

29. Dorothy Solinger, "The potential for urban unrest," in David Shambaugh (ed.), *Is China Unstable?* (Washington, D.C.: Sigur Center for Asian Studies, George Washington University, 1998).

reason for concern. China's 20th-century history is marked by instances of intellectuals and workers joining together in political movements that have destabilized regimes and caused profound changes, as witnessed in the May Fourth movement and, most importantly, the establishment of the Chinese Communist Party itself.

Like the efforts to control the Internet, it is unlikely the party-state will succeed in totally suppressing the efforts of non-establishment intellectuals to join with other social groups. The leaders of these efforts came of age during the Cultural Revolution. They became workers when their education was interrupted or were sent-down youth during the Cultural Revolution. Having been forced to labour in factories and fields, they had contacts with ordinary working people, which their intellectual predecessors and the younger intellectuals did not have. Moreover, because they had become totally disillusioned with their political leaders and the political system during the Cultural Revolution, their generation tends to question everything. Consequently, they express more independence than intellectuals of other generations. While most intellectuals and students in the 1990s appear to have become apolitical or more interested in making money, the politically engaged members of the Cultural Revolution generation have been the most active in joining with other social groups in common cause.

While the Jiang leadership in the 1990s has tolerated a variety of voices, it has not let any of them organize into political groupings. Moreover, it has only briefly tolerated public political discourse. Still, political ideas, ranging from Maoist to liberal to moral leftist, continue to be discussed internally in establishment intellectual and policy circles. Perhaps as the price for continuing these discussions, members of the intellectual establishment have stayed clear of any contact with non-establishment democratic and labour activists.

Intellectuals and Students at the End of the Century

China's zig-zag, contradictory treatment of intellectuals in the 1990s reveals that while some leaders, including Jiang,[30] may agree with the intellectuals on the need for political reforms to deal with problems provoked by the economic reforms, they are hesitant to move actively in this direction. They fear not only social unrest but also a Soviet-style scenario in which both they and the Leninist party-state would be replaced. Consequently, though the party-state's control weakened further in the 1990s as a result of accelerating market reforms, growing involvement with the outside world and its continuing withdrawal from most areas of daily life, it continues to suppress any action that it considers a political threat.

30. Jiang Zemin, "Hold high the great banner of Deng Xiaoping theory for an all-round advancement of the cause of building socialism with Chinese characteristics into the 21st century," report delivered at the 15th National Congress of the Communist Party of China on 12 September 1997, *Beijing Review*, 6–12 October 1997, pp. 10–33.

As yet, the Jiang government has not been confronted with massive student demonstrations on the scale of those in 1989 or even in 1986. Not only have students become more politically quiescent since the Tiananmen Square demonstration, the Jiang government has pre-empted such protests by detaining or arresting potential instigators and equipping the People's Armed Police with non-lethal weapons so that it will be able to deal with demonstrations much more effectively than was the case in 1989. The party-state has been successful so far in suppressing any intellectual and student challenges on sensitive anniversaries or during visits by Western leaders, by putting controversial intellectuals and students under surveillance, house arrest or detention, and preventing students from gathering outside their universities. The party-state's precautions and increased ability to suppress such protests will lessen their threat. The one exception was the two-day outburst of anti-Americanism in May 1999 following the NATO accidental bombing of the Chinese embassy in Belgrade.

The party-state's major concern at the end of the century was to prevent the emergence of underground intellectual–worker alliances to surface as a political movement that could ultimately overthrow the regime. Despite the small number of intellectuals engaged in such activities, the potential for demonstrations led by intellectuals that might spread to disaffected workers is real. When *falungong* practitioners suddenly appeared in front of the government's headquarters in Beijing on 25 April 1999, the party-state also became increasingly concerned with the emergence of religious sects that could similarly undermine the Party. But if China's leaders have learned any lesson from 4 June, it should be that gradually building political institutions, such as a genuine legislature, competitive elections, independent unions and the rule of law, allowing freedom of expression and association, provides disaffected elements, such as laid-off workers, politically-engaged intellectuals and the alienated, with less destabilizing means to express their grievances and seek redress than through demonstrations and mass protests.

It is still unclear whether the signs of a political spring in summer and autumn 1998 with the discussions of political reforms or the signs of winter in late 1998 with the suppression of non-establishment intellectuals will prevail. Nevertheless, there is no question that most Chinese intellectuals and students in the 1990s enjoyed more individual and intellectual freedoms, access to foreign counterparts and a more pluralistic cultural environment than at any other time in the history of the PRC. And the Jiang leadership appeared willing to tolerate political discourse among establishment intellectuals that did not directly challenge its authority or move far beyond establishment circles.

Art in China since 1949

Michael Sullivan

Since the Communists came to power in 1949 Chinese art has seen extraordinary changes. For 30 years, the Party apparatus and its Marxist-Maoist ideology exerted so tight a control over cultural life that it is natural for the art of that period to be viewed primarily as a reflection or expression of political forces. To some degree that is unavoidable, and it is the approach taken by the authors of two important books on post-1949 Chinese art, while Jerome Silbergeld's monograph on the Sichuan eccentric painter Li Huasheng is a fascinating study of the way in which these forces affected the life and work of an individual artist.[1]

Mao Zedong's "Talks on Literature and Art" delivered in Yan'an in 1942 had laid down the principles on which the arts were to "serve the people." The Party did not wait for the declaration of the PRC to put them into effect. In July 1949 the First National Congress of Literary and Art Workers was held, an event crucial for the integration of the arts into the system, during which Mao instructed all "progressive cultural workers" to serve the cause of revolution and mass education. Not to offer one's talents to society was sheer selfishness. The appeal was hard to resist. Many artists, including cosmopolitan painters and sculptors such as Pang Xunqin, Wu Zuoren and Liu Kaiqu, who had trained in France, were prepared to give up their independence (for which there was in any case no market) for the economic security and sense of dedication to a cause that the new regime offered.

This was initially made easier by the tolerant policy of the authorities towards established artists. Xu Beihong, for example, was appointed Chairman of the Artists' Association, to be followed after his early death in 1953 by the grand old man of traditional painting, Qi Baishi. The actual power in the Association was of course held by a core of Yan'an-trained Party men.

In the early 1950s, Western-style artists were sent for training, or retraining, to the Soviet Union and eastern bloc countries, while Soviet Socialist Realism was taught by visiting professors in the Academies, most notably by the Moscow Academiciam Konstantin Maksimov, who arrived in Beijing early in 1955. Even after the break with the Soviet Union in 1958–59, Soviet Socialist Realism continued to be a powerful propaganda tool, and eventually, after Mao died, it was turned by artists against its promoters to expose the horrors of the Cultural Revolution.

At the same time, mass education during the 1950s and early 1960s vastly expanded the social base from which art and artists could

1. Ellen Laing, *The Winking Owl: Art in the People's Republic of China* (Berkeley: University of California Press, 1984), and Julia Andrews, *Painters and Politics in the People's Republic of China, 1949–1979* (Berkeley: University of California Press, 1994); and Jerome Silbergeld with Gong Jisui, *Contradictions: Artistic Life, the Socialist State, and the Painter Li Huasheng* (Seattle: University of Washington Press, 1993).

spring. The Party made strenuous attempts to foster a peasant art movement, basing it on the few places in China, notably Huxian in Shaanxi, which did actually have some "peasant art." Art teachers were sent into the countryside to teach the peasants, but eventually what began as a mass movement faded away, and today practically no one visits the peasant art museums. Yet the movement did not die out completely, and in 1998 recent, more sophisticated work by Huxian artists was being promoted as part of the ideological backlash against the movements that had developed in the last two decades.[2]

During the 1950s debate was intense about the relative merits of oil painting and traditional *guohua*. One powerful group led by Jiang Feng, head of the Party group in the Central Academy, advocated the abandonment of *guohua* as bourgeois, elitist and of no use in a revolutionary society.[3] Opposed to him were, on the one hand, Maoist theorists such as Cai Ruohong, who urged that it be "reformed," cleansed of its conventional repertory and thus adapted to depict modern life, while on the other, leading *guohua* masters, including Fu Baoshi and Pan Tianshou, insisted that its essential qualities must be preserved. The debate, although carried on for the most part over the heads of the artists themselves, did inject an element of not wholly unhealthy tension into the art world, while it challenged the proponents of *guohua* to experiment in developing the medium and its techniques to show that it could depict the modern world.

Experiments along these lines had been made by Xu Beihong and Jiang Zhaohe in the 1940s, but now they were carried much further, by an ever-increasing number of ink painters that included Li Keran, Guan Shanyue, Song Wenzhi and Qian Songyan. Even the scholar and connoisseur Wu Hufan, under pressure from Party officials to politicize his art, celebrated China's first atomic bomb test of 1965 in a hanging scroll in the traditional style.[4] The debate about the validity and future of ink painting has never died down, and may never be resolved: it was, for instance, the topic of an international symposium held in Shanghai as recently as October 1998.[5]

During the 1950s and 1960s the greatest emphasis was upon figure painting, where Western, and chiefly Soviet, models had to compete with the Dunhuang frescoes as sources of style and technique. There was also a huge official demand for monumental sculpture on the Soviet model, and a dearth of trained sculptors. Art was classified as "harmful" (nudes, abstractions, expressionist works, for example); "good" (revolutionary art in all its forms); or "not harmful" (landscapes and still lives). Pure

2. See Liao Kaiming, "Content good: form beautiful. Selected Works from the new farmers' painting," *Meishu*, No. 9 (1998), pp. 6–8.
3. This issue is discussed in detail in the chapter "The politicisation of *guohua*," in Andrews, *Painters and Politics*, pp. 176–200.
4. Illustrated in *ibid*. Fig. 108.
5. The symposium, held in conjunction with the Second Shanghai Biennale, was sponsored by the Shanghai Art Museum and funded by the Annie Wong Art Foundation in Hong Kong.

landscapes were permitted, as showing love of country, so long as one didn't do too many of them. Western art was seen through Soviet eyes. Wu Guanzhong, returning from Europe to teach at the Central Academy, was forbidden to mention Cézanne; while as a precaution he destroyed all the nudes he had painted in Paris.[6]

It may seem surprising that in this atmosphere artists produced any good work at all. But these conditions created security and plenty of work for them, while the range of acceptable subject-matter was greatly extended. During the more relaxed periods – 1956 to early 1957, 1962–63, 1972 to early 1973, for example – major artists such as Li Keran, Pan Tianshou and Li Kuchan showed remarkable vigour and spontaneity in their *guohua*, although far too much of their time and energy was spent on routine assignments and public projects such as the huge paintings the established *guohua* masters executed in 1959 for public buildings in Beijing.[7]

The years 1973 to 1976 were a period of ever increasing misery for artists under the cultural tyranny of Jiang Qing. On 8 January 1976, Zhou Enlai, whom many had looked on as their protector, died, and the last flicker of light seemed to go out of the world of art – although at the May Qingming Festival a massive demonstration in Zhou's memory was accompanied by an outpouring of poetry, painting and graphic work which for the first time since 1949 was an entirely spontaneous (though momentary) expression of deeply-held feeling and emotion.[8] Yet when in September of that year, a month after the death of Mao, the Gang of Four were arrested, national rejoicing was not accompanied by any outburst of free expression in the arts. In a famous cartoon of 1979, Liao Bingxiong depicts himself, his shell broken open, so paralysed by 30 years of control that he cannot move.[9]

Between 1977 and 1979 there was a feeble thaw, while victimized artists were slowly rehabilitated. Participants in the officially sponsored New Spring Art Exhibition (*Xinchun huazhan*), held in February 1979, ranged from old masters such as Liu Haisu (82) and Pang Xunqin (70) to recent graduates who included Feng Guodong (31) and were soon to become leaders in the influential Beijing Oil Painting Research Association (Beijing youhua yanjiuhui). Political protest was not yet an element in this movement, but when in the same year the Stars (*Xingxing pai*) hung their first, unauthorized, exhibition on the railings of Beihai Park, a

6. His bitter experiences, when he was told to go home and study socialist realism and then come back and teach, are told in his biography by Chai Mo, *Yuan liao caihong* (*The Consummation of the Rainbow*) (Beijing: People's Cultural Publishing House, 1997).

7. It must be emphasized, however, that pressure from Party hard-liners was never quite removed. The bedraggled but defiant eagles of Pan Tianshou's last years, for example, show his state of mind, while his early death in 1973 was the direct result of harassment by Jiang Qing and her supporters. His work was included posthumously in the notorious Black Painting Exhibition held in Beijing in February/March 1974.

8. Some of the art produced during those crucial days was belatedly reproduced in *Meishu*, Nos. 8–12 (1979).

9. See Michael Sullivan, *Art and Artists of Twentieth Century China* (Berkeley: University of California Press, 1996), Plate 63.

new and far more disturbing element appeared in the art world.[10] So successful were they that in the following year the National Gallery of Art gave them space for their second exhibition. Although the group soon dissolved, and most of its leading members later sought refuge abroad, a page had turned. In spite of intermittent waves of oppression, the art world of post-Mao China would never be the same again.

The significance of the Stars' exhibitions of 1979 and 1980 lay partly in the fact that some of the exhibits were daringly ambiguous in their meaning (Wang Keping's sculptured Mao-like head, for example) but even more in the fact that, for the first time since 1949, a group of young artists and poets were acting together outside the artistic establishment. This led the way for a growing number of independent groups, beginning with the Contemporaries (*Tongdairen*), who exhibited in Beijing in October 1980; they included oil painters who later became well-known: Wang Huaiqing, Sun Weimin and Zhang Hongtu. The fact that several of them were influenced by Matisse and Klimt[11] shows how quickly, once the doors began to open, Western Post-Impressionist art had been taken up. Indeed, the early 1980s was a time when artists and writers seized avidly on everything Western, ancient and modern, that was flooding into China. It is little wonder that they were as bewildered as they were stimulated by the plethora of artistic ideas, forms and styles that confronted them. That the authorities likewise were often at a loss as to how to deal with this new situation is reflected in the frequent changes of cultural policy throughout the 1980s.

The "New Wave," as it came to be called, of the early 1980s saw some astonishing things, not least the beginning of the Avant-Garde, many performances, and the exhibition in 1984 in Shanghai of Yan Li's Surrealist works. In 1985 there emerged for exhibition purposes a number of independent groups, such as the Shanghai Young Artists Group, the first sign of that city's rebirth as a cultural centre; the Half-way There Group, chiefly middle-aged Soviet-trained artists trying with little success to establish their credentials in a new era; and the New Space Group, who painted stylized figures in cool colours, influenced by Edward Hopper.

The first independent art magazine, *Zhongguo meishu bao*, was also founded in 1985, edited by the Beijing critic Li Xianting. It covered all the new trends while paying lip-service to the authorities. The Sixth National Art Exhibition in the same year showed a range of work wider than anything that had been seen since 1949. In the meantime, regional schools of art were taking on a character of their own: for example, realistic oil painters including Luo Gongliu and Chen Danqing based in

10. See Zhang Tsong-zung, *The Stars: Ten Years* (Hong Kong: Hanart Z, 1989), which includes Geremie Barmé's critical overview "Arrière-pensée on an Avant-Garde." When I asked Jiang Feng why the gallery had given space to the Stars, he said that the aim was to show the artists how mistaken they were, and that their show would be ignored by the public. In fact, it drew crowds, and 70% of the comments in the albums provided by the gallery were favourable.

11. Their work is discussed and illustrated in *Meishu zuopin*, No. 7 (Beijing, 1981), and in Joan Lebold Cohen, *The New Chinese Painting 1949–1986* (New York: Harry N. Abrams, 1987), pp. 76–81.

Sichuan who found their subject-matter in Tibet and the Borderlands, their poetic realism in the style of Andrew Wyeth;[12] and, by contrast, the "heavy colour" decorative style developed by Ding Shaoguang and others in Yunnan.[13]

Before this buoyant mood could be expressed, however, artists had to get the poison out of their system. This was done first by an officially-encouraged campaign of cartoons satirizing the Gang of Four,[14] and then in the "literature and art of the wounded," or "scar art" of the early 1980s, when artists used the style of Soviet Socialist Realism both to reveal society as it really is and to recall the horrors of the Cultural Revolution years – a powerful example being Chen Conglin's "Snow on X Month, X Day, 1968," depicting the aftermath of bloody factional fighting in Sichuan.[15] The sense of loss and alienation felt by many found expression in the Obscure (menglong) school of poetry, and in art that showed depersonalized figures, often faceless or in back view, with beyond them empty, limitless space. The cultural authorities naturally condemned these haunting works, and these artists, as "negative."

Most striking at that time was the subversion of the big character poster of the Cultural Revolution by Gu Wenda, whose Installations embraced huge characters miswritten, deformed or crossed out. Xu Bing's Installation *Xishijian*, "A Mirror to Analyse the World," which came to be known as "The Book of Heaven," *Tianshu*, comprised long sheets of paper draped over the gallery, on which were printed by hand from wooden blocks thousands of characters, each an invention of the artist.[16] Thus did Gu Wenda and Xu Bing mock the meaninglessness of the written word, and the futility of human endeavour, in Communist society.[17] Even more radical was the "Xiamen Dada" group, launched by Huang Yongping who, proclaiming the end of art, logically concluded their 1986 exhibition by publicly burning all the exhibits.[18]

In 1986 Li Xianting was already planning a major exhibition of Avant-Garde art, which was shelved later that year when the campaign against "bourgeois liberalization" clamped down on experimental forms in the arts. But by 1988 controls had loosened and artists were testing the

12. For a number of typical works, see Tao Yongbai, *1700–1985: Oil Painting in China* (Shanghai: Jiangsu Art Publishing House, 1988).
13. See Joan Lebold Cohen, *Yunnan: A Renaissance in Chinese Painting* (Minneapolis: Fingerhut Group, 1988).
14. These were, so far as I know, never published in China, but one of them is reproduced in my *Art and Artists of Twentieth Century China*, Plate 62.
15. See *Ibid.* Fig. 22.8.
16. Since the *Tianshu* has been exhibited in the West, it has acquired a number of new meanings; but that the original meaning and purpose of the work was, indirectly at least, political, was expressed in a letter from Xu Bing to me in September 1997, in which he wrote, "The Tian Shu was originally created out of an anxiety over the sense of loss I felt towards my culture and personal situation that prompted me to seek anwers to some meaningful questions."
17. A good introduction to the now extensive literature on Xu Bing and Gu Wenda is Oscar Ho and T.Z. Zhang (Zhang Tsong-zung), *Desire for Words: An Exhibition of Installation Works by Xu Bing and Gu Wenda* (Hong Kong: Hong Kong Arts Centre, 1992).
18. On Huang Yongpin's Dadaist activities, see Valerie C. Doran (ed.), *China's New Art: Post-1989* (Hong Kong: Hanart TZ Gallery, 1993), pp. xvi and xciii, and Figs. 99 and 100.

waters once more. In November of that year the Central Academy organized the first exhibition entirely devoted to the Nude, showing over 150 works ranging from salon-style academicism (Jin Shangyi, Lin Gang, for example) to the crudest Expressionism (Shang Yang, Xie Dong-ming).[19] In February 1989 a more progressive group staged the long-postponed Avant-Garde Exhibition, made notorious when one of the artists, Xiao Lu, daughter of Xiao Feng, shattered with two pistol shots the mirror in her Installation "Conversation" that separated two figures who were clearly not communicating with each other.[20] Official toleration had reached breaking point. The exhibition was closed down after a few days and stringent regulations were put into force to vet all works submitted for exhibition before they could be shown.

But the pressure for more freedom was still building up, culminating in the month-long occupation of Tiananmen Square (May to early June 1989), its brutal dispersal by the army, and the destruction by tanks of the huge styrofoam statue of the Spirit of Democracy that had been made by students at the Central Academy of Art, with the active support of many of its teachers, and carried in sections for erection on the Square. A month later the Seventh National Art Exhibition went ahead. Since many of the leading artists refused to submit works, or had sought refuge abroad, this was the opportunity for unknown artists from the provincial schools, who carried off most of the prizes.[21] Meanwhile the process had begun of weeding out, interrogating and punishing artists who had taken part in, or supported, the Tiananmen Square occupation.

At this stage, and for a year at least, it seemed that, with its leaders abroad or silenced, the modern movement had died, and with it all the creative energy and hopes of the 1980s. How could the artists cope with this? The manner in which they did is a story at least as extraordinary as that of the movements of the 1980s.

A key factor in the revival of art was the fact that by the early 1990s the spirit of free enterprise had emerged, as artists once forced to sell their work through their unit in exchange for a small percentage were now selling directly, at first chiefly to foreigners in Beijing whose enthusiasm for every new thing gave them great encouragement. No such paths to fortune were open to writers, who were almost entirely dependent on a shrinking domestic market. In December 1989 the *China Daily* reported that there were no less than 250 "art galleries" in the capital, although most consisted of a single artist trying to sell his or her work through a friend who acted as "agent." The export of oil paintings for sale was encouraged as a valuable source of foreign exchange, while an increasing number of galleries, chiefly in New York, were opening to sell the new Chinese art. Before the end of the decade, Wu Guanzhong's paintings were fetching high prices on the international market, Huang Yongyu,

19. See Tang Shisheng and Gan Wuyan (eds.), *Works of the Chinese Nude Oils Exhibition* (Guilin: Guangxi People's Publishing House, 1988).
20. Illustrated in Sullivan, *Art and Artists of Twentieth Century China*, Fig. 256.
21. Prize-winning works from this exhibition are reproduced in *Meishu*, Nos. 7, 8, 9, and 10 (1979), with a full list in No. 11.

satirical poet and cartoonist who had become a much-sought-after painter in Hong Kong, had built himself a house outside Beijing, while Wang Huaiqing, an oil painter who had long worked in relative obscurity in Beijing, had come under contract to a Taipei gallery, and his prices had soared. Meanwhile, new commercial galleries such as Karen Smith's CourtYard Gallery and Brian Wallace's Red Gate Gallery in Beijing, and Lorenz Helbling's ShangArt in Shanghai, were now for the first time providing valuable outlets for the many new young artists.

The free economic climate undoubtedly contributed to the growing confidence of independent artists who were successfully creating an art world outside the official establishment. On 2 June 1990, *Wenyi bao* signalled an official return to "Marxist values in art," but the artists heeded it not. On the contrary, the years 1990–92 saw a remarkable outburst of creative activity, as artists responded to the tragic events of 1989 and the attempt to reimpose control in an astonishing variety of ways. At the same time that Xu Bing was being officially condemned for the *Tianshu*, he and his assistants were engaged on his enterprise labelled "Ghosts pounding the Wall" – taking rubbings from the rough stone surfaces of a tower on the Great Wall and mounting them as a huge Installation that could be interpreted on many symbolic levels, not only as a reflection on the Wall, its history and meaning but, as with the *Tianshu*, a comment on the futility of human endeavour.

In 1992, Li Xianting, with Zhang Tsong-zung (Johnson Zhang), Director of the Hanart TZ Gallery in Hong Kong, planned an ambitious exhibition of the work produced since 1989 by the more adventurous, experimental and unreconciled artists.[22] Because these works could not be shown in China, the landmark exhibition was held in Hong Kong in January–February 1993, and later shown in Europe, Australia and America. The organizers divided the works into six main categories, covering the main aspects of the Avant-Garde in the early 1990s: Political Pop, including pictures of Mao, part nostalgic, part satirical, part influenced by Pop Art, by Wang Guangyi, Yu Youhan, Li Shan, Geng Jianyi and others; Cynical Realism, including Fang Lijun's comic but frightening cadres, and Liu Wei's equally repellent "Revolutionary Family" series; the Wounded Romantic Spirit, such as Xia Xiaowan's agonized figures suggesting the influence of Heironymus Bosch and Max Ernst; Emotional Bondage, Fetishism and Sado-Masochism, including Gu Dexin's viscera in coloured plastic and Zeng Fanzhi's nightmare "Hospital" triptych; Ritual and Purgation – Endgame Art[23] (Installations, including the work of Gu Wenda and Xu Bing); and Introspection and Retreat into Formalism – New Abstract Art, including works by Shang Yang, Wang Chuan and others, in a variety of forms, some decorative, some sculptural.

Although these labels were somewhat arbitrary, and certainly trendy,

22. See Li Xianting, "Major trends in the development of contemporary Chinese art," in Doran, *China's New Art*, pp. x–xxii.
23. This is Li Xianting's label for a collection of works that included Xu Bing's *Tianshu* and Holy Scriptures in Braille, Gu Wenda's "Oedipus Refound Complex" series and the New Analysts Group's charts and mathematical formulae.

they do give some indication of the ways in which artists were satirizing the revived Mao cult and Party cultural dictatorship, exposing the sickness of modern Chinese urban society, and proclaiming their response to the corrupting influence of burgeoning consumerism. The idealism of the mid-1980s had gone and the artists' targets were less obviously political, as they wrestled with issues of personal identity, the purpose and language of art, and the freedom and insecurity that the erratic loosening of Party controls now offered them.

The most direct way to establish their identity, and attract attention in an increasingly competitive milieu, was through the now widely fashionable forms of Happenings, Performances and Installations, which, however perverse or eccentric, were essentially creative. The appeal of Installations was obvious: they were not directed at any particular political target; the artist could fill a whole gallery with a single work; there was no limit to the ideas, forms and materials set out, which might include the latest information technology, computer monitors, television screens and so on; and the meaning was often controversial. There were no objective standards by which they could be evaluated: they could only be described.[24] One critic wrote how Performance artists "used their bodies as objects of physical and psychological mutilation in order to awaken public consciousness of human dignity" – although as with Performances in the West, the viewers' response was often limited, confused or even hostile.[25]

By the mid-1990s Chinese art had changed almost beyond recognition. Mainstream officially approved art continued to flourish, as can be seen from the pages of *Meishu*. In 1996 a working conference of artists and writers gave a Report to the Fifth Central Committee of the 14th Congress of the CCP, condemning the new tendencies and stressing the importance of "spiritual civilization." In December 1996 the "First Academic Exhibition of Chinese Contemporary Art 96–97" was banned on the eve of its opening on the grounds that the permit had not been applied for in time. The real reasons were the sponsorship from outside the PRC, and the presence of several exhibits, notably those by Deng Jianjin (nudes caged, or in the early stages of decay) and Shi Lei (dismembered bodies, gaping mouths), which critics might well have dismissed as merely sick, although the artists claim that they reflect the problems plaguing Chinese society: cynical materialism, corruption, violence, drug abuse, unemployment. But official control, as always, was erratic. When in that same year the Shanghai Art Museum, not to be outdone by Venice and São Paolo, held its first Biennale, the wide range of works included a number of Installations, of which the most sensational was Gu Wenda's "American,

24. See Wang Lin, "Installation and Chinese experience," *Meishu yanjiu (Art Research)*, No. 3 (1998), pp. 44–46.
25. If it is true that, as Hou Hanru put it, "Performance ... is certainly the most direct way to express the real situation of human beings living in a culturally, politically and morally alienating society," one may wonder why reactions are often so confused and hostile. See his "Beyond the cynical: China's Avant-Garde in the 1990s," *Art Asia Pacific*, Vol. 3, No. 1 (1996), pp. 42–51.

Italian and Dutch Branch Works" created almost entirely from human hair glued to hanging sheets of paper.[26] The artist's title for this work was intentionally enigmatic.

While the cultural authorities were unpredictably oppressive, leading modernists showed much uncertainty about just where they stood in relation to art and society. In interviews in 1998[27] the painter Guo Wei claimed that his aim was to "paint for society's benefit," while Zhou Zhunya said his was to "promote a healthier point of view in the Chinese people." In the idealistic 1980s such statements would have been taken at their face value. In the 1990s, if not merely self-seeking, they suggest that the artist's duty is to force people to look the sickness of Chinese society in the face. Mao Yan claimed, on the same occasion, that "the individual voluntarily subordinates his or her desires to the good of society as a whole"; yet he also said that Chinese artists wanted to "invent their own art" and "to search for a Chinese art that is individualistic." How these opposing aims were to be reconciled is not clear. The confusion of values was further exacerbated by the rapid commercialization of the art world, already referred to above. This has led to a demand on the part of the new entrepreneurial class for two very different kinds of art. On the one hand, they want academic, salon-style oil paintings (including nudes) to decorate their offices, the demand for which is met by a number of technically accomplished artists such as Wang Yidong, Chen Yiming and Yang Feiyun; on the other, often these same patrons want Chinese ink painting to give them a veneer of traditional culture. This is a stimulus to the new literati painting, *xin wenren hua*,[28] most of which is dull and repetitive, or betrays a technical incompetence due to lack of rigorous training with the brush that is passed off as spontaneity.

Between these two poles there is little room, in mainland China at least, for the public display, or private or commercial acquisition, of experimental art or the Avant-Garde. The survival of this movement depends chiefly upon Chinese collectors in Hong Kong and Taipei, the interest and patronage of foreigner visitors to the PRC, and the handful of commercial galleries run by foreigners. However, the reins are a good deal looser than they were. Today, the cultural authorities do not bear down on the artists as heavily as they did before. There is no longer any need to make propaganda for the government because, as Guo Wei put it, "the government handles its socialist propaganda itself. So long as you conduct your own affairs [that is, keep out of politics], the government will not interfere with you too much," although, he goes on, "there is still a small element of control in participating in government

26. See *Shanghai Biennale* (Shanghai: Shanghai Art Museum, 1996), Plates 104–106.
27. See "The faces of China's future," *Limn: Magazine of International Design*, No. 2 (1998), pp. 12–23. This issue also contains two articles on post-1989 Chinese art: Charles Egan, "The future of new Chinese art" (pp. 4–11), and Britta Erickson, "Made in China: is there a market for new Chinese art?" (pp. 24–30).
28. For an objective look at the *Xin wenren hua*, see Francesca dal Lago, "New literati painting," *Art Asia Pacific*, No. 19 (1998), pp. 32–34.

exhibitions."[29] But, as Zhou Chunya pointed out in the interview cited above, this is no different from the situation for artists in San Francisco.

By the late 1990s the artists who had fled abroad and those who had stayed in China were slowly being drawn together once more. The former were exhibiting in China, notably at the Second Shanghai Biennale of 1998, where the work of Gu Wenda (New York), Zeng Youhe (Honolulu), Liu Guosong (Taipei) and Wucius Wong (Hong Kong) were displayed. Meanwhile the latter were showing their work in Hong Kong, Taiwan, Europe and America. Some expatriates, such as Yan Yanping on Long Island and Qu Leilei in London, expressed a greater nostalgia, and perhaps a deeper appreciation, for the roots of Chinese culture as they explored the pictorial and semantic power of the Chinese character rather than deconstructing it, as Gu Wenda and Xu Bing had done. At the same time, modernists in the PRC wanted desperately to create works that, while expressing Chinese feelings and experience, would bring them into the international world of art. For these artists the cultural frontiers of Chinese art were dissolving. It was natural for them to feel that the question of "what is Chinese art" was becoming unanswerable, and to search for the meaning and purpose of art in their own imaginative creations.

Yet the debates that have animated the Chinese art world for almost a century will not simply go away. Although many artists and critics would claim that the old *guohua–xihua* dichotomy had been nullified by the increasing popularity of mixing media and techniques from China and the West, there survives the nagging feeling that ink painting is Chinese, oils and acrylics are foreign, and that it is even the patriotic duty of the artist to express Chinese feelings in a Chinese way. The declared intention of the organizers of the second Shanghai Biennale was to stress the central role of ink painting and to demonstrate its wide range of expressive possibilities. This may well account for Gu Wenda's rejection, in his Installation for that exhibition, of the materials he had been working with in New York, such as condoms, sanitary napkins and the sweepings from the hairdresser's floor, and executing his monumental pseudo-characters in ink on paper, floating them in the clouds above a vestigial traditional landscape.

With so many new artists appearing on the scene as the end of the century approaches, and so vast a range of responses to the present condition of Chinese society, it is much more difficult than it was in 1989 to summarize the main tendencies. In spite of the fact that artists have a freedom and prospect of wealth that they have never known before, and the doors to the West are wide open, all is not well. While the great majority of artists paint unashamedly for the market-place and adjust their considerable technical skills accordingly, many of those who resist that temptation feel resentment towards, and even alienation from the mass of the people whose problems and anxieties they feel they are expressing. The result is that the Avant-Garde, speaking only to other artists, a small

29. "The faces of China's future," p. 22.

circle of their friends and a few students in the big metropolitan centres, feel marginalized – a far cry indeed from their central role in 1989.[30] They have been castigated, even by some moderately "progressive" critics such as Cao Yiqiang, a young professor in the National Academy, Hangzhou, for their rejection of all tradition; by ignoring the past, these critics claim, they are giving up the very foundation on which the art of today and of the future is built.

In the meantime, such issues as the responsibility of the artist, national versus international style, and the role and future of ink painting are hotly debated. None of these issues was resolved – indeed, how could they be? – but the intensity of the debate, and the degree of commitment of the artists who are not simply bent on amassing a fortune, suggests that Chinese art at the end of the century, for all its confusion of aims, forms and techniques, is in a vigorous state.

30. See Fan Jingzhong, Cao Yiqiang, Huang Zhuang and Yan Shanchun, "The pessimism in art of ours," *Meishu yanjiu*, No. 1 (1997), pp. 19–21.

Literary Decorum or Carnivalistic Grotesque: Literature in the People's Republic of China after 50 Years*

Bonnie S. McDougall

The profound silence that followed immediately after the 4 June massacres in 1989 was short-lived. As it became clear that the regime would stay in power, writers reacted as opportunity and circumstances allowed. Dissident writers associated with the protest movement were in danger of arrest and imprisonment: Duo Duo[1] only just managed to get his flight to London on 4 June, joining those like Bei Dao[2] who were already abroad and had no choice but to remain. Writers in high positions were also vulnerable: Wang Meng[3] was forced to resign as Minister of Culture in 1989 and dropped from the Party's Central Committee at the 1992 Party Congress. Less prominent writers waited for a more propitious time to publish; younger writers barely paused.

An anxious period followed where prospects for easing political tension and returning to economic growth were uncertain. Deng Xiaoping's January 1992 Southern Tour finally confirmed the policy for the decade: economic liberalization (affecting also culture and education) was stepped up, while political liberalization was limited to restricting the influence of the old left.[4] The responsibility of editors, publishers and critics to maintain political, moral and aesthetic decorum was subverted by pressures to make money, if not to get rich then simply to survive. Political issues became more narrowly defined: as long as they stopped short of advocating its overthrow, writers could choose to support the Party or to ignore it.[5] In the summer of 1992, Li Ruihuan, in charge of ideological work at the Politburo, urged freedom from censorship for literary and artistic works that did not break the law, and recognition that

* I am most grateful to Chen Maiping, Anders Hansson, Michel Hockx, Kam Louie and Tommy McClellan for their generous assistance on this article.

1. Male; b. 1951.

2. Male; b. 1949; a co-founder of the original *Jintian* (*Today*) in 1978 and its revival in 1990.

3. Male; b. 1934. As Minister of Culture from 1986 to 1989, he retains the privileges of a minister and is still vice-president of the Chinese Writers' Association and the Federation of Writers and Artists. For his resignation, see Richard Baum, *Burying Mao: Chinese Politics in the Age of Deng Xiaoping* (Princeton: Princeton University Press, 1994), pp. 295, 316 and 364.

4. *Ibid.* pp. 372–74. For an overview of the pre-1990 economic reforms that gave greater autonomy to state enterprises, see Donald Hay *et al.*, *Economic Reform and State-Owned Enterprises in China, 1979–1987* (Oxford: Clarendon Press, 1994), pp. 3–39 and 83–113; for limits to the scope of the reforms in practice, see pp. 281–83. For the declining power of the Writers' Association, see Hong Zicheng, *Zhongguo dangdai wenxue gaishuo* (*An Outline of Contemporary Chinese Literature*) (Hong Kong: Qingwen shushi, 1997), pp. 163–65.

5. On the gap between official rhetoric and social practice in the early 1990s, see Tony Saich, "Discos and dictatorship: party-state and society relations in the People's Republic of China," in Jeffrey N. Wasserstrom and Elizabeth J. Perry (eds.), *Popular Protest and Political Culture in Modern China* (Boulder: Westview Press, rev. ed., 1994), pp. 246–267.

the function of literature and the arts was not political indoctrination but included entertainment and aesthetic appreciation.[6]

Writers might have rejoiced were it not for two other factors: potential or actual loss of personal material security (salaries and welfare benefits as full-time writers or cultural functionaries) plus the dwindling attention of readers. Although a larger proportion of the population was literate and urban-based than ever before,[7] these potential readers faced a unprecedented range of entertainment and information choices, from domestic and imported popular fiction, films and television to sport, shopping, travel and even for a few millions the Internet. Poetry and drama drifted towards the margins as fiction became the favoured genre, a trend intensified by the adaptation of short stories and novels into films and television dramas. The renewed prestige that writers had enjoyed briefly in the late 1970s and early 1980s, speaking out on behalf of the educated urban population against the Cultural Revolution and re-creating the intellectual hero in fiction,[8] was undermined as incomes rose and modernization penetrated every corner of people's lives; the new cultural heroes were pop stars or enterprise millionaires.

Countering the general enthusiasm for popular commercial culture, the Sixth Plenum of the 14th Party Congress in October 1996 reasserted the Party's intention to control "spiritual civilization," targeting literature and the arts, the mass media, and public morals in general.[9] To reinforce the message, the Sixth Congress of the Federation of Writers and Artists (the first since 1984) was held in December along with the Fifth Congress of the Writers' Association.[10] Most professional writers have chosen to remain affiliated with the national, provincial or municipal branches of the Writers' Association; some also have day jobs in the cultural and educational establishment. A very small number of literary writers can afford to be freelance; a few have at least temporarily abandoned literature for business.

In the new fragmented, multi-dimensional space where political repression co-exists with cultural diversity, the effects can be paradoxical. A recent report notes that Shanghai's relatively efficient cultural bureaucracy is a real hindrance to theatre artists, compared with the administrative muddle of overlapping national, municipal and army agencies in Beijing which allows the Central Experimental Theatre to

6. Baum, *Burying Mao*, p. 356.
7. Richard Kirkby, "Dilemmas of urbanization: review and prospects," in Dennis Dwyer (ed.), *China: The Next Decade* (London: Longman, 1994), pp. 128–155.
8. For the self-promotion of writers in this period, see Bonnie S. McDougall, "Self-narrative as group discourse: female subjectivity in Wang Anyi's fiction," *Asian Studies Review*, Vol. 19, No. 2 (November 1995), pp. 1–24; see also Jing Wang, *High Culture Fever: Policies, Aesthetics, and Ideology in Deng's China* (Berkeley: University of California Press, 1996), pp. 114–16.
9. For the impact on television, see Michael Keane, "Television and moral development in China," *Asian Studies Review*, Vol. 22, No. 4 (December 1998), pp. 475–503.
10. Helmut Martin, " 'Cultural China': irritation and expectations at the end of an era," in Maurice Brosseau *et al.* (eds.), *China Review 1997* (Hong Kong: Chinese University Press, 1997), pp. 277–326, esp. pp. 295–98.

flourish.[11] Editors, distributors and mediators, through whom censorship has functioned since 1949,[12] no longer displace general readers as the primary consumers of literary works,[13] but censorship is still exercised. When Mo Yan[14] received the Great Writers literary prize in 1996 for *Feng ru fei tun* (*Full Breasts and Fat Buttocks*), some of the judges such as Su Tong[15] and Wang Zengqi[16] warned readers not to be put off by the crudity of the title, but the novel was still criticized and its publication halted. Globalization enables PRC writers to publish abroad, and younger writers even appear in exile publications;[17] but works by dissidents abroad are still banned, while foreign literary, academic and commercial influences are largely unrestricted.

Younger writers probably believe that the economic and social changes effected in the 1990s are irreversible; it is doubtful that older writers share their views. Inevitably, there is some nostalgia for the status and rewards formerly bestowed on establishment writers.[18] As always, no matter what problems writers face, there is no shortage of volunteers to fill whatever space is made available. The main differences between 1949 and 1999 for those considering a literary career are relative safety and a range of choices; although greatly weakened, the party-state cultural apparatus established in 1949 remains virtually intact at the end of the century.

From the middle of the 1980s to the present, fiction has been the main site of literary experimentation and commercialization.[19] Liu Suola[20] and Xu Xing[21] are said to have introduced disruptive discourse in 1985, but were unkindly dubbed "Yuppie modernists" for their depictions of privileged youth afflicted by ennui. At the same time, Can Xue[22]

11. Pamela Yatsko, "Arrested artistry," *Far Eastern Economic Review*, 27 August 1998, p. 48.
12. Michael Schoenhals, "Media censorship in the People's Republic of China," and Bonnie S. McDougall, "Censorship and self-censorship in contemporary Chinese literature," in Susan Whitfield (ed.), *After the Event: Human Rights and Their Future in China* (London: Wellsweep Press, 1993), pp. 61–72 and 73–90.
13. Bonnie S. McDougall, "Writing self: author/audience complicity in modern Chinese fiction," *Archiv Orientalni*, Vol. 64, No. 2 (1996), pp. 245–268.
14. Male; b. 1956; best known for his 1987 novel *Hong gaoliang jiazu* (*The Red Sorghum Clan*), adapted by Zhang Yimou for his first film as a director.
15. Male; b. 1963; best known for his 1987 novella "Qi-qie cheng qun" ("A crowd of wives and concubines"), filmed by Zhang Yimou as *Raise the Red Lantern*.
16. Male; 1920–97.
17. For example, Bei Cun (male; b. 1965) and Zhu Wen (male; b. 1967) in *Jintian*.
18. Jing Wang, *High Culture Fever*, p. 265. It must be remembered that the vast majority of writers since 1949 have supported the regime, and even during the Cultural Revolution there were many willing to accept the risks for the sake of the rewards.
19. Wu Yiqin, *Zhongguo dangdai xin chao xiaoshuo lun* (*On Contemporary New Wave Chinese Fiction*) (Nanjing: Jiangsu wenyi chubanshe, 1997); Jin Han, *Zhongguo dangdai xiaoshuo shi* (*A History of Contemporary Chinese Fiction*) (Hangzhou: Hangzhou daxue chubanshe, rev. ed., 1997); and Chen Xiaoming, *Wubian de tiaozhan* (*The Boundless Challenge*) (Changchun: Shidai wenyi chubanshe, 1993). The terminology employed by Chinese critics (experimental, avant-garde, new wave, modernist or post-modern) is generally time-relative.
20. Female; b. 1955; has lived abroad since 1988.
21. Male; b. 1956; one of the few writers to have returned to China since 1989.
22. Female; b. 1953.

pioneered a radical disordering in time and space, incorporating fantasy and dreams, irrational logic, and metaphors of sexual depravity and violence, in works that offered a challenge to both the literary and political status quo. Ma Yuan[23] developed a playfully inventive narrative style in stories like the 1987 "You shen" ("A wandering spirit"), where the author intervenes with intertextual references to his own work and Bei Dao's poetry. His tendency towards surrealism is more pronounced in the 1986 novella "Xugou" ("Fabrication"); partly set in a leper colony, it explores the theme of lost identity in a bleak environment punctuated with episodes of pathetic bestiality. Yu Hua[24] focused variously on cruelty, cannibalism, self-mutilation, rape, revenge and madness; his stories seemed calculated to repel but nevertheless won a diverse audience including literary critics and scholars who read them as political allegories. Leaning in another direction altogether, Chi Li[25] depicted the everyday rigours of ordinary urban life.

As literature for many readers became no more than a commodity, writers learned to make choices between the security of a state salary and elite readership, going for a middle-of-the-range audience or appealing directly to the mass market. For example, an experienced writer could earn 1,000 *yuan* per script for the television skits (*xiaopin*) which became immensely popular in the early 1990s; small wonder that even a famous writer like Liu Xinwu[26] succumbed. While Zhang Kangkang[27] and Wang Anyi[28] explored the social and subjective realms of educated women, Zhang Xianliang[29] and Liu Heng[30] wrote best-sellers describing primitive forms of masculinity and impotence as personal crises as well as political allegory, and Su Tong and Mo Yan moved from nativist writing towards melodrama with eventful plots, powerful characters, and graphic depictions of sex and violence. In commercial terms, all were outclassed by Wang Shuo,[31] whose tales of urban delinquency from the perspective of the delinquents were sophisticated enough to be published in the literary journals, reaching the attention of critics who typically ignored other forms of popular fiction such as martial arts epics, romances and science fiction.

A conspicuous feature of post-1989 fiction is the absence of overt political campaigns (the Party campaigning against writers, writers campaigning against the Party), while the political messages prevalent in the 1980s are harder to find or decipher. Yu Hua's post-1989 stories, such as "Huozhe" ("Living," 1992, filmed by Zhang Yimou in 1993), are distinctly less brutal than his earlier work; Can Xue's new stories are

23. Male; b. 1953; stopped writing in 1987.
24. Male; b. 1960; now freelance.
25. Female; b. 1957.
26. Male; b. 1942.
27. Female; b. 1950.
28. Female; b. 1954.
29. Male; b. 1936; one of the first novelists to achieve overseas success; now in business.
30. Male; b. 1954; his novella "Fuxi Fuxi" was filmed by Zhang Yimou under the title *Judou*.
31. Male; b. 1958; now freelance.

similarly less surreal. Mo Yan's 1990 "Shen liao" ("Divine discourse"), which relates the eccentric personal habits of a wealthy landowner in pre-1949 China, appears to have no contemporary relevance;[32] his 1993 story "Ling yao" ("The cure"), on the other hand, which is set in the 1940s, can be read as referring to the frequency of executions in the 1980s and the widespread belief that the victims' internal organs are used for transplants; otherwise there would be no point in updating Lu Xun's famous 1919 story "Yao" ("Medicine") on the same subject. Some writers, like Han Dong[33] and Zhu Wen, choose individual realms of discourse and hence social marginalization.[34] Chen Ran's[35] 1992 novella "Zuichun li de yangguang" ("Sunshine between the lips") plays on the small details of sexual encounters and their symbolic meanings, announcing at the beginning of the story the narrator's total lack of interest in the outside world; the "private life" in her novel *Siren shenghuo* (*Private Life*, 1995) depicts an existence untrammeled by events or restraints.

The subject matter of contemporary fiction falls into several overlapping categories: modern social history; life in the countryside, including among ethnic minorities; urban life and modernization; Educated Youth and the Cultural Revolution; and human nature, identity and gender. An outstanding chronicle of contemporary urban life is the 1993 *Fei du* (The *Ruined Capital*) by Jia Pingwa.[36] This novel is set in Xi'an, here designated by its alternate name Xijing in a well-established metaphor indicating China; much is made of its recent faked antiquity for tourist consumption as well as its feeble attempts at modernization. Its leading characters are local cultural heroes who play the role of traditional literati at the same time as they indulge in morally dubious business enterprises and extra-marital affairs. Modelled on a Qing dynasty best-seller, *Jin ping mei* (*Golden Lotus*), it displays great interest in its characters' sex lives, but its descriptions of sexual activity are interrupted by a row of blank squares with the number of characters "deleted by the author" in brackets. Its leisurely, affable narrative and its acute detail on urban life still pleased general readers; the novel was a huge commercial success that mocked commercialism at the same time as it attacked the complacency of China's cultural and political elites, and the controversy around it as both an allegory and an example of contemporary decadence presumably boosted sales further.[37]

---

32. D. D. Wang nevertheless finds allegory in this story; see David Der-wei Wang (ed.), *Running Wild: New Chinese Writers* (New York: Columbia University Press, 1994), p. 255.
  33. Male; b. 1965.
  34. Chen Xiaoming, *Shengyu de xiangxiang: jiushi niandai de wenxue xushi yu wenhua weiji* (*The Residual Imagination: Literary Narrative and Cultural Crisis in the 90s*) (Beijing: Huayi chubanshe, 1997).
  35. Female; b. 1962; editor at Zuojia chubanshe (Writers' Press).
  36. Male; b. 1952.
  37. For the controversy see Wang Yiyan, "Jia Pingwa's *Feidu*: elegy for Chinese high culture," *Journal of the Oriental Society of Australia*, Vols. 27 and 28 (1995–96), pp. 165–194. Jia Pingwa's next novel, *Tumen* (*Earthen Doors*, 1996), is said to be a sign of his gratitude for his subsequent re-acceptance as an approved writer; see Martin, " 'Cultural China'," p. 295.

At the other end of the social scale are Wang Shuo's tales of the big city. Wang Shuo's fame began with the 1984 "Kongzhong xiaojie" ("Air hostess"), a conventional tale of a doomed love affair; its characteristic innovation is the social status of the protagonist-narrator, a demobilized drifter who cannot find a place in society. Within a few years, the drifter had turned into a fully-fledged hooligan or con-man in works like "Wanzhu" ("The operators," 1987), his first novel *Wanr de jiu shi xintiao* (*Playing for Thrills*, 1988) and *Qianwan bie ba wo dang ren* (*Don't Take Me for a Man*, 1989). At the same time, his language loosened to the extent that some passages of dialogue in contemporary urban slang are almost incomprehensible to outsiders, while injections of political jargon go beyond Ah Cheng's subtle ironies to straightforward farce. A key word in his work is "play" (*wan*, also meaning games or tricks), and Wang Shuo also plays with the reader's expectations. *Playing for Thrills*, for example, mixes the conventions of a thriller with knowing literary devices such as extended dream sequences, fanciful descriptions of people and places, parodic references to established writers, anti-climatic disclosure of information, passages hinting at hidden depths and a final authorial intervention professing boredom with the absurd, convoluted plot and its picaresque (but not villainous) protagonist. Among the gang members' less attractive attributes are their double standards: while sexually predatory men are glorified, sexually active women are treated as sluts (the only one of these woman to be given a major role is revealed – that is, excused – as a victim of child abuse).[38] Despite auto-biographical elements in the characterization, Wang Shuo is not semi-literate as his protagonist-narrator Fang Yan claims to be, but a fully professional writer who has found that streetwise humour with touches of sentimentality engages a wide range of readers. Wang Meng's support for Wang Shuo's refusal to observe literary decorum or public morality caused a minor scandal in 1993.[39]

Contemporary rural China is depicted in Mo Yan's 1987 *Tiantang suantai zhi ge* (*The Garlic Ballads*), about three families who take part in riots over the local authorities' corruption and decadence. The heroine, who claims her sexual freedom at the cost of repeated beatings from her father and brothers, finally commits suicide, while the two heroes, representing different types of male resistance to oppression, only barely manage to survive to the end of the story. A traditional touch to the narrative is given by short verses at the head of each chapter, attributed to the local storyteller commenting on the action. There is an unremitting emphasis throughout on lacerated flesh, excrement, noxious insects, pain and humiliation, much of it inflicted on the peasants by the local authorities, some of it by themselves.

A Bakhtinian metaphor particularly relevant to this kind of fiction is the carnival: "Debasement and mockery are idealised in a special

38. Xiao Yuan, *Wang Shuo zai pipan* (*A Further Criticism of Wang Shuo*) (Changsha: Hunan chubanshe, 1993).
39. See Wang Meng, "Duobi chonggao" ("Avoiding loftiness"), *Dushu*, January 1993; reprinted in several collections of readers', critics' and writers' opinions on Wang Shuo.

carnivalistic image, the grotesque body ... Thus carnival ... banishes fear of individual pain and death, for 'the grotesque body is cosmic and universal' ..."[40] "If Socialist Realist art ... emphasises the clean, closed-off, and narcissistic body, the art of the grotesque stresses change, mediation, and the ability to surprise."[41] Writers whose work could be described as carnivalistic in this sense include Ma Yuan, Can Xue, Yu Hua and Mo Yan; Su Tong's post-1989 novel *Mi* (*Rice*) is a powerful example. Set in the 1920s and 1930s in a small town outside Shanghai against a background of rural poverty and urban gangsterism, the story relates the reversal of social hierarchies as a peasant takes over a prosperous rice shop. The protagonist's forms of play, however, involve cruelty and degradation; other episodes include incest and a young boy's murder of his sister. Bodies are minutely described as orifices for inappropriate functions and as subject to internal decay from venereal disease and starvation; dialogue is mainly in the form of obscene abuse. There are no redeeming characters or hope for the future; neither city nor countryside offer comfort or sanctuary. Press reactions quoted on the cover praise the novel for its completeness and integrity, its imagination and honesty, and its seething energy and anger, but the descriptions of violence, rage and pain take the novel beyond realism.

Characteristics of carnivalism in fiction also include "extraordinary situations, extreme frankness of speech, journeys to the underworld or heaven, dialogues in the other world and in extreme or liminal situations, ... and circumstances temporarily free from quotidian consequences and social positions in which people can discover and articulate their most fundamental belief and the sense of their lives."[42] Many 1990s writers engage with themes or images of memory, dreams, hallucination, myth and the supernatural. Su Tong's shorter fiction, whether set in the recent past or in the present, in the countryside or in towns, features characters who are barely affected by politics or modernization; their family-based plots, sometimes labelled "pseudo-genealogies," are overtly mythic.

At the opposite end of the spectrum to carnivalistic writing is literary decorum. Although welcomed by the authorities and suited to the tastes of more conventional readers, writing in this mode is less apt to attract critical attention. Wang Anyi's "Shushu de gushi" ("Uncle's tale," 1990) combines a cool demolition of a 1980s literary myth (the heroic rehabilitation of a former rightist writer, possibly modelled on Zhang Xianliang) with an artful play on the equally clichéd fictional device of a framed narration. Chi Li writes on the work and home lives of urban workers, setting out anti-romantic attitudes towards love and marriage;[43] she is often grouped with the prize-winning Fang Fang,[44] but since the latter

40. Gary Saul Morson and Caryl Emerson, *Mikhail Bakhtin: Creation of a Prosaics* (Stanford: Stanford University Press, 1990), p. 444.
41. *Ibid.* p. 449.
42. *Ibid.* pp. 465–66.
43. I find it difficult to agree with J. Wang's claim that writers and readers of neo-realistic fiction by writers like Chi Li are "profoundly deceitful": see Jing Wang, *High Culture Fever*, pp. 268–270.
44. Female; b. 1955.

favours melodrama and the supernatural, the two have little in common apart from being female, living in Wuhan, and enjoying careers as professional writers. Li Rui's[45] *Jiu zhi* (*The Old Address*) is a sober, unembellished account of a provincial clan from the late 1920s to the present, based on his own family history.

Readers in and outside China tend to assume that writers in their work testify (intentionally or otherwise) as witnesses to real events or situations, so that readers may understand them more fully or more deeply. In a broad sense, some literary works may give readers a sense of apprehending truths about the world, but what writers say in and about their work is not the kind of evidence that would stand up in court. The new fiction is just as unreliable, in this sense, as the socialist realism that preceded it, or the modernist literature of the 1930s and 1940s.

Nevertheless, it has been argued that the current trends are directly related to "reality which is already too grotesque and bizarre,"[46] although it could just as well be argued that the chief characteristic of the period since 1985 is widespread prosperity, and that "the grotesque and bizarre" is more characteristic of earlier periods in PRC history. The prevalence of violent crime, drug addiction, abduction of women and children, prostitution and official corruption was a common topic of discussion in the 1990s; however, works written in the 1990s but set in earlier periods both before and after 1949, when crime is supposed not to have been as serious, depict an equally chaotic and violent society.

An alternative way of reading post-1985 fiction is to see the world it creates as a construct in writers' mentalities. For example, women are routinely battered, raped, commit suicide or are horribly killed in stories by male writers but come to less harm in the hands of women writers.[47] "Guidi shang de yueguang" ("Moonlight over the field of ghosts") by Yang Zhengguan[48] is a rare case where the wife kills the husband rather than vice versa; his "Gan gou" ("The dry ravine"), on the incest and murder of a sister by her brother, is more typical of the period. More generally, the spectacle of fathers killing children, children killing fathers, and brothers killing brothers and sisters; maggots and lice, suppurating sores and rotting limbs; a pervasive stench of excrement and filth; foul and abusive language: all occur in post-1985 fiction with a frequency higher than in the real world of whatever period. Writing about literature in the Soviet Union under Stalin, Bakhtin idealized the potential of fiction as a celebration of chaos, a carnival of reversed hierarchies and disorder, a market place where popular culture drives out the elites. In 1990s China, writers' own sense of dispossession – their loss of an assured role

45. Male; b. 1950; an editor at *Shanxi wenxue* (*Shanxi Literature*).
46. Wang, *Running Wild*, p. 244.
47. Lu Tonglin characterizes the late 1980s as misogynous; see *Misogyny, Cultural Nihilism, and Oppositional Politics: Contemporary Chinese Experimental Fiction* (Stanford: Stanford University Press, 1995). The same phenomenon is observable in May Fourth fiction at a reduced level of brutality; see Bonnie S. McDougall, "Disappearing women and disappearing men in May Fourth narrative," *Asian Studies Review*, Vol. 22, No. 4 (December 1998), pp. 427–458.
48. Male; b. 1957.

in a stable political and social hierarchy – along with the degrading need to compete in an open market[49] give rise to mixed feelings of liberation and anxiety. As barriers come down, literary decorum is relegated to older and female writers.[50] (Writers are still mostly male, and the "hot" new tendencies are mostly associated with young male writers.)

Much post-1985 fiction requires considerable commitment from its audience; reading it can be a disturbing experience. Some commentators, on the other hand, find it exhilarating, and defend its brutality as metaphorical or as a victory for free speech.[51] In "Zhuojian" ("In flagrante delicto"), Li Peifu[52] describes a husband spying on his wife: accompanied by his brother, he finds her in bed with another man; they see the man give her 1,000 *yuan* to break off their affair, and his brother then persuades the husband to let him (the brother) sleep with her for 60 *yuan*. At first numbed by the night's events, the husband finally returns home swearing to kill his wife. D. D. Wang finds both irony and sensuality in this story: "through muffled laughter it permits a word on behalf of the libidinal needs and perverse hopes of the people," although the wife is presumably murdered at the end of the story.[53] Brutality is also highly marketable, and not only to middle or lowbrow readers: if the elite reading public (intellectuals, cultural bureaucrats and politicians) demanded or expected refined proletarian heroes in the 1960s and early to mid-1970s, disillusioned intellectuals in the late 1970s and early 1980s, and sex and violence in the late 1980s and 1990s, this is what writers delivered. We can learn from this kind of fiction what is discursively acceptable in contemporary China, and deduce from its fragmentation the fragility but persistence of central control; home readers find in it the pleasure of recognition, while non-Chinese readers learn about the small events of daily life. It is difficult to maintain that it gives unique insights into any of these areas.

China's failure to gain a Nobel Prize for Literature has been debated by PRC supporters and detractors over the past few years, although the reasons have more to do with the nature of the Swedish Academy than the merits of Chinese writers or China's international standing. The question why the PRC has failed to produce great writers is a false one, however, since there is no formula, regardless of national will or

49. Writing about rural markets in the aftermath of the 1978 reforms, Skinner noted that although in general the situation in urban areas had improved more than in the countryside, urban intellectuals still felt aggrieved that the gap was not wider in their favour; late Qing Confucian bureaucrats and PRC Marxist intellectuals shared an elite distrust of free markets. G. William Skinner, "Rural marketing in China: repression and revival," *The China Quarterly*, No. 103 (September 1985), pp. 393–413, esp. p. 393.

50. Can Xue and Fang Fang share male writers' obsession with family violence.

51. See prefaces to Wang, *Running Wild* and other anthologies by Howard Goldblatt, Henry Zhao and Jing Wang. Jing Wang also offers a powerful defence along these lines in *High Culture Fever*, p. 258. Her contention (pp. 269–271) that the training-ground for hooligans was the Cultural Revolution and their appearance was due to the post-1978 open economy is, however, misleading; hooliganism was present throughout the whole period, but it was not advisable to include hooligans as characters in fiction, let alone as leading characters until the 1980s (with rare exceptions, e.g. Bei Dao's CR hooligan in "Bodong" ("Waves")).

52. Male; b. 1950.

53. Wang, *Running Wild*, p. 255.

resources. It is tempting to blame the PRC for its promotion of poor writing over the past 50 years but less plausible to praise it for such good writing as has appeared, such as the obscure (*menglong*) poetry written during the Cultural Revolution.

By the end of the 1990s, when social mobility, disposable incomes and the free flow of ideas and information among the population in general were at unprecedented levels, most professional writers (Chen Naishan being the main exception) still preferred to depict melancholy, corruption (moral and material) and decay. The same phenomenon is observable in Taiwan and Western countries. Like politicians, writers are given to claiming to speak on behalf of the masses, culture or even civilization as we know it. At times the claim has validity; the pessimistic voices in 1980s China can be seen as justified in the wake of continuing repression since 1989, and writers in the late 1990s might well feel gloom at the prospects for the coming decades. As the Chinese readership becomes more socially diverse and less subject to domination by elite interests, however, readers also welcome writers who make no pretence to social leadership.

Index

Lightning Source UK Ltd.
Milton Keynes UK
UKOW050947131212

203611UK00002B/55/A